T0330235

Explorations in Environmental and Natural Resource Economics

NEW HORIZONS IN ENVIRONMENTAL ECONOMICS

Series Editors: Wallace E. Oates, *Professor of Economics, University of Maryland, USA* and Henk Folmer, *Professor of General Economics, Wageningen University and Professor of Environmental Economics, Tilburg University, The Netherlands*

This important series is designed to make a significant contribution to the development of the principles and practices of environmental economics. It includes both theoretical and empirical work. International in scope, it addresses issues of current and future concern in both East and West and in developed and developing countries.

The main purpose of the series is to create a forum for the publication of high quality work and to show how economic analysis can make a contribution to understanding and resolving the environmental problems confronting the world in the twenty-first century.

Recent titles in the series include:

The Greening of Markets
Product Competition, Pollution and Policy Making in a Duopoly
Michael Kuhn

Managing Wetlands for Private and Social Good
Theory, Policy and Cases from Australia
Stuart M. Whitten and Jeff Bennett

Amenities and Rural Development
Theory, Methods and Public Policy
Edited by Gary Paul Green, Steven C. Deller and David W. Marcouiller

The Evolution of Markets for Water
Theory and Practice in Australia
Edited by Jeff Bennett

Integrated Assessment and Management of Public Resources
Edited by Joseph C. Cooper, Federico Perali and Marcella Veronesi

Climate Change and the Economics of the World's Fisheries
Examples of Small Pelagic Stocks
Edited by Rögnvaldur Hannesson, Manuel Barange and Samuel F. Herrick Jr

The Theory and Practice of Environmental and Resource Economics
Edited by Thomas Aronsson, Roger Axelsson and Runar Brännlund

The International Yearbook of Environmental and Resource Economics 2006/2007
A Survey of Current Issues
Edited by Tom Tietenberg and Henk Folmer

Choice Modelling and the Transfer of Environmental Values
Edited by John Rolfe and Jeff Bennett

The Impact of Climate Change on Regional Systems
A Comprehensive Analysis of California
Edited by Joel Smith and Robert Mendelsohn

Explorations in Environmental and Natural Resource Economics
Essays in Honor of Gardner M. Brown, Jr
Edited by Robert Halvorsen and David F. Layton

Explorations in Environmental and Natural Resource Economics

Essays in Honor of Gardner M. Brown, Jr

Edited by

Robert Halvorsen

Professor of Economics, University of Washington, Seattle, USA

David F. Layton

Associate Professor of Public Affairs, University of Washington, Seattle, USA

NEW HORIZONS IN ENVIRONMENTAL ECONOMICS

Edward Elgar
Cheltenham, UK • Northampton, MA, USA

Published by
Edward Elgar Publishing Limited
Glensanda House
Montpellier Parade
Cheltenham
Glos GL50 1UA
UK

Edward Elgar Publishing, Inc.
136 West Street
Suite 202
Northampton
Massachusetts 01060
USA

A catalogue record for this book
is available from the British Library

Library of Congress Cataloguing in Publication Data
Explorations in environmental and natural resource economics : essays in honor of Gardner M. Brown, Jr. / edited by Robert Halvorsen and David Layton.
    p. cm.—(New horizons in environmental economics)
  Includes bibliographical references and index.
    1. Environmental economics. 2. Economic development—Environmental aspects. 3. Natural resources—Management. I. Brown, Gardner Mallard. II. Halvorsen, Robert. III. Layton, David, F., 1967– IV. Series.
HD75.6.E99 2006
333.7—dc22   2006041093

ISBN-13: 978 1 84542 184 7
ISBN-10: 1 84542 184 1

Printed and bound in Great Britain by MPG Books Ltd, Bodmin, Cornwall

For
Pranee and Chaiyo
and
Naomi and Neeta

Contents

Contributors

Robert T. Deacon, Department of Economics, University of California, Santa Barbara

Charles M. Fulcher, National Marine Fisheries Service, Woods Hole

Michael Hanemann, Department of Agricultural and Resource Economics, University of California, Berkeley

Ronald N. Johnson, San Diego

Catherine L. Kling, Department of Economics, Iowa State University

David F. Layton, Daniel J. Evans School of Public Affairs, University of Washington

S. Todd Lee, National Marine Fisheries Service, Seattle

Dean Lueck, Department of Agricultural and Resource Economics, University of Arizona

Jeffrey A. Michael, Honors College, Towson University

Craig Mohn, Department of Agricultural and Resource Economics, University of California, Berkeley

Catherine S. Norman, Department of Economics, University of California, Santa Barbara

Raymond B. Palmquist, Department of Economics, North Carolina State University

Gregory M. Parkhurst, Department of Agricultural Economics, Mississippi State University

Mark L. Plummer, NOAA Fisheries, Seattle

Robert Rowthorn, Faculty of Economics, University of Cambridge

James N. Sanchirico, Resources for the Future, Washington, DC.

Jason F. Shogren, Department of Economics and Finance, University of Wyoming

Martin L. Weitzman, Department of Economics, Harvard University

James E. Wilen, Department of Agricultural and Resource Economics, University of California, Davis

Jinhua Zhao, Department of Economics, Iowa State University

Foreword

We thank the University of Washington Department of Economics for sponsoring 'Frontiers in Natural Resource and Environmental Economics', a conference in honor of Gardner M. Brown, Jr., that led to this book. In particular, we thank Richard Parks for his efforts in planning a wonderful event and helping to lay the foundation for this book; Neil Bruce, who supported and encouraged us to plan a conference worthy of Gardner's career; and Gary Waterman who helped to make the event, and in turn this book, a reality. Gardner Brown has contributed to his department, university, and profession in every way possible – as a leader, scholar, teacher, mentor, and friend. We know that we speak for his many colleagues, and the authors of these chapters, when we thank him for the opportunity to share his passion for environmental and natural resource economics.

Robert Halvorsen
David F. Layton

Introduction

GARDNER MALLARD BROWN, JR

Gardner Brown's career of more than 40 years spans fundamental changes in how human beings use and view the resources and services provided by the earth's natural systems. His first interest in the field began with a summer internship in the late 1950s at the then recently formed Resources for the Future with John Krutilla. Then, questions of fundamental resource scarcity were drivers of the nascent field. His work and interests today reflect how dramatically the world's problems have changed, focusing on problems such as global environmental change and antibiotic resistance. Of course Gardner has always been quick to note the important new directions in the field, while promoting a rare kind of rigorous economics that engages both economists and non-economists alike.

Gardner began his career as an academic economist with the completion of his dissertation in 1964 under Michael Brewer, Julius Margolis, and S.V. Ciriacy-Wantrup. When he took his first, and only, academic position in the Department of Economics at the University of Washington, the field of natural resource economics was new and just establishing its identity. When Gardner began publishing, and making his way on the tenure track, there was no Endangered Species Act, no Environmental Protection Agency. From the beginning, Gardner decided to let his deep environmental interests drive his selection of research problems. Just as importantly he committed himself to simultaneously making his economics rigorous. He was among the first natural resource economists to embrace the recently developed techniques in dynamic optimization. Even though no one has ever accused him of being a 'Chicagoan', Gardner recognized early the need to engage the fundamental importance of property rights while eschewing an attendant philosophy he found distasteful. He has always exhibited a rare combination of an absolute unwillingness to let the field dictate his choice of problems with an equal commitment to embracing the fundamental tools and ideas of economics. This is how Gardner published in the leading journals of the field such as *The American Economic Review*, *The Review of Economics and Statistics*, and the *Journal of Political Economy*, on topics such as the value of shoreline and ducks. This is how he has emerged as an economist's economist while engaging important scholars outside of the Economics profession.

Gardner has often been the first, or among the first, to tackle emerging environmental problems or apply new approaches. His work on the valuation of migratory waterfowl is one of the earliest uses of the contingent valuation method. His work on antibiotic resistance precedes that of any other economist. He was the first to seriously employ ecological predator–prey systems and metapopulation models in economics. His work thrives on learning from other disciplines. He then transforms his experiences into something new and important and shares it back. This is no doubt why he has been asked to serve on four different National Academy of Sciences panels (Outer-Continental Shelf, Fisheries, Endangered Species, Cumulative Environmental Effects of Oil and Gas Activities on Alaska's North Slope) and the National Science Board Task Force on Global Biodiversity. It is this range and depth of work that inspires the contributors to this volume.

EXPLORATIONS IN ENVIRONMENTAL AND NATURAL RESOURCE ECONOMICS

This volume contains three sections, each of which represents a major thrust of Gardner's research and policy interests. The first section covers the conservation of biological resources. Gardner's work in this area is seminal and widely respected in the Economics discipline, but its impact has been equally great in the areas of conservation biology and policy. Notably, Gardner's work has cross-fertilized both economics and conservation biology by introducing important ideas from both to each other. In the first chapter of this volume, Wilen and Sanchirico extend the bioeconomic metapopulation model first introduced by Gardner and discuss its implications for the recent and on-going policy debates regarding the formation of marine reserves. At about the same time as his introduction of the metapopulation model, Gardner also introduced models of the optimal use of antibiotics in the face of evolving bacterial resistance. In Chapter 2, Robert Rowthorn extends this important line of work by developing models of treatment for a susceptible–infected–susceptible disease under budget constraints. In Chapter 3, Parkhurst and Shogren use experimental approaches to examine how voluntary compensation incentives can be structured so as to yield spatially complex patterns of protected lands such as habitat corridors via decentralized compensation schemes. In Chapter 4, Lueck and Michael examine the incentives present in the Endangered Species Act and its implications for forest management by both private and public landowners.

The next section of this volume considers issues centered on questions of resource modeling, growth, and environmental quality. Gardner has always been fundamentally interested in models and the stories and agendas that underlie them. The first two chapters in this section ask whether the presumed stories that underlie two received empirical regularities should be accepted as known fact. Both find that the underlying stories are not nearly as strong as some would suggest and that getting the stories right may bear importantly on policy. In Chapter 5, Deacon and Norman consider whether the 'income growth drives pollution reduction' story of the environmental Kuznets curve holds up, or whether there are other forces at work besides income growth. In Chapter 6, Ronald Johnson considers whether the standard explanations for the 'curse of natural resources' have explanatory power in explaining the relationship between state-level economic growth and natural resources in the United States. The second half of this section engages what some might see as the essential Gardner Brown research style: developing novel dynamic optimization models of resource use. The two chapters here take the opportunity to highlight the seemingly fractured nature of the optimal resource use canon and show how the differences are more apparent than real. In Chapter 7, Martin Weitzman shows how one can unify the traditional Faustmann model of forest rotation and the workhorse fisheries models. In Chapter 8, Mark Plummer considers a related problem in unifying the traditional dynamic optimization models for the utilization of non-renewable resources and renewable resources. Simply put, Weitzman integrates the economics of fishing and forestry and Plummer integrates the economics of fishing and mining.

The final section of this volume relates to Gardner's abiding interest in non-market valuation. Gardner's work in this area began in the 1960s and continues today. In his research, Gardner has been at the forefront of applying techniques ranging from open-ended Contingent Valuation methods, to Stated Preference methods, to hedonic methods, in addition to developing the Hedonic Travel Cost model. This section, like Gardner's research, illustrates a range of approaches and his penchant for both theory and empirical application. In Chapter 9, Zhao and Kling develop a theory of welfare measurement for consumers facing dynamic decisions under uncertainty. In Chapter 10, Mohn and Hanemann extend and apply the Kuhn–Tucker model to valuing recreational fishing, a recent addition to the family of models available for revealed preference non-market valuation. In Chapter 11, Palmquist and Fulcher take a fresh look at one of Gardner's seminal applications, valuing shoreline as a residential amenity. In Chapter 12, Layton and Lee show how Stated Preference ratings data can be used for valuation within the framework and assumptions of the neoclassical Random Utility model.

We anticipate that the reader will find in these 12 chapters what we see in the more than 40 years of Gardner M. Brown, Jr's career: a willingness to engage important environmental and natural resource problems using the instrument of economics, and a commitment to developing economic models up to the task of addressing important environmental problems. Together these make a legacy of scholarship.

PART I

Conservation of biological resources

1. Bioeconomics of metapopulations: sinks, sources and optimal closures

James E. Wilen and James N. Sanchirico

1 INTRODUCTION

In his long and distinguished career, Gardner Brown has exhibited a level of creativity that few other resource economists can claim to approach. He has been the first to recognize and introduce a number of issues, concepts and important policy problems that have subsequently been folded into the mainstream. Among these one can highlight his work on calibrated and simulated bioeconomic modeling (Brown and Hammack, 1973), hedonic travel cost modeling (Brown and Mendelsohn, 1984), and antibiotic resistance (Laxminarayan and Brown, 2001; Brown and Layton, 1996). We choose to highlight and celebrate another first, namely his work that introduces metapopulation biology (Brown and Roughgarden) to the field of renewable resource economics.

Gardner's paper with J. Roughgarden in 1997, *Ecological Economics*, is entitled 'A metapopulation model with private property and a common pool'. Prior to this paper, virtually all treatments of fisheries population dynamics in economics used the simplified lumped parameter 'whole population' paradigm to depict a renewable resource. The whole population model has been well mined for interesting results, and it is the basis for important conclusions about renewable resource management that link the fundamental problem to capital theory, including the early work by Brown in 1974. At the same time, biologists have begun to incorporate a new understanding of the role of space and spatial processes into population dynamics. The most prominent version of these new models is the so-called 'metapopulation model', which represents whole populations as consisting of subpopulations linked by spatial processes. The Brown and Roughgarden paper utilizes a metapopulation depiction of a marine resource in order to explore the management implications of a biological system with explicit spatial structure.

In this chapter we discuss the metapopulation framework for depicting renewable resources, discuss recent scientific findings about spatial

3

processes, and then highlight some particular findings regarding source/
sink structures. We then present an alternative metapopulation system
that incorporates source/sink mechanisms and discuss its implications
for resource management. We focus particularly on conditions that
suggest spatial closure policies. This focus highlights the current interest
in marine reserves, but it places reserves in the context of economically
optimal policies for fisheries management rather than justifying reserves
by appealing to other non-fisheries benefits (Neubert, 2003; Sanchirico
et al., 2006).

2 METAPOPULATIONS AND SPATIAL PROCESSES

Over the past couple of decades, in particular, marine scientists have made
important breakthroughs in understanding how abundance is distributed
in the world's oceans. An important finding is that populations are not
homogenously distributed 'whole populations' but rather patchy subpopulations or metapopulations. Moreover, subpopulations appear to be linked
by spatial processes that operate on various time and spatial scales. At one
extreme are large-scale and slow processes such as the Pacific Decadal
Oscillation, which is believed to affect whole assemblages in the North
Pacific ocean ecosystem (Hare and Francis, 1995). During some periods
lasting a decade or two, temperature, wind, and sea surface conditions favor
certain species, and then conditions flip to favor other assemblages. This is
one reason for apparent long cycles in salmon and crab abundance off
Alaska (Hare *et al.*, 1999). These long cycles may also explain the evolu-
tionary strategy adopted by many rockfish populations off the lower
Pacific. Many rockfish species have successful recruitments only once or
twice per decade (Warner and Hughes, 1988), but they are slow-growing
and extremely long-lived, attributes that allow them to survive through
several macro-scale ecosystem condition shifts.

In addition to ecosystem-wide interdecadal forces, coastal ecosystems
are also affected by more familiar interannual forces such as El Niños and
La Niñas (Lenarz *et al.*, 1995). These affect smaller regions from year to
year in dramatic ways by influencing upwelling events that lie at the base of
the oceanic food web (Yoklavich *et al.*, 1996). Finally, oceans and populations are affected by local small-scale events such as wind, temperature, and
currents that also distribute nutrients up and down the coast in ways that
may depend upon circumstances lasting a few days or even hours. There is
some evidence that year class strength for some intertidal organisms (such
as urchins) depends upon favorable or unfavorable conditions that occur
over a window of only a few days (Wing *et al.*, 1998). Of critical importance

are wind and current conditions that either sweep larvae into suitable habitat or sweep them out to the open sea where they simply die without settling.

Interestingly, much of our increased understanding of these forces has emerged, not as directed scientific effort to understand metapopulations and the oceanographic forces that link them per se, but as indirect knowledge spinoffs from efforts to predict weather. For example, the large-scale buoy system distributed across the Pacific that was put in place in the early 1990s to predict El Niños has helped us understand much more about oceanographic circulation and its role in producing favorable and unfavorable upwelling conditions. Local weather prediction has relied on coastal radar systems, which have in turn been used to observe and measure sea surface and local circulation patterns. Some of our understanding of the patchy distribution of abundance has come from conventional fisheries-oriented trawl survey work, but other information has come from bathyspheric mapping and remote vehicle sensing whose original purpose was exploration for undersea minerals.

The key importance of this new observation-based paradigm shift is that it draws attention to the role of space in population dynamics, and the role of spatial/dynamic processes as forces governing linked spatial metapopulation systems. From a policy perspective, admitting the importance of space also opens up a host of new policy questions. For example, how should we manage a system of linked subpopulations? What are the possibilities for spatially designated policy instruments as opposed to whole fishery instruments? What information is needed to implement spatial management and are the gains worth the transactions costs? If spatial instruments may be used, what special enforcement and monitoring problems are raised and how can systems be designed to decentralize?

The Brown/Roughgarden (BR) paper (1997) represents the first attempt to examine the bioeconomic implications of the new metapopulation paradigm for fisheries. Their paper represents a significant departure from the mainstream of renewable resource economics, because it depicts a population not as a conventional whole population, but as a system of subpopulations linked by a spatial process. In the next section we discuss the innovations in the BR paper and summarize their conclusions.

3   THE BROWN/ROUGHGARDEN METAPOPULATION MODEL

The BR model depicts a benthic organism population (barnacles) that is characterized by spatially distinct and discrete patches of habitat. Adults inhabit the habitat and essentially fill up suitable space (Roughgarden and Iwasa, 1986). The adults in each patch are subject to natural and fishing mortality. In addition, larvae that settle into the patch replenish the adult population. The larvae are produced in proportion to the total adults in the entire metapopulation of linked patches. The larvae collect in a larval pool and then are distributed back to the patches or subjected to natural mortality. Settlement in each patch depends inversely upon the number of adults, depicting a situation where there is a limited amount of available space upon which larvae may settle.

Let $N_i(t)$ be the number of adults in patch i, the population dynamics of which are governed by

$$\dot{N_i}(t) = F_i(N_i, L) \equiv L(t)[A_i - a_i N_i(t)] - \mu_i N_i(t) - h_i(t) \quad i = 1, 2 \ldots m. \tag{1.1}$$

The first term in brackets is the total larval settlement into patch i, assumed dependent on total space not occupied by existing adults, and the last two terms are natural and fishing mortality rates, respectively. There are m patches in the metapopulation system, linked via their individual and joint dependence upon the larval pool. In each patch, settlement depends not only on the total number of larvae available in the larval pool, but also on the space available for settlement. The parameter A_i represents space available in patch i and the parameter a_i represents the rate of occupation by adults. The dynamics of the larval pool are governed by

$$\dot{L}(t) = \sum_{i=1}^{m} n_i N_i(t) - L \sum_{i=1}^{m} [A_i - a_i N_i(t)] - vL. \tag{1.2}$$

The first term is the total number of larvae produced, assumed proportional and additive to the total adults in the system, with patch-specific production coefficients n_i. The second term represents losses due to settlement into available space in the subpopulation patches and the last term is natural mortality of larvae.

The BR paper embeds the metapopulation description above into a simple bioeconomic model that allows harvesting of barnacles from each patch. The objective function is

$$J = \max \int_0^\infty \sum_{i=1}^{m} P_i h_i(t) e^{-\rho t} dt, \tag{1.3}$$

namely, maximize discounted harvesting revenues from all patches by choosing appropriate harvesting strategies for each patch. In this formulation there are no density-dependent harvesting costs, and the problem is formally a linear control problem subject to the $m + 1$ state equations in (1.2) and (1.3) above.

BR show that there is a steady state harvest equilibrium implied in a one patch system that is consistent with intuition. In particular, one can solve for the values of the adult and larval population in terms of biological parameters and the discount rate. As is common for models without density dependent costs, the equilibrium does not depend upon the price level in the one patch case. Instead, the equilibrium depends upon a tradeoff between the discount rate and the two own biological interest rates associated with the adult and larval net growth processes. The authors' more surprising conclusion is associated with the multiple patch system, for which they conclude that it is only optimal to harvest from one patch. This result, they suggest, is due to a non-convexity in the production system. In particular, they show that the marginal product of adults in total larval production is increasing, suggesting that a form of 'specialization and trade' among and between patches may be optimal.

4   METAPOPULATIONS AND DISPERSAL MECHANISMS

While a common pool larvae/adult system is a compelling description of benthic metapopulations such as barnacles, there are several other alternative hypotheses about spatial/dynamic mechanisms that are also plausible. Indeed, the accumulating evidence from oceanographic studies, population abundance surveys, and ecological theory hints at a range of possibilities. For example, some suggest that connectivity between patches in a metapopulation is due to adult movement. Adults may move from one patch to another, for example, as relative densities change and conditions become crowded. In other metapopulations, connectivity results from larval dispersal as in BR. But even with larval dispersal, patterns other than implied by the common pool assumption may exist. For example, some suggest that dominant coastal circulation direction (advection) during larval transport phases may be important. Other evidence points to coastal geography, with some evidence that promontories act to deflect dominant currents, causing eddies and gyres that retain larvae. Then, during relaxation events, larvae retained are redistributed back to coastal habitats. And there is disagreement among scientists about whether larvae are simply passively transported by oceanographic forces, or whether they act 'purposefully' to determine their ultimate settlement location, by moving up and down the water column, and so on.

Early metapopulation models by Levin (1960) and Pulliam (1988) begin with simple linear structures that admit a range of connectivity mechanisms. For example, consider the system depicted by

$$\dot{N}_i(t) = f_i[N_i(t)] + \sum_{j=1}^{m} b_{ij} N_j(t) - h_i(t) \quad i = 1, 2, \ldots m, \tag{1.4}$$

where the first term is the own growth for patch i, the second term is net dispersal into and out of patch i, and the last term is harvest in patch i. By appropriate choices of the dispersal parameters, one can depict a range of options. For example, a simple depiction a density dependent dispersal process would be

$$\sum_{j=1}^{m} b_{ij} N_j(t) \equiv b(N_1 - N_i) + b(N_2 - N_i) + \ldots + b(N_m - N_i)$$

$$i = 1, 2, \ldots m. \tag{1.5a}$$

In this system, net dispersal into and out of patch i would be the sum of pairwise dispersals from other patches. Patches in which the population densities are high relative to patch i would contribute adult migration whereas populations with lower adult density would absorb emigration from patch i. Since this is a system, we would have similar dispersal functions for the other patches. In addition, there are some 'adding up' conditions for the linked patches to account for the fact that adults arriving into patch i from patch j must also show up in the population dynamics equation for patch j as adults departing patch j for patch i.

The linear metapopulation model can also be used to depict other more structured dispersal systems that incorporate directional gradients associated with oceanographic forces. For example, consider a system with patches ordered from uppermost to lowermost in a geographically stratified system. Then we might have something like

$$\dot{N}_1(t) = f_1[N_1(t)] - b_1 N_1(t)$$
$$\dot{N}_2(t) = f_2[N_2(t)] + b_2 N_1(t)$$

$$\cdot$$
$$\cdot$$
$$\cdot$$

$$\dot{N}_{\dot{m}}(t) = f_m[N_m(t)] + b_m N_1(t). \tag{1.5b}$$

In this system, patch 1 acts as a source, feeding adults or larvae into the other patches below it in a manner that depends upon density in patch 1.

Again, an adding up restriction would be implied in that the sum of arrivals into sinks could not exceed the total of departures from the source. This configuration is capable of depicting a rich variety of sink/source systems, including multiple sources, linked and independent subsystems, gyres and eddies, and so on (Sanchirico and Wilen, 1999).

How would a system characterized by these additive spatial/dynamic processes be optimally managed? The bioeconomic objective can be written as

$$J = \max \int_0^\infty \sum_{i=1}^m \{P_i - [c_i/N_i(t)]\} h_i(t) e^{-\rho t} dt \qquad (1.6)$$

s.t. $\dot{N}_i(t) = f_i[N_i(t)] + \sum_{j=1}^m b_{ij} N_j(t) - h_i(t) \quad i = 1, 2, \ldots m.$

In this framework, net profits from each patch depend upon stock-dependent costs, with cost coefficients c_i as well as possibly patch-dependent prices P_i.

This general system is a linear control problem and hence we assume a control set with upper and lower bounds for the harvest rates. We also assume that parametric conditions on the control set and structure of the problem are such as to guarantee that a fully interior solution exists in which it is feasible to harvest from each patch if that is optimal. Then the procedure used to determine the optimal strategy is to solve for the conditions that hold at the fully interior singular steady state. At this equilibrium, the switching functions and their derivatives are zero and the Pontryagin conditions for the co-state and state equations hold (see Sanchirico and Wilen, 2005). While the details are tedious, the equations describing steady state biomass levels can be summarized as:

$$\phi_i(N_i) \equiv (\rho - F_i(N_i))(P_i - c_i/N_i) - (c_i/N_i)F_i(N_i) =$$

$$(c_i/N_i^2)\sum_{j=1}^{j=m} b_{ij} N_j + \sum_{j=1}^{j=m} (P_j - c_j/N_j) b_{ji} \quad i = 1, 2, \ldots m. \qquad (1.7)$$

The interpretation of these is as follows. First, the LHS of the equality is simply the condition that defines the optimal biomass associated with a single non-spatial patch. As Clark (1980) has shown, when this LHS is set equal to zero, a steady state is defined that just brings into balance the marginal liquidation gain that one might earn from a one unit reduction in the steady state biomass, with the sustained losses associated with that once and for all reduction in the steady state. In the spatial system, this is

modified by all of the terms on the RHS, the whole of which account for
the affects of the biomass change in patch i on system-wide profits reflected
through dispersal. There are two terms on the RHS. The first represents the
change in patch i costs associated with the net change in dispersal into
patch i that is induced by sum of all of the pairwise dispersal changes. The
second term sums up the impact of a marginal change in patch i biomass
on profits in all of the other linked patches, weighted by the marginal profit
of those physical changes.

Note that (1.7) is a system and hence impacts on patch i profits will also
appear in all of the other linked patches in the most general integrated
system. But in special cases (for example, a sink/source case in which
patches are linked in a unidirectional manner) the details and linkages that
appear on the RHS will depend upon the structure of dispersal. We illustrate this with the special case of a two-patch sink/source system next.

5   A TWO-PATCH SOURCE/SINK SYSTEM

Consider a two-patch version of the system in (1.5b) with patch 1 a source
and a downstream patch 2 the sink so that

$$\dot{N}_1(t) = r_1 N_1(t)[1 - N_1(t)/K_1] - bN_1(t) - h_1(t)$$

$$\dot{N}_2(t) = r_2 N_2(t)[1 - N_2(t)/K_2] + bN_1(t) - h_2(t). \tag{1.8}$$

This system is a special case of the more general system depicted above
in (1.6) and (1.7), with parametric assumptions for the dispersal system
$-b_{11} = b = b_{21}$ and $b_{12} = 0 = b_{22}$. Using these parametric assumptions
in (1.7), we have

$$\phi(N_1) = b(P_2 - P_1) - b(c_2/N_2)$$

$$\phi(N_2) = bc_2(N_1/N_2^2). \tag{1.9}$$

Of interest here is how the optimal biomass levels compare with the reference case where the two patches are independent and unconnected with
dispersal. In the case of independent patches, optimal equilibrium biomass
levels must satisfy $\phi(N_1) = 0 = \phi(N_2)$. Consider the situation first where
prices are the same in both patches so that the first LHS term in the equation for optimal source biomass drops out. Then, since $\phi(N_j)$ is upward
sloping for relevant levels of biomass, (1.9) suggests that the biomass will
be lower in the source and higher in the sink than in the situation without

connectivity. This seems counterintuitive at first blush, but it is actually capturing the pure effect that dispersal is having on biomass flows between patches. Because dispersal out of the source acts to reduce the effective net intrinsic growth rate in the source, it shifts the net-of-dispersal yield curve downward and to the left as in the upper-left panel of Figure 1.1. This alone results in a ceteris paribus lower optimal biomass in the source than would be the case without leakage. In the sink, dispersal acts to shift the yield curve upwards in an amount depending upon the magnitude of the flow as in the upper-right panel of Figure 1.1. This yield curve shift has a similar effect, but with a higher equilibrium biomass indicated. Thus the overall effect of unidirectional dispersal is to shift the equilibrium yield curves in ways that favor shifting harvesting from the source to the sink. The joint equilibrium involves a relatively low level of harvest and high biomass in the source, and relatively high level of harvest and biomass in the sink.

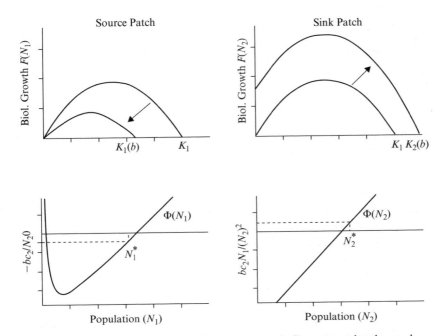

Note: The graph is derived analytically but drawn numerically to ensure that the panels are all on the same scale. The notation $K_1(b)$ denotes the endogenous carrying capacity in the patch given a positive dispersal rate. Note the $K_2(b)$ is drawn for the optimal level of dispersal when the source biomass is N_1^*.

Figure 1.1   Source/sink optimal population levels

The above 'flow effect' of source/sink dispersal seems intuitive on its own, but an additional question is: how do various parametric assumptions associated with economic conditions affect the optimal policies? We would expect, for example, that there are possibilities in which the 'economic gradient' (direction of net profitability) aligns with the 'biological gradient' (direction of dispersal flow), and other circumstances in which they are opposed. In particular, with a source/sink system, the dispersal always flows in a particular direction, from source to sink(s). But net profitability may be arrayed in that same spatial pattern, or it may line up in an opposite pattern, to take two polar extremes. What happens as it becomes relatively more (or less) profitable to harvest in the sink (or source)?

Consider differences in unit cost coefficients first. These might differ if different patches had different seabed conditions, or different prevailing currents or winds, or were different distances from port, and so on. Note first from (1.7) and (1.9) that the source cost coefficient c_1 appears only in the equation including $\phi(N_1)$ whereas the sink cost coefficient c_2 appears in the equation $\phi(N_2)$ and in both of the RHS parts of the equation (1.9) defining optimal biomass levels for the source/sink system. Understanding how higher costs in the source affect the system is straightforward. First, as c_1 gets larger, the $\phi(N_1)$ shifts, causing higher values for the equilibrium source biomass, ceteris paribus. But the optimal sink biomass is linked to the source biomass via the second equation in (1.9). In particular, as the source biomass goes up with the shift in $\phi(N_1)$, the sink biomass must also equilibrate at a higher biomass. So, as source costs rise, the biomass in both patches rises. The case with the cost coefficient c_2 is not easy to infer intuitively, and in fact comparative statics analysis suggests that the manner in which c_2 affects biomass levels is ambiguous.

How do ex-vessel price levels (and differences) matter? We note, first, that with the system of independent patches and density-dependent costs, raising the price reduces the equilibrium biomass, other things equal. The price level in the source patch enters the first equation in (1.9) only and in a manner that has a consistent sign, so that, as source patch prices rise, biomass in the source patch will fall unambiguously. This effect then feeds into the second equation in (1.9) in a direct manner, so that the effect of a source patch price rise on the sink biomass is to cause equilibrium biomass to fall. The impact of a price change in the sink is more complicated since the sink price appears in both $\phi(N_2)$ directly as well as indirectly in the source equation in (1.9). The fact that the sink price affects the whole system simultaneously makes the comparative statics implication of sink patch rises ambiguous on both equilibrium biomass levels.

6 OPTIMAL CLOSURES

Over the past decade or so, there has been a groundswell of support by marine ecologists and biologists for the use of permanent spatial closures to manage fisheries systems. Although there are now hundreds of articles on marine reserves, there are lingering controversies about what impacts they might have and whether they might be useful substitutes for conventional methods of fisheries management. The scientific consensus that seems to be developing is roughly as follows (National Academy of Sciences, 2001). First, closed areas are likely to be useful for producing what we might call 'posterity benefits' associated simply with protecting intact marine ecosystems. This is intuitive and based on similar reasoning for protecting our systems of terrestrial parks. Second, in some circumstances closed areas may also enhance fisheries by producing higher yields, but the circumstances are more circumscribed than researchers first believed. In particular, fisheries yield in whole metapopulations may increase with spatial closures when the reserve-designate has been dramatically over-harvested in the first place (Sanchirico and Wilen, 2001). In that case, there is both a small opportunity cost to closing a patch, and a high potential gain from spillovers into remaining open areas. In a real sense, of course, this result is more suggestive that an overharvested system would benefit from any effort reduction, rather than arguing the case for spatial closures per se.

Most of the literature on marine reserves utilizes biological rather than bioeconomic models, and hence the questions asked and the frameworks used to address them reflect biological perspectives. For example, the focus on whether reserves can produce *yield* increases as opposed to increases in fisheries' *economic returns* is a product of a modeling framework that ignores economics. This distinction is more than simply arguing that biological quantities ought to be expressed in dollars. For example, virtually all biological modeling of marine reserves ignores the fact that there will be a behavioral response to reserve creation as fishermen relocate to other patches. Most biological models either assume that displaced effort just goes away (thereby underestimating costs) or that it displaces proportionately or in some other ad hoc way.

The BR paper lays some important foundations for (largely subsequent) papers that addressed marine reserves but within a bioeconomic framework. First of all, they are among the first to cast a fisheries model within a metapopulation framework. This is important because one cannot address the economics of marine reserves without taking an explicitly spatial framework, and the metapopulation framework is arguably the obvious place to start. Second, they frame their problem by asking questions about how to make optimal choices to manage a spatial system. This pedagogical approach differs from prior biological modeling work, which, for the most part, simulates a limited number of options and then compares. Finally, they raise important questions about how spatial processes combine with economic processes and how outcomes are dictated by bioeconomic conditions instead of simply biological conditions.

While not necessarily intended to inform the debate on reserves at the time, the BR paper nevertheless reaches the intriguing conclusion that, in a metapopulation system, it may be optimal to close one or more patches to harvesting. This is intriguing because it suggests that marine reserves may logically emerge out of a problem formulation that asks the question: how do we optimally manage a spatially explicit metapopulation? The result that closures may sometime be optimal in a very general fisheries optimization setting is more appealing than the typical approach in the literature, which asks: under what circumstances can we improve on a status quo by closing an area?

The BR conclusion is actually more provocative and perhaps even more appealing to supporters of marine reserves in that it argues that closing all but one patch is optimal. They attribute this result to a feature of their metapopulation structure, namely the fact that there is a non-convexity in the larval production function. But there are other reasons why closures might be optimal, even in a system that is well behaved and concave. A most basic circumstance is when a parametric corner solution is indicated. For example, consider the simple one-patch model with density-dependent costs. We know that the optimal steady-state biomass is an increasing function of the cost/price ratio, depicted in our system as a rightward shift of the $\phi(N_i)$function. But as the cost/price ratio increases, it reaches a critical level at which the implied optimal biomass is the carrying capacity biomass. This is an example of a parametric corner solution, where cost/price ratios dictate a complete closure (or, alternatively, that the fishery is not feasible to begin harvesting).

In a linked system, such as our sink/source system, it seems intuitive that we might find a similar result. Of particular interest is the question: when is it optimal to close the source patch and leave only the sink open to exploitation? In a real sense, this is a bioeconomic condition that ecologists are searching for when they advocate marine reserves as fisheries management tools. A translation of their quest to show that closed areas actually may enhance a fishery is the question: when is a source closure optimal in the sense of yielding the highest present value rents from a linked system?

We can answer that question graphically in the context of our sink/source example in Figure 1.2. Note that we are looking for conditions that dictate that the optimal biomass in the source is equal to $\hat{N}_1 = K_1[1 - (b/r_1)]$, the biomass at which potential yield from the source is zero. First, consider a

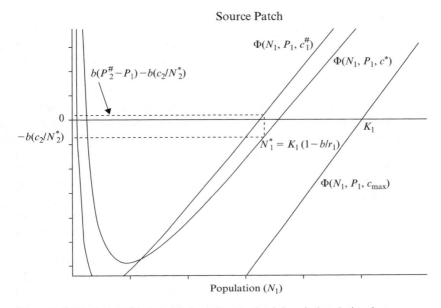

Source Patch

$$\Phi(N_1, P_1, c_1^{\#})$$

$$\Phi(N_1, P_1, c^*)$$

$$b(P_2^{\#} - P_1) - b(c_2/N_2^*)$$

$$-b(c_2/N_2^*)$$

$$K_1$$

$$N_1^* = K_1(1 - b/r_1)$$

$$\Phi(N_1, P_1, c_{max})$$

Population (N_1)

Note: $P_2^{\#} > P_1$ where $P_2^{\#}$ is the critical cost level in the sink such that closing the source patch to fishing is optimal. c_{max} is the cost level with no dispersal such that the optimal catch in the source is equal to zero. $c^* < c_{max}$ and is the critical cost level with dispersal such that a closing the source patch is optimal. $c^{\#} < c^*$.

Figure 1.2   Optimal closure of the source patch

cost c_{max} such that, at that cost, the optimal biomass is at the single patch carrying capacity biomass K_1. This is depicted in Figure 1.2 by the function $\phi(N_1, P_1, c_{max})$ intersecting the axis at K_1. But the actual optimal biomass in the sink/source case is one depicted by a level for which $\phi(N_1, P_1, c_1) = b(P_2 - P_1) - b(c_2/N_2)$. Suppose, first, that prices in the two patches are equal so that the RHS is negative. Then, graphically, optimal biomass occurs at a level for which the $\phi(N_1, P_1, c_1^*)$ function is negative and equal to $-b(c_2/N_2)$ at the indicated optimal value. But, from Figure 1.2, this must be on a $\phi(N_1, P_1, c_1^*)$ function that is shifted to the left of the $\phi(N_1, P_1, c_{max})$ function. This points to an interesting conclusion, namely, that, with dispersal, one would choose optimally to close a source at lower costs than without dispersal. This amplifies the obvious point that dispersal makes the shadow value of biomass in the source higher because of its role as a feeder population to the sink, justifying closure at lower cost levels.

Similar conclusions emerge out of investigating how other parameters affect decisions to close the source patch optimally. One would expect, for example, that, as prices in the sink patch are larger than prices in the source patch, it becomes increasingly desirable to close the source. This is indeed the case as illustrated by Figure 1.2. Suppose, first, that prices in each patch are equal. Then we have the case just discussed, for which it is optimal to close the source at a price less than c_{max}. Now, assume that ex-vessel prices in the sink are higher than in the source, so that $P_2^\# > P_1$, and by an amount large enough to make the RHS of the source equilibrium condition in (1.9) positive. Then there is a critical cost coefficient $c_1^\#$ such that $\phi(N_1, P_1^\#, c_1^\#)$ intersects that positive RHS value in equation (1.9) exactly at the carrying capacity for the source. This intersection and equilibrium occurs at a cost coefficient $c_1^\#$ which is even smaller than that for the case with equal prices discussed above. Thus the conclusion is that, the higher are the prices in the sink, the lower is the corresponding critical cost coefficient that supports closing the source patch. Again, this amplifies common sense since a higher sink price increases the shadow value of dispersal out of the source and into the sink.

In summary, Brown/Roughgarden suggest that it may be optimal to refrain from harvesting all patches in a metapopulation or, in other words, to leave a large part of a population as a reserve. Their analysis is carried out under the assumption of a common larval pool, with increasing returns to larval production. As we show here, these conclusions that lead to spatial closures as optimal polices do not necessarily require non-convexities in the production function of the system. Instead, closures may be optimal as corner solutions when there is heterogeneity in bioeconomic parameters. Intuitively, high costs and/or low prices tend toward corner solution outcomes. More interestingly, the effect of dispersal is to widen the range of parameters for which corner solution closures are optimal (Sanchirico *et al.*, 2006). With dispersal, cutoff costs at which it is optimal to close a source are lower than without dispersal. Similarly, there is a minimum price that just makes fishing a source feasible; that minimum is higher with dispersal than without. Correspondingly, dispersal may make the minimum price that leaves it feasible to fish a sink lower than would otherwise be without dispersal. Higher sink prices may also outweigh higher source prices as determinants of optimal source closures.

7 SUMMARY AND CONCLUSIONS

One of the more appealing aspects of natural resource economics is that it gives economists the opportunity to explore how other companion disciplines understand biophysical natural resource processes. Renewable resource economists have extracted a number of important conclusions from simple models of biological growth over the past 50 years, beginning with important early work by Scott Gordon and Anthony Scott. But the field of biology has moved forward, and new views of biological processes are increasingly spatial. The Brown/Roughgarden paper is thus a welcome introduction to metapopulation dynamics and the implications for managing renewable resources whose dynamics are governed by spatial as well as dynamic processes.

In this chapter we revisit the main theme introduced by Brown/ Roughgarden, namely, how should we manage a spatially linked metapopulation in order to maximize system-wide rents? In contrast to Brown/ Roughgarden, who focus on a common pool larval dispersal process, we focus on a process with advective character, or dispersal dependent upon dominant oceanographic forces. In our simple structure, this implies a source subpopulation that is assumed located up-current of a sink subpopulation. The first question we address is how the standard single-patch fisheries' optimality conditions are modified with sink/source dispersal. The answer is intuitive; single-patch conditions are modified by accounting for the role that spillover (via dispersal) plays in generating net benefits in the sink, and net costs in the source. Ceteris paribus, optimal management of a sink/source system calls for relatively more biomass in the sink and less in the source, capitalizing on the natural direction of the flow of dispersal. Changing economic parameters modifies this basic tendency, in a manner that depends upon whether biological and economic gradients align or not. For example, raising the source cost or reducing the source price increases the shadow value of dispersal, giving rise to economic forces that amplify the basic biological forces to send dispersal from the source to the sink. Raising sink costs or reducing sink prices is ambiguous, reflecting that fact that the overall impact depends upon opposing forces, namely biological forces sending dispersal from the source to the sink, countered by economic forces that actually make it desirable (if not feasible) to send dispersal away from the lower profit sink patch.

This chapter also revisits another Brown/Roughgarden result, namely the potential optimality of a full closure in one or more patches. Brown/Roughgarden reach the conclusion that it may be optimal to close multiple patches when there are non-convexities in the larval production function. We introduce another possibility, namely that closures may be optimal as 'corner solutions' where costs are too high or prices too low to justify harvesting in the source patch. As we demonstrate, there are critical values for costs and prices that dictate optimal closures of the source. With dispersal, it is optimal to close the source at a cost that is lower (or price that is higher) than would otherwise be the case if the patches were unconnected by dispersal. Again, this indicates that optimality in a metapopulation depends upon bioeconomic factors, including the dispersal rate and direction of flow. The more significant a source is in feeding larvae to a sink, the higher the shadow value of dispersal, and the wider the range of parameters that will justify full closure of the source.

These results and the results from the original Brown/Roughgarden paper just begin to scratch the surface about how to optimally manage spatially connected metapopulation systems. This is more than an interesting academic exercise because scientists are rapidly accumulating broader and deeper understanding about marine spatial/dynamic processes. At the same time, there have been innovations in tracking and monitoring technology that allow fishing vessels to be monitored continuously over time and space. Thus it will not be too far in the distant future that managers will be able to manage at finer levels of spatial and temporal resolution that take advantage of our new understanding of metapopulation dynamics.

REFERENCES

Brown, Gardner (1974), 'An optimal program for managing common property resources with congestion externalities', *Journal of Political Economy*, **82** (1), 163–73.

Brown, Gardner and Judd Hammack (1973), 'Dynamic economic management of migratory waterfowl', *Review of Economics and Statistics*, **55** (1), 73–82.

Brown, Gardner and David Layton (1996), 'Resistance economics: social cost and the evolution of antibiotic resistance', *Environment and Development Economics*, **1** (3), 349–55.

Brown, Gardner and Robert Mendelsohn (1984), 'The hedonic travel cost method', *Review of Economics and Statistics*, **66** (1), 427–33.

Brown, Gardner and Jonathon Roughgarden (1997), 'A metapopulation model with private property and a common pool', *Ecological Economics*, **22** (1), 65–71.

Clark, Colin W. (1990), *Mathematical Bioeconomics: The Optimal Management of Renewable Resources*, 2nd edn, Wiley: New York.

Hare, S.R. and R.C. Francis (1995), 'Climate change and salmon production in the Northeast Pacific Ocean', *Can. Spec. Pub. Fish. Aquatic Science*, 121.

Hare, S.R., N.J. Mantua and R.C. Francis (1999), 'Inverse production regimes: Alaskan and West Coast salmon', *Fisheries*, **24** (1), 6–14.

Laxminarayan, Ramanan and Gardner Brown (2001), 'Economics of antibiotic resistance: a theory of optimal use', *Journal of Environmental Economics and Management*, **42** (2), 183–206.

Lenarz, W.H., D. VanTresca, W.M. Graham, F.B. Schwing and F.P. Chavez (1995), 'Explorations of El Niño and associated biological population dynamics off central California', *California Cooperative Oceanic Fisheries Investigations Reports*, **36**, 106–19.

Levin, S.A. (1960), 'Dispersion and population interactions', *American Naturalist*, **108**, 207–27.

Levin, S.A. (1976), 'Population dynamic models in heterogeneous environments', *Annual Review Ecolog. Systems*, **7**, 287–310.

National Academy of Sciences, National Research Council (2001), *Marine Protected Areas: Tools for Sustaining Marine Ecosystems*, Washington, DC: National Academy Press.

Neubert, M.G. (2003), 'Marine reserves and optimal harvesting', *Ecology Letters*, **6** (9), 843–9.

Pulliam, H.R. (1988), 'Sources, sinks and population regulation', *American Naturalist*, **132**, 652–61.

Roughgarden, J. and Y. Iwasa. (1986), 'Dynamics of a metapopulation with space-limited subpopulations', *Theoretical Population Biology*, **29**, 235–61.

Sanchirico, J.N. and J. Wilen (1999), 'Bioeconomics of spatial exploitation in a patchy environment', *Journal of Environmental Economics and Management*, **37**, 129–50.

Sanchirico, J.N. and J. Wilen (2001), 'A bioeconomic model of marine reserve creation', *Journal of Environmental Economics and Management*, **42**, 257–76.

Sanchirico, J.N. and J. Wilen (2005), 'Optimal management of renewable resources: matching policy scope to ecosystem scale', *Journal of Environmental Economics and Management*, **50** (1), 23–46.

Sanchirico, J.N., U. Malvadkar, A. Hastings and J. Wilen (2006), 'When are no-take zones an economically optimal strategy?', *Ecological Applications* (in press).

Warner, R.R. and T.P. Hughes (1988), 'The population dynamics of reef fishes', *Proceedings of the 6th International Coral Reef Symposium*, **1**, 149–55.

Wing, S.R., L.W. Botsford, S.V. Ralston and J.L. Largier (1998), 'Meroplanktonic distribution and circulation in a coastal retention zone of the northern California upwelling system', *Limnology and Oceanography*, **43**, 1710–21.

Yoklavich, M.M., V.J. Loeb, M. Nishimoto and B. Daly (1996), 'Nearshore assemblages of larval rockfishes and their physical environment off central California during an extended El Niño event, 1991–1993', *Fishery Bulletin*, **94**, 766–82.

2. The optimal treatment of disease under a budget constraint

Robert Rowthorn

This chapter is concerned with the optimum treatment profile for an SIS disease. With this type of disease every individual who is not currently infected is susceptible to future infection. Thus an individual who catches an infection and is later cured goes through the cycle: susceptible–infected–susceptible. We assume that there is one population, one type of infection and one form of treatment. The problem is to determine what fraction of infected persons should receive treatment at each moment of time. Such a problem has already been analysed in an interesting article by Lightwood and Goldman (2002). These authors find the optimal treament path under the assumption that the medical authorities operate without an explicit budget constraint. The sole objective of the authorities is to maximize the discounted sum of social benefits minus costs. The aim of this chapter is to extend the work of Lightwood and Goldman by analysing the effect of an explicit budget constraint on optimal behaviour.

This is a realistic extension since in practice the medical authorities will normally be subject to some form of budget constraint. This chapter also draws on Laxminarayan and Rowthorn (2002). Two types of constraint are considered. In the first case, the medical authorities receive an initial endowment which they can spend or invest as they like. In the second case, there is a fixed ceiling on the rate of expenditure on treatment, and money that is not spent at one time cannot be used to supplement expenditure at another time. This reduces the degree of intemporal flexibility as compared to the first case. One striking feature of the analysis is that optimal paths involve extreme choices. At any moment, either no-one at all should be treated or else treatment should be at the maximum level that is allowed. In the unconstrained problem, there is at most one regime switch on an optimal path. This accords with the findings of Lightwood and Goldman. In the constrained problem, there may be up to two switches.

The structure of the chapter is as follows. The first section considers optimization in the absence of an explicit budget constraint. The subsequent sections extend this analysis by introducing different kinds of budget constraint. The chapter concludes with a numerical example which compares constrained and unconstrained solutions and highlights their key features.

1 NO BUDGET CONSTRAINT

The problem is to choose a trajectory for the control variable f so as to maximize the following discounted integral:

$$V = \int_0^\infty e^{-\delta t}[p(N-I) - cfI]dt, \qquad (2.1)$$

where N is total population, I is the number of people who are infected, p is the social value attached to good health, c is the cost of treatment and $f \in [0,1]$ is the proportion of infected people who are currently receiving treatment.

The dynamics of infection are given by the following SIS-style equation

$$\dot{I} = [\beta(N-I) - \tau - \alpha f]I, \qquad (2.2)$$

where β indicates the infectivity of the disease, τ is the rate of spontaneous recovery in the absence of treatment and α indicates the speed at which treatment induces recovery. The initial level of infection $I_0 \in (0, N)$ is exogenously given.

The current value Hamiltonian for the above problem is

$$\tilde{H} = p(N-I) - cfI + m[\beta(N-I) - \tau - \alpha f]I, \qquad (2.3)$$

where m is the shadow price of infection. The first order conditions for a maximum are

$$f \begin{Bmatrix} = 0 \\ \in [0,1] \\ = 1 \end{Bmatrix} \text{ as } m \begin{Bmatrix} > \\ = \\ < \end{Bmatrix} - \frac{c}{\alpha}, \qquad (2.4)$$

$$\dot{m} = \delta m - \frac{\partial \tilde{H}}{\partial I}$$
$$= \delta m + p + (c + \alpha m)f - m(\beta N - \tau) + 2m\beta I. \qquad (2.5)$$

Interior Segment

Consider a path which satisfies the above first order conditions. Suppose that $f \in (0,1)$ over an open segment of this path. Within this segment it must be the case that $c + \alpha m = 0$ and hence

$$m = -\frac{c}{\alpha}. \tag{2.6}$$

Differentiating, it follows that

$$\dot{m} = 0. \tag{2.7}$$

Hence, from (2.5)

$$\delta m + p + (c + \alpha m)f - m(\beta N - \tau) + 2m\beta I = 0. \tag{2.8}$$

Eliminating m we obtain

$$\delta(-c/\alpha) + p - (-c/\alpha)(\beta N - \tau) + (-c/\alpha)2\beta I = 0, \tag{2.9}$$

which yields the stationary solution

$$I^* = \frac{\alpha p + c(\beta N - \delta - \tau)}{2c\beta}. \tag{2.10}$$

At a stationary point $\dot{I} = 0$. Hence from (2.2) and the above equation it follows that $f = f^*$ where

$$f^* = \frac{c(\beta N - \tau + \delta) - \alpha p}{2c\alpha}. \tag{2.11}$$

The shadow price is given by

$$m^* = -\frac{c}{\alpha}. \tag{2.12}$$

Thus, if there is an open segment over which $f \in (0,1)$, then within this segment $f = f^*$, $I = I^*$ and $m = m^*$. Note that the value of f^* given by equation (2.4) may lie outside the interval $[0,1]$ and may therefore be infeasible. In this case, there is no open segment along which $f \in (0,1)$.

Boundary Solutions

Boundary solutions occur when f takes the extreme value 0 or 1. Let us consider these cases individually.

If $m > m^* = -\frac{c}{\alpha}$ then $f = 0$ and

$$\dot{I} = [\beta(N - I) - \tau]I, \tag{2.13}$$

$$\dot{m} = p + m[2\beta I + \delta + \tau - \beta N]. \tag{2.14}$$

The curve $\dot{I} = 0$ is then given by

$$I = N - \tau/\beta \tag{2.15}$$

and $\dot{m} = 0$ is given by

$$m = \frac{-p}{2\beta I + \delta + \tau - \beta N}. \tag{2.16}$$

The above equations yield the unique fixed point $P^H = (I^H, m^H)$ where

$$I^H = N - \tau/\beta, \tag{2.17}$$

$$m^H = \frac{-p}{\beta N + \delta - \tau}. \tag{2.18}$$

If $m < m^* = -\frac{c}{\alpha}$ then $f = 1$ and

$$\dot{I} = [\beta(N - 1) - \tau - \alpha]I, \tag{2.19}$$

$$\dot{m} = p + c + m[2\beta I + \delta + \tau + \alpha - \beta N]. \tag{2.20}$$

The curve $\dot{I} = 0$ is given by

$$I = N - (\tau + \alpha)/\beta, \tag{2.21}$$

and $\dot{m} = 0$ is given by

$$m = \frac{-(p + c)}{2\beta I + \delta + \tau + \alpha - \beta N}. \tag{2.22}$$

The above equations yield the unique fixed point $P^L = (I^L, m^L)$ where

$$I^L = N - (\tau + \alpha)/\beta, \tag{2.23}$$

$$m^L = \frac{-(p + c)}{\beta N + \delta - \tau - \alpha}. \tag{2.24}$$

Note that the point $P^* = (I^*, m^*)$ lies on the intersection of the curves for $\dot{m} = 0$ as given by equations (2.16) and (2.22).

Phase Diagram

Figure 2.1 shows the phase diagram in (I, m) space. For $m > m^*$ it is always the case that $f = 0$ and behaviour is therefore determined by equations (2.13) and (2.14). For $m < m^*$ it is always the case that $f = 1$ and behavior is determined by equations (2.19) and (2.20). Perturbing these equations, we obtain the directions of movement shown in the diagram.

To find the optimum solution we begin by noting that this is an infinite horizon autonomous problem. Apart from the discount factor under the integral, the time variable does not enter explicitly into any of the functions, equations or constraints. In such a problem the current shadow price is a single-valued function $m(I)$ of the state variable.[1] This implies that no optimum path can zig-zag back on itself so as to achieve two distinct values of m for the same value of I. Thus an optimal path f can never switch from 0 to 1 or vice versa at any point that lies between I^L and I^H. However, it is permissible for such a switch to occur outside of this range. It is clear from Figure 2.1 that at most one switch can occur on an optimal path. Finally, the point $P = (I^*, m^*)$ cannot be reached by a path which does not zig-zag back on itself and hence it cannot be optimal either to remain at this point or converge to it.

The above analysis severely limits the number of candidates for an optimal path. Potential solutions can be classified into four basic types. In the first type $f = 0$ always. In the second type there exists a switch point I^s which is less that I^L and is such that $f = 1$ for $I < I^s$ and $f = 0$ for $I > I^s$. Paths of these types converge to the point $P^H = (I^H, m^H)$ where no-one is

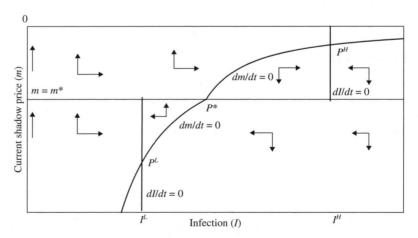

Figure 2.1   Phase diagram: unconstrained case

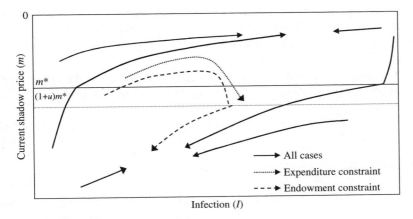

Figure 2.2   Potential optimal paths

treated. In the third type there exists a switch point $I^s > I^H$ such that $f = 0$ for $I > I^s$ and $f = 0$ for $I < I^s$. Finally, there is a fourth type in which $f = 1$ always. In solutions of the third and fourth types every path must eventually converge to the point $P^L = (I^L, m^L)$ where all infected persons receive treatment. The general form of these candidate solutions is indicated by the solid curves in Figure 2.2. Given the parameter values of the problem, it is a simple matter to determine by means of numerical computation what, if any, is the best switch point for each type of solution. Having done so, the optimal solution is then found by choosing the type that yields the highest value of V.

2   BUDGET CONSTRAINT

Two types of budget constraint will be considered. In the first case, the medical authorities receive an initial endowment which they can spend as they like. In the second case, there is a fixed ceiling on the rate of expenditure on treatment, and money that is not spent at one time cannot be used to supplement expenditure at another time. This reduces the degree of intemporal flexibility as compared to the first case.

2.1   Initial Endowment

Suppose the medical authority is given an initial endowment K_0 which it invests at a constant interest rate δ. All future expenditures are financed by drawing upon the accumulated funds in the endowment. Thus expenditure must satisfy the intertemporal budget constraint $K_0 \geq \int_0^\infty e^{-\delta t} cfI dt$. This constraint can be expressed in the alternative form $\int_0^\infty e^{-\delta t}[\delta K_0 - cfI] dt \geq 0$.

The problem is to maximize the integral (1) subject to the above constraint. This is equivalent to maximizing the following integral:

$$\int_0^\infty e^{-\delta t}[p(N-I) - cfI] dt + u \int_0^\infty e^{-\delta t}[\delta K_0 - cfI] dt, \qquad (2.25)$$

subject to the complementary slack conditions

$$u \geq 0, \int_0^\infty e^{-\delta t}[\delta K - cfI] \geq 0, u \int_0^\infty e^{-\delta t}[\delta K_0 - cfI] = 0. \qquad (2.26)$$

As before the state equation is

$$\dot{I} = [\beta(N-I) - \tau - \alpha f]I \qquad (2.27)$$

and the initial condition is $I(0) = I_0 \in (0, N)$.

The Hamiltonian for this problem is

$$\tilde{H} = p(N-I) - cfI + m[\beta(N-I) - \tau - \alpha f]I + u(\delta K_0 - cfI), \qquad (2.28)$$

where u is a constant whose value is not yet known. The first order conditions for an optimum are as follows:

$$f \begin{Bmatrix} = 0 \\ \in [0, 1] \\ = 1 \end{Bmatrix} \text{ as } m \begin{Bmatrix} > \\ = \\ < \end{Bmatrix} - \frac{(1+u)c}{\alpha} = (1+u)m^* \qquad (2.29)$$

$$\dot{m} = \delta m - \frac{\partial \tilde{H}}{\partial I}$$
$$= \delta m + p + [(1+u)c + \alpha m]f - m(\beta N - \tau) + 2m\beta I. \qquad (2.30)$$

These equations are similar to those derived in the unconstrained case.

Phase diagram

The phase diagram is similar to that for the unconstrained case. The only difference is that c is replaced by $(1+u)c$ and hence m^* is replaced by $(1+u)m^*$. To find the optimum solution we begin by noting that this is not an autonomous problem since the constraints may vary over the course of time as the endowment accumulates or runs down.[2] Thus, on the optimum path, the current shadow price may not be a single-valued function $m(I)$ of the state variable. This path may therefore zig-zag back on itself in (I, m) space. Thus f can switch from 0 to 1 within the range (I^L, I^H), which is forbidden in the unconstrained case. Such a switch can only occur when $m = (1 + u)m^*$. The resulting path is illustrated by the dashed line in Figure 2.2. The optimum path may also be similar in character to one of the paths obtained in the unconstrained case. Such paths contain at most one switch point.

2.2 Expenditure Limit

Suppose there is a fixed ceiling M on the rate of expenditure on treatment. Money that is not spent now cannot be accumulated to supplement expenditure in the future. This implies that $M > cfI$. To allow for this constraint we modify the Hamiltonian so as to form the Lagrangean,

$$L = p(N - I) - cfI + m[\beta(N - I) - \tau - \alpha f]I + w(M - cfI), \quad (2.31)$$

which is to be maximized subject to the complementary slack condition

$$w \geq 0, \ (M - cfI) \geq 0, \ w(M - cfI) = 0, \quad (2.32)$$

where w is a function of time. As always the state equation is

$$\dot{I} = [\beta(N - I) - \tau - \alpha f]I. \quad (2.33)$$

The costate equation is

$$\dot{m} = \delta m - \frac{\partial L}{\partial I}$$
$$= \delta m + p + ((1 + w)c + \alpha m)f - m(\beta N - \tau) + 2m\beta I \quad (2.34)$$

and the control variable f satisfies the following conditions:

$$f \begin{cases} = 0 \\ \epsilon [0, \frac{M}{cI}] \\ = \min(1, \frac{M}{cI}) \end{cases} \text{ as } m \begin{cases} > \\ = \\ < \end{cases} - \frac{(1 + w)c}{\alpha} = (1 + w)m^*. \quad (2.35)$$

Suppose that the above condition is satisfied. If $m > (1 + w)m^*$ then $f = 0$. Under these conditions $M - cfI > 0$ and hence $w = 0$. Thus $m > m^*$. Conversely, if $m > m^*$ then $m > (1 + w)m^*$ and hence $f = 0$. If $f = \min(1, \frac{M}{cI})$

then $m \le (1+w)m^*$ and hence $m < m^*$. Conversely, suppose that $m < m^*$. If $w = 0$ then $m < -(1+w)m^*$ and hence $f = \min(1, \frac{M}{ci})$. If $w > 0$ then it is also the case that $f = \min(1, \frac{M}{ci})$. Thus, condition (2.35) can be written as follows

$$f \begin{Bmatrix} = 0 \\ \in [0, \frac{M}{ci}] \\ = \min(1, \frac{M}{ci}) \end{Bmatrix} \text{ as } m \begin{Bmatrix} > \\ = \\ < \end{Bmatrix} - \frac{c}{\alpha} = m^* \tag{2.36}$$

Interior segment

Consider a path that satisfies the above first order conditions. Suppose that $f \in (0, \frac{M}{ci})$ over an open segment of this path. From the complementary slack conditions it follows that $w = 0$ within this segment and hence

$$m = m^* = -\frac{c}{\alpha}. \tag{2.37}$$

Differentiating, within the open segment it follows that

$$\dot{m} = 0. \tag{2.38}$$

Since $w = 0$ equation (2.34) can be written

$$\dot{m} = \delta m + p + (c + \alpha m)f - m(\beta N - \tau) + 2m\beta I, \tag{2.39}$$

which is the same as in the unconstrained case. As before, combining these equations with (2.2) yields $f = f^*$. The interior segment once again consists of the single point $P^* = (I^*, m^*)$. And as before there is no optimal path that leads to this point nor is it optimal to remain at this point.

Boundary solutions

Boundary solutions occur when f takes the extreme value 0 or $\min(1, \frac{M}{ci})$. Let us consider these two cases.

If $m > m^* = -c/\alpha$ then $f = 0$ and the analysis is the same as in the unconstrained case. In particular, the curve $\dot{m} = 0$ is given by equation (2.14). However, if $m < m^*$ then $f = \min(1, \frac{M}{ci})$ and

$$\dot{I} = [\beta(N - I) - \tau]I - \alpha \min(I, \frac{M}{c}). \tag{2.40}$$

The nature of the fixed points of this differential equation depends on the parameters of the model. Suppose that $(N - \tau/\beta)^2 > \frac{4\alpha M}{\beta c}$ and $\frac{M}{c} > I^L = N - \frac{\tau}{\beta} - \frac{\alpha}{\beta}$. In this case there are three fixed points I^L, I^{ML} and I^{MH}, where

$$I^{ML} = \frac{N - \tau/\beta - \sqrt{(N - \tau/\beta^2)} - \frac{4\alpha M}{\beta c}}{2},$$ (2.41)

$$I^{MH} = \frac{N - \tau/\beta + \sqrt{(N - \tau/\beta^2)} - \frac{4\alpha M}{\beta c}}{2}.$$ (2.42)

It is easily shown that $I^L < I^{ML} < I^{MH}$. The middle of these points is unstable and the other two are stable. Note that $I^{MH} < I^H$.

Phase diagram

For $m > m^*$ the phase diagram in (I, m) space is the same as in the unconstrained case. To complete the phase diagram for $m < m^*$ would require a knowledge of w that is not available. However, it is possible to construct a partial phase diagram which contains sufficient information to restrict the range of potential optimal paths to a workable set. The nature of this set depends on the parameter values of the model and on the amount of money available in the budget. As an illustration, suppose that $I^L < I^{ML} < I^* < I^{MH}$. Under these conditions the partial phase diagram has the form shown in Figure 2.3. As in the unconstrained case, this is an infinite horizon, autonomous problem, so the optimal path cannot zig-zag back on itself, since this would yield multiple values for $m(I)$. For $I \in [I^L, I^{ML}]$ and $I \in [I^{MH}, I^H]$ the optimal path cannot cross over the line $m = m^*$ since that would imply a backward zig-zag in the path, which is forbidden. However, the figure is consistent with a limited number of cross-overs elsewhere. For example, the optimum path may cross in a downward direction in the range

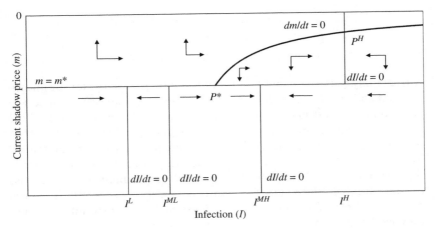

Figure 2.3   Partial phase diagram: constrained case

$[I^L, I^{MH}]$. From the figure one can see that there can be at most one upward and one downward cross-over on an optimum path. An upward cross-over may be followed by a downward cross-over, but the reverse order is not allowed. The general character of the permissible candidates for the optimal path is illustrated in Figure 2.2. The dashed line indicates a type of candidate solution that is unique to the case of an expenditure constraint. Paths of the type indicated by the solid curves in this diagram are also permitted. As before, an upward cross-over indicates a switch from maximum to zero treatment, whereas a downward cross-over indicates a switch from zero to maximum treatment. Note that Figure 2.3 has been derived on the assumption that $I^L < I^{ML} < I^* < I^{MH}$. However, similar diagrams can be obtained using other parameter combinations. In each case, candidates for the optimum path involve at most two switches of regime. Moreover, in the case of two switches, this must take the form of maximum treatment followed by no treatment followed by maxium treatment once again.

3   A SIMPLE PROCEDURE

It is often difficult to know in advance whether or nor a particular endowment or expenditure constraint will turn out to be binding. Moreover, the behaviour of w will not generally be known until after the optimum solution has as been found. These difficulties can be avoided by reformulating the problem as follows. From the preceding discussion, we know that the optimum path is always of the following form:

$$\text{for } t \in (0, t_1): f = \text{maximum allowed,}$$
$$\text{for } t \in (t_1, t_2): f = 0,$$
$$\text{for } t \in (t_2, \infty): f = \text{maximum allowed,}$$

where it may be the case that $t_1 = 0$ and/or $t_2 = \infty$. This is true for the unconstrained and constrained problems. Using standard methods of numerical approximation and knowledge of the parameter values, we can find the values of t_1 and t_2 that maximize the integral $\int_0^\infty e^{-\delta t}[p(N - I) - cfI]dt$ subject to the relevant constraint. It is not possible to evaluate an integral over an infinite horizon, so the standard procedure is to maximize $\int_0^T e^{-\delta t}[p(N - I) - cfI]dt$ where T is some large number. In the case of an initial endowment, the constraint will then be of the form $K_0 \geq \int_0^T e^{-\delta t}cfI dt$, and in the case of an expenditure constraint the condition will be $cfI \leq M$.

4   A NUMERICAL EXAMPLE

Figure 2.4 shows the optimal paths in a specific numerical example. Starting from an initial infection level $I_0 = 0.5$ the socially optimum policy in this example is to treat every infected person at all times. This is the unconstrained case. Along this path the infection level is gradually brought down to an asymptotic limit of 0.125. The value of the programme in this case is $V = 6.53$. The figure also shows what happens if treatment is financed from the proceeds of an initial endowment $K_0 = 0.5$. In this case the optimum policy is to treat no-one at all for a time. During this period infection becomes more widespread but simultaneously the unspent endowment accumulates. Despite the increase in infection, the point is eventually reached after nearly 10 units of time where the endowment has accumulated sufficient funds to treat all sick people in perpetuity. At this point, there is a switch to $f = 1$ and the infection rate is brought down again to the unconstrained limit of 0.125. The value of the programme in this case is $V = 4.22$. Thus the existence of an endowment constraint does not affect the long-term amount of infection, but it does impose a social cost as infection increases to a very high level during the initial period when there is no treatment. The figure also shows the optimal path when there is an upper limit on expenditure of the form $M = 0.05$. On this path, the stream of expenditure has a discounted sum equal to 0.5, which is exactly the same as in the endowment case. Over the long run, therefore, the cost of the two paths is identical. Along the expenditure-constrained path, infection stabilizes at the very high level of 0.75 and the value of the programme is $V = 2.93$. Thus the inflexibility imposed by setting a fixed expenditure limit is very costly in

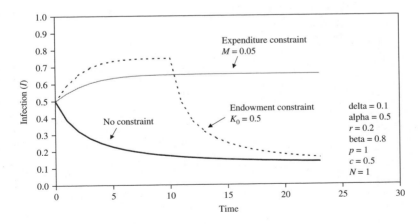

Figure 2.4   Optimum paths compared

social terms. It means less infection in the short run than in the endowment case, but much higher infection in the long run. By refusing to allow the medical authorities to hoard funds, the expenditure limit prevents the eventual big push that allows infection to be brought under control.

Figure 2.5 illustrates a quite different outcome. The basic parameters underlying this simulation are the same as in the previous case, but the constraints are different and there is a different starting point. As before, the discounted sum of expenditures is identical along the two constrained paths, and once again the endowment yields a much higher social value than the expenditure constraint. In the unconstrained case, the optimal policy is to treat all infected people at all times ($f = 1$). Under this policy, infection rises gradually towards 0.125 and the social value of the programme is $V = 8.85$. When an upper limit is imposed on expenditure, there is initially an explosion in infection because there is not enough money to treat everyone. The number of people infected eventually stabilizes when it reaches 0.71. The social value of this programme is 5.90. In the case of an endowment constraint, the optimum policy is to exhaust the endowment within ten units of time. During the initial period every sick person is treated, but at the end of the period all treatment is abruptly halted. After the cessation of treatment the level of infection rises even faster than in the previous case and eventually stabilizes at 0.75. The social value of this programme is $V = 7.45$. Thus the inflexibility imposed by setting a fixed expenditure limit is very costly in social terms. It means a lot more infection in the short run than in the endowment case, in return for only a little less infection in the long run.

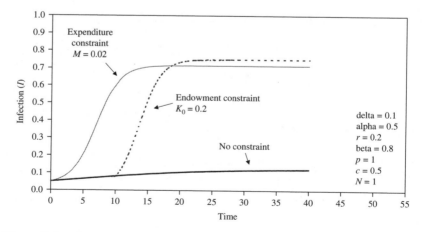

Figure 2.5   Optimum paths compared

5   CONCLUSIONS

This chapter has derived the following results. If there are funds available, it is never optimal to deny treatment to a nonzero fraction of the infected population. Under these conditions, the optimal policy is to treat no-one at all or to treat as many infected persons as the budget allows. If there is no budget constraint, the optimal policy requires that either no infected person is treated or all such persons are treated. Moreover, there are at most two switches from zero to maximum treatment or vice versa. If a budget constraint must be imposed it is better for it to be in the form of a capital endowment rather than an expenditure limit. The former provides an intertemporal flexibility that is not permitted with a strict expenditure limit. Such flexibility may be of great social value.

NOTES

1. See the appendix.
2. The problem can be converted into autonomous form by including the value of the endowment K as a second state variable. The shadow price m is then a function of both I and K. It is therefore no longer a single-valued function of I alone.

REFERENCES

Goldman, S.M. and J. Lightwood (2002), 'Cost optimization in the SIS model of infectious disease with treatment', *Topics in Economic Analysis & Policy*, **2** (1), Article 4, http:/www.bepress.com/bejeap/topics/vol2/iss 1/art4.
Laxminarayan, R. and R.E. Rowthorn (2002), 'Globalization and disease spillovers', working paper, Resources for the Future, Washington, DC.

APPENDIX: THE SHADOW PRICE IN AN AUTONOMOUS, INFINITE HORIZON MODEL

Consider the following autonomous, infinite horizon, optimization problem. Let

$$V(x_0, t_0) = \max_{u(.)} \int_{t_0}^{\infty} e^{-\delta t} g(x(t), u(t)) dt, \qquad (2.43)$$

such that

$$\dot{x} = h(x(t), u(t)) \qquad (2.44)$$

and $u(t) \in \Omega$, $x(t) \in \Pi$ and $x(t_0) = x_0$. In this problem, apart from the discount factor under the integral, the time variable does not enter explicitly into any of the functions or equations. Moreover, the constraints on u and x are time-invariant.

The above problem can be written in the alternative form: find

$$V(x_0, t_0) = e^{-\delta t_0} \max_{u(.)} \int_0^{\infty} e^{-\delta t} g(x(t), u(t)) dt, \qquad (2.45)$$

such that

$$\dot{x} = h(x(t), u(t)) \qquad (2.46)$$

and $u(t) \in \Omega$, $x(t) \in \Pi$ and $x(0) = x_0$. It is obvious that

$$V(x_0, t_0) = e^{-\delta t_0} V(x_0, 0). \qquad (2.47)$$

Along an optimal path, the current shadow prices satisfy the following equations:

$$m(x_0, 0) = \frac{\partial V(x_0, 0)}{\partial x_0} \qquad (2.48)$$

$$m(x_0, t_0) = \frac{e^{\delta t_0} \partial V(x_0, t_0)}{\partial x_0}. \qquad (2.49)$$

Hence

$$m(x_0, t_0) = m(x_0, 0). \qquad (2.50)$$

Thus the current shadow price depends only on the contemporary value of the state variable. It does not depend explicitly on time and can be expressed as follows:

$$m(x_0, t_0) = m(x_0), \qquad (2.51)$$

where $m(x_0)$ is a single-valued function. This function must be single-valued since the maximum value of the integral in (2.45) is unique.

3. Coordinating conservation on private lands

Gregory M. Parkhurst and Jason F. Shogren

1 INTRODUCTION

In the 1930s, conservationist Aldo Leopold argued a key to conservation was to compensate landowners for their efforts to protect nature on private lands. He said conservation 'ultimately boil[s] down to reward the private landowner who conserves the public interest' (see Bean, 1999; Innes *et al.*, 1998). Compensation can be used to create an incentive to encourage landowners to maintain their land in an undeveloped state or to mitigate the environmental impact of development by helping the landowner meet maintenance and restoration costs of environmentally sensitive areas. Compensation aligns a landowner's private incentives with the social desire to create nature reserves that shelter species at risk. In the United States, compensation also reduces the odds that a landowner might claim a Fifth Amendment 'taking': private property taken for a public use, without just reimbursement. Landowners with a financial stake in conservation should provide more environmental stewardship.

Today, the US Fish and Wildlife Service and many state agencies have designed compensation programs to reduce the risk of defensive habitat destruction by providing landowners with regulatory relief in the event that restrictions are levied against their land (for example, Safe Harbor Plans and Habitat Conservation Plans in the Endangered Species Act (ESA) of 1973; see Bean, 1998). Compensation takes the form of grants, loans, cash payments, and tax allowances offered by federal, state, or nonprofit organizations (Parkhurst and Shogren, 2005). These programs are funded by numerous methods, including tax revenue, lottery funds, and special permits. A good example is the Idaho Department of Fish and Game's (IDFG) Habitat Improvement Program (HIP). The HIP is a cost share program that allocates funds for improvements on both private and public lands. Recognizing the role landowners play in providing habitat for upland game and wild birds, the primary objective of HIP is to encourage private landowners to invest in habitat restoration and enhancement projects that increases the populations of wild birds (IDFG, 2000). Landowners enter into an agreement that specifies the requirements to maintain the land for a decade or more; in return, the IDFG reimburses up to 75 percent of the landowner's costs, 37.5 percent for projects on lands enrolled in the CRP (Conservation Reserve Program), with a maximum of $2000 per project.

But landowner compensation itself does not guarantee the creation of habitat most suitable for species protection. Landowners still have no incentive to coordinate their land retirement decisions to create, say, one contiguous reserve that falls across property lines or to create optimal habitat configurations within their own property lines. Fragmented retirement decisions will affect species that prosper within a large habitat (for example, northern spotted owl, red-cockaded woodpecker, grizzly bears). Most voluntary compensation programs are not designed to directly address the biologist's concern that landowners may not coordinate conservation efforts to create a contiguous reserve that falls across property lines or within their own property (see Brown and Shogren, 1998). Conservation biologists argue that many species face extinction due to fragmented habitat on both public and private lands. Habitat fragments are either too small to provide species with the physical and biological landscape characteristics necessary for survival and breeding, or they are too isolated from other fragments, causing species 'bottlenecks', which increases susceptibility to changes in its environment (for example, Saunders *et al.*, 1991). 'Bottlenecks' emerge from inbreeding and the term refers to reduced chromosomes types in a species' DNA. But biologists also point out that *how* one reconfigured fragmented habitat matters because different species thrive under different spatial habitat designs (for example, Noss, 1993).

Given limited conservation dollars, designing a compensation mechanism that can voluntarily create contiguous habitats that minimize edge effects increases the odds of species survival. The *agglomeration bonus* is an incentive mechanism designed to address the question of contiguous habitat reserves across distinct private land holdings. The bonus creates incentives for landowners to coordinate conservation decisions (Smith and Shogren, 2002; Parkhurst *et al.*, 2002). A regulator offers each landowner (i) a schedule specifying compensation for retired acres, and (ii) an agglomeration bonus to induce coordinated acre retirement to create one large habitat preserve across common borders. The bonus pays the landowner extra for each border shared by two conserved acres, regardless of whether the border is solely on his own land or on both his and his neighbor's land. Each landowner is being rewarded for the specific parcel retired, and for the *shared border*. The bonus creates a network externality between the landowners. Now, each landowner's conservation payment depends on their conserved acres, their neighbors' conserved acres, and the location of all conserved acres within the landscape.

The agglomeration bonus, however, creates a classic coordination problem: the existence of multiple Nash equilibria (Schelling, 1960). Now each landowner must choose between a high risk–high reward strategy for which earnings depend on other landowners' choices (that is, payoff dominant strategy) or a safe bet strategy that earns fewer profits but depends less on the actions of others (that is, risk dominant strategy), or some strategy in-between (Harsanyi and Selten, 1988). The combinations of conservation strategies create multiple Nash equilibria, only one of which is the first best outcome of a contiguous habitat. Failure to coordinate actions results in both fewer financial gains to landowners and greater fragmentation of critical habitat.

This chapter examines how individuals voluntarily coordinate their land conservation actions when presented with the agglomeration bonus incentive mechanism. We design an experiment that uses a spatially explicit grid game (see Figure 3.1). Here four neighboring landowners each

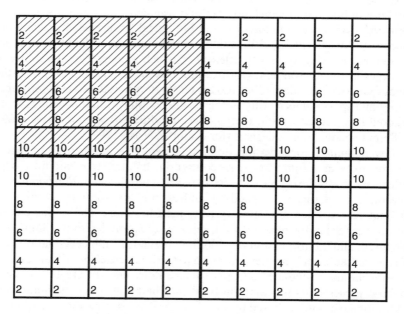

Note: The above grid represents four private landholdings of 25 parcels each. The patterned area represents one landowner's land holdings; productive values are monotonically decreasing as cells move away from the center row.

Figure 3.1   10 × 10 land grid

independently chose which productive land units he or she will 'retire' for habitat conservation given a specific (but unstated) conservation target – a habitat corridor, core, cross, and four-corners. Overall, our results suggest the agglomeration bonus was most effective at inducing people to play the payoff dominant strategy in the habitat corridor: 83 percent of the rounds by experienced subjects, which is comparable to a 82 percent success rate obtained in earlier work using the traditional normal form matrix game.[1] Coordination to the core and cross was more difficult because each player needed to coordinate with the three other players. Voluntarily creating isolated corners was relatively straightforward.

2 AGGLOMERATION BONUS AND SPATIAL CONSERVATION TARGETS

Assume a regulatory agency identifies both the land desired for conservation and the habitat configuration (for example, core or corner). They design an agglomeration bonus mechanism to create incentives to persuade each landowner to conserve the parcels that achieve the conservation objective. This mechanism has individual subsidies paid to landowners on a per conserved acre basis, and can be attached to a common border between two conserved parcels either within or across landowner holdings so that landowners can receive an additional payment when two conserved acres share a common border. The bonus can also be attached to the border of a land characteristic such as national forest land or a river or other land attribute so landowners receive an additional payment when their conserved land borders a desired land attribute such as a river. The value of the various subsidies can differ and the magnitude of each subsidy will depend on the productive value of the land. Although the values of the various subsidies can differ across subsidy type, the subsidy value does not differ across landowners. For example, if the per acre subsidy is set at $10, every parcel set aside for habitat by every landowner would earn the same $10 per conserved parcel subsidy.

Our agglomeration bonus is a subsidy menu mechanism with four specific subsidies: (1) a *per conserved habitat acre subsidy*, S_H; (2) an *own shared border subsidy*, S_{OB}; the landowner receives a subsidy for every border shared between two of his own conserved acres (see Figure 3.2a); (3) a *row shared border subsidy*, S_{RB}; a landowner receives a subsidy for every border shared by one of his habitat acres and a habitat acre of the row neighboring landowner (Figure 3.2b); and (4) a *column shared border subsidy*, S_{CB}; a landowner earns a subsidy for every border shared by one of his habitat acres and a habitat acre of the column neighbor

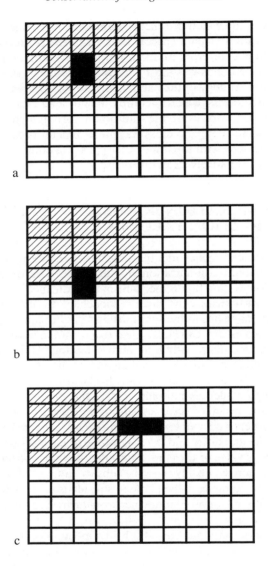

Notes:
a. With an *own shared border subsidy*, S_{OB}, the landowner receives a subsidy for every border shared between two of his own conserved acres.
b. With a *row shared border subsidy*, S_{RB}, a landowner receives a subsidy for every border shared by one of his habitat acres and a habitat acre of the row neighboring landowner.
c. With a *column shared border subsidy*, S_{CB}, a landowner earns a subsidy for every border shared by one of his habitat acres and a habitat acre of the column neighbor.

Figure 3.2   Border bonuses

(Figure 3.2c). These subsidies can be positive, negative or zero, and depend on productive values and desired configuration and location of the habitat.

The subsidy menu serves two main purposes: to make voluntary conservation profitable, and to create a network externality between landowners' conservation decisions. The conservation objectives create a network externality between landowners' conservation patches in which landowners act as if they were cooperating by locating their retired parcels on common borders to earn maximum profits. Now a landowner's conserved habitat depends on his own conservation and on the conservation decisions of his neighboring landowners.

The agglomeration bonus can then be configured to provide incentives to create the desired conservation target. Specific guidelines have been proposed to design habitat preserves for land sensitive species: the species distribution should be across its entire range; larger habitat preserves are preferred to smaller preserves; the less distance between preserves the better; coordinating conservation to create one large habitat preserve is preferred to numerous smaller fragmented preserves; two habitat fragments should be linked with a conservation corridor of like habitat; and habitat blocks that are protected from human interaction are preferred (see Noss, 1993; Hof and Bevers, 1998).

We consider four conservation targets: a core, corridor, cross, and four-corners, illustrated in Figure 3.3. First, some species thrive within one large habitat *core* (for example, northern spotted owl, red-cockaded woodpecker, grizzly bears). A large core minimizes edge effects. Second, species benefit from access to a long habitat *corridor* that allows movement from reserve to reserve (for example, wolves, elk), increasing the species' probability of survival by reducing the likelihood of a 'bottleneck' (Beier and Noss, 1998). Third, some experts believe the good strategy for some species is to design a lengthy corridor with a habitat *cross* or rest area along the path which facilitates both residence along the path and migration between larger habitat parcels (for example, grizzly bear). Adding a cross to a corridor can lower rates of natural and anthropogenic risks in what have been called 'genetic sinks', for example exposure to edge-inhabiting predators, diseases carried by domestic animals, and poaching, which increase the longer the corridor (McKenzie, 2003). Stepping stone habitat patches, either unconnected or connected by shorter habitat corridors, is one way to protect species (Simberloff *et al.*, 1992). Fourth, those species susceptible to diseases are better managed as metapopulations in isolated conservation *corners* (for example, bison, prairie dogs, black-footed ferrets). Species susceptible to diseases should be managed as metapopulations with isolated habitat areas that meet a minimum population size or core area; for

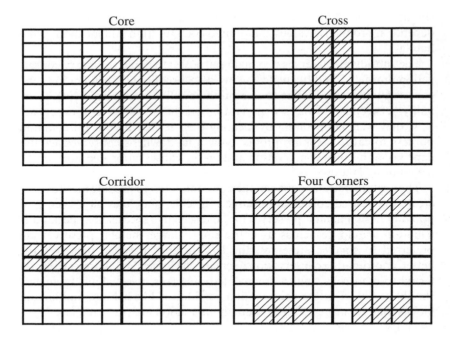

Figure 3.3   Conservation targets

example, black-footed ferret or the black-tailed prairie dog populations affected by the plague (BFFRIT, 2002).

3   EXPERIMENTAL DESIGN: THE GRID GAME

In a companion paper examining group behavior we describe the spatial grid experimental design in detail (see Parkhurst and Shogren, 2004). Here we summarize the key elements of the experimental design. The design has 10 structural elements: land grid, players/matching, conservation targets and treatments, subsidy menu, strategies, calculator, communication, information, history, and procedures.[2]

- *The land grid.* Figure 3.1 illustrates our spatial 10×10 land grid, divided into four symmetric landholdings. Each 5×5 landholding has 25 productive cells: 5 cells valued at \$2 (row 1), \$4 (row 2), \$6 (row 3), \$8 (row 4), and \$10 (row 5, common border).

- *Number of players and random matching.* Eight subjects participated in a session. Each subject was randomly assigned into anonymous groups of four before the beginning of each round.
- *Conservation targets and treatments.* We examine the conservation targets: a corridor, core, cross, and corner. In sessions 1–7, we used an ABA treatment design (for example, core–corridor–core). In sessions 8–10, we used an AB treatment design.[3] Each target had 10 rounds. In sessions 1–7, subjects played 30 rounds (ABA: $10 \times 3 = 30$). In sessions 8–10, subjects participated in 20 rounds (AB: $10 \times 2 = 20$).
- *Subsidy menus and maximum number of retired acres.* Table 3.1 shows the agglomeration bonus subsidy menu for each conservation

Table 3.1   *Treatments and sessions: four treatments, Corridor, Core, Corner and Cross*

Sessions		Per brown cell Subsidy ($)	Own border bonus ($)	Row border bonus ($)	Column border bonus ($)	Number of participants (rounds)
1&2	Corridor	3	8	16	0	16 (10)
	Core	3	16	13	8	16 (10)
	Corridor	3	8	16	0	16 (10)
3&4	Core	3	16	13	8	16 (10)
	Corridor	3	8	16	0	16 (10)
	Core	3	16	13	8	16 (10)
5&6	Core	3	16	13	8	16 (10)
	Corner	3	8	−5	−5	16 (10)
	Core	3	16	13	8	16 (10)
7	Corner	3	8	−5	−5	8 (10)
	Core	3	16	13	8	8 (10)
	Corner	3	8	−5	−5	8 (10)
8	Corner	3	8	−5	−5	8 (10)
	Core	3	16	13	8	8 (10)
9&10	Corner	3	8	−5	−5	16 (10)
	Cross	3	19	16	16	16 (10)

Note: The agglomeration bonus menu is presented for each treatment.

treatment and order of treatments in sessions. Subjects had a sheet detailing the subsidy values for each of the four individual subsidies and included the land values for the entire 10×10 grid.

- *Strategies – brown out cells*. A subject could either leave his cells *green*, in which case they earned the value in the cell, or he could *brown out* cells, which means he earns the subsidies and forgoes the productive value. For the cross, core, and corner targets, subjects could brown out a maximum of six cells; for the corridor target, a maximum of five cells could be browned out. Note each subject has tens of thousands of strategies to choose from; for example, each subject has 68 406 strategy choices for the corridor treatment, implying $(68\,406)$ possible group outcomes.[4]

- *Nash equilibria*. The grid game is a supermodular game: one can order elements in the strategy space of the players and strategic complementarity exists between players' actions (Milgrom and Roberts, 1990). Multiple Nash equilibria arise in supermodular games, and these equilibria can be Pareto ranked. In the corridor target, for example, about 9400 Nash equilibria exist (97^2). Figure 3.4 illustrates five different classes of Nash equilibria and provides examples of each for the corridor target. The Pareto dominant Nash equilibrium is when all four players coordinate their actions along the common row border and each earns maximum payoffs of 227 computer dollars. Four classes are Pareto-dominated equilibria with payoffs of 213, 207, 195, and 191 computer dollars; the 191 payoff equilibrium is the risk-dominant equilibrium. The take-home pay transfer rate was \$1 per 100 computer dollar.

- *Calculator*. In place of a specific normal form payoff matrix, we provided a 10×10 *grid calculator* to aid the subjects in calculating potential profits associated with different actions. The grid calculator allowed the subject to calculate the potential profits derived from different land retirement configurations created by him and the other three players.

- *Communication*. Each subject could send one non-binding, unstructured cheap talk message per round. Subjects had two minutes to send messages, use the calculator, and send their choices.

- *Public and private information*. After all four subject's choices were submitted, the resulting grid was presented to the group. The subjects' 5×5 grid of values, the maximum allowed number of brown cells, a message box, and the grid calculator came up on the computer screen and players chose the cells to brown out. Subjects had common knowledge regarding payoffs and strategies. Each subject's individual payoffs and accumulated payoffs were private information.

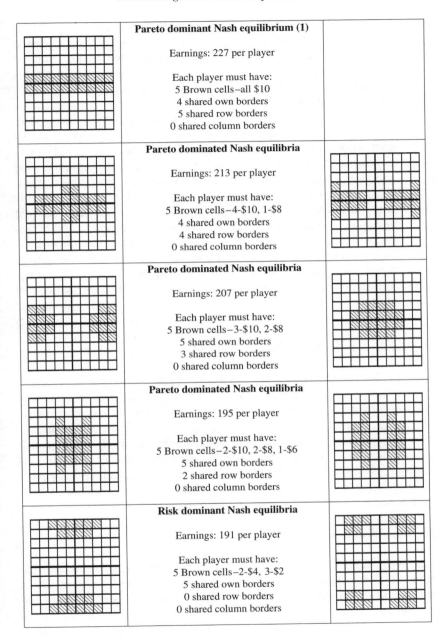

	Pareto dominant Nash equilibrium (1) Earnings: 227 per player Each player must have: 5 Brown cells–all $10 4 shared own borders 5 shared row borders 0 shared column borders	
	Pareto dominated Nash equilibria Earnings: 213 per player Each player must have: 5 Brown cells–4-$10, 1-$8 4 shared own borders 4 shared row borders 0 shared column borders	
	Pareto dominated Nash equilibria Earnings: 207 per player Each player must have: 5 Brown cells–3-$10, 2-$8 5 shared own borders 3 shared row borders 0 shared column borders	
	Pareto dominated Nash equilibria Earnings: 195 per player Each player must have: 5 Brown cells–2-$10, 2-$8, 1-$6 5 shared own borders 2 shared row borders 0 shared column borders	
	Risk dominant Nash equilibria Earnings: 191 per player Each player must have: 5 Brown cells–2-$4, 3-$2 5 shared own borders 0 shared row borders 0 shared column borders	

Figure 3.4   Grid game Nash equilibria

- *History box and record sheet.* To help subjects keep track of past play and past payoffs, we provided (1) a *history box* for each player, showing the actual spatial configuration created in all previous rounds; and (2) a record sheet, in which each subject wrote down his own and the other group members' choice of strategies and associated payoffs in previous rounds.
- *Procedures.* All experiments were run on computers. Subjects were not told about the conservation targets and all wording in the instructions and on the computer screens was context-free. Following standard protocol, subjects were recruited campus wide and were told to report at a computer lab at a given time. Experimental instructions were provided to each of the participants and the monitor read them out loud while the subjects followed along. Subjects could ask basic questions about experimental procedures. The monitor walked subjects through two practice rounds. The monitor then handed out the agglomeration bonus subsidy menu, each subject entered his or her name and student ID number into the computer, the computer randomly assigned the subjects to groups of four, and the experiment began.

4   RESULTS FOR INDIVIDUAL BEHAVIOR

We focus here on individual play and discuss the results in four stages. First, we review the observed behavior at the individual level. Next we establish the persistence of this behavior in the steady state. Finally, we test formerly the significance of these results on complexity, experience, and coordination exposure using conditional probit analysis. We separate individual outcomes into three classes: the payoff dominant strategy, second best contiguous habitat strategies, and third best-fragmented habitat strategies.[5] Table 3.2 shows strategy choices by treatment for all and subsets of individual observed behavior.[6] We now summarize our key findings.

Individual Behavior

Corridor   Table 3.2 shows individual play by session and for all observations for the corridor. For all observations, we observe 83 percent chose the payoff-dominant conservation strategy, 2 percent second best, and 15 percent fragmented habitat strategies. For subjects in the initial rounds (1–10), the payoff-dominant strategy was played 61 percent of the time, second best strategies 4 percent, and fragmented habitat strategies 35 percent. In rounds 11–20, 86 percent of strategy choices was the

Table 3.2   Conservation strategies by treatment

Incentive design	Individual strategy choice		
	Payoff dominant conservation strategy (%)	Non-optimal contiguous habitat strategy (%)	Fragmented habitat strategy (%)
Corridor (all)	397 (83)	11 (2)	72 (15)
1,2 rounds 1–10	98 (61)	7 (4)	55 (35)
3,4 rounds 11–20	139 (86)	4 (3)	17 (11)
1,2 rounds 21–30	160 (100)	0	0
Core (all)	495 (52)	204 (21)	261 (27)
3,4 rounds 1–10	85 (53)	29 (18)	46 (29)
5,6 rounds 1–10	98 (61)	24 (15)	38 (24)
1,2 rounds 11–20	6 (4)	104 (65)	50 (31)
7,8 rounds 11–20	12 (8)	43 (27)	105 (65)
3,4 rounds 21–30	157 (98)	2 (1)	1 (1)
5,6 rounds 21–30	137 (86)	2 (1)	21 (13)
Cross	62 (39)	64 (40)	34 (21)
9,10 rounds 11–20	62 (39)	64 (40)	34 (21)
	Optimal conservation configuration (%)	Non-optimal, four isolated habitat reserves (%)	More or less than four isolated habitat reserves (%)
Corners (all)	449 (80)	50 (9)	61 (11)
7,8 rounds 1–10	118 (74)	24 (15)	18 (11)
9,10 rounds 1–10	115 (72)	18 (11)	27 (17)
5,6 rounds 11–20	146 (91)	7 (4.5)	7 (4.5)
7 rounds 21–30	70 (88)	1 (1)	9 (11)

payoff-dominant strategy, with 3 percent to second best strategies, and 11 percent to fragmented strategies. For experienced subjects, we see a 100 percent optimal payoff-dominant strategy.[7]

Core   For the core treatment, we examine all observations and how initial experience affects core. For all observations, Table 3.2 indicates 52 percent optimal core, 21 percent second best, and 27 fragmented strategies. In rounds 1–10, the strategy choices were 57 percent optimal core strategy, 17 percent second best strategies, and 26 percent fragmented strategies. For rounds 11–20, 6 percent choose the payoff-dominant core strategy, 46 percent second best strategies, and 48 percent fragmented strategies. Experienced subjects in the core treatment chose the payoff-dominant core strategy 92 percent, second best strategies 1 percent, and fragmented strategies 7 percent. For corridor-experienced subjects (rounds 11–20), we see 4 percent payoff-dominant core, 65 percent second best, and 31 percent fragmented strategies. In rounds 21–30, corridor 98 percent of experienced subjects played the payoff-dominant strategy. For corner-experienced subjects, we find 8 percent optimal core strategy, 27 percent second best, and 65 percent fragmented strategies. These proportions increased for corner experienced subjects in rounds 21–30: 86 percent payoff dominant strategy, 1 percent second best strategies and 13 percent fragmented strategies.[8]

Cross   For the cross treatment, all observations come from rounds 11–20. We see 39 percent payoff-dominant cross strategy, 40 percent second best habitat strategies, and 21 percent fragmented habitat strategies.

Corner   For all observations, Table 3.2 shows 80 percent the dominant corner strategy, 9 percent second best four isolated habitat strategies, and 11 percent strategies that result in more-or-less-than four habitat reserves. In initial rounds (1–10), we see 73 percent play the dominant corner strategy and 13 percent second best strategies. For rounds 11–20, 91 percent play the dominant corner strategy, and in rounds 21–30, 88 percent of experienced subjects choose the dominant strategy.

The experimental data indicate that the agglomeration bonus can be used to create land configurations with mixed success. We now formally state our first result.

Result 1

(a) In initial rounds (1–10), the agglomeration bonus was the most successful in inducing individuals to play the payoff-dominant strategy for the corner conservation objective. (b) Overall, when the complexity of the coordination problem increases in the sense that all four players must coordinate to maximize payoffs (core treatment), play of the payoff-dominant strategy decreases. However, in initial rounds and for experienced individuals, no statistical difference exists: play of the payoff-dominant strategy is not statistically different. (c) Subjects exposed to the cooperating conservation objective (corridor) tended to choose the payoff-dominant or second best strategies in the core treatment more often relative to subjects exposed to the non-cooperating corner conservation objectives. Increased play of fragmented habitat strategies following the corner conservation objective was more pervasive for both core experienced and core inexperienced individuals.

Support   We formally test Result 1(a), differences in the play of the payoff-dominant strategy, X, across treatments in rounds 1–10, using a Fisher's exact test.[9] The null hypothesis in the Fisher's exact test is that the probability of choosing the payoff-dominant strategy is equal across treatments.[10] We reject the null hypothesis for comparisons between the corner and core (*p-value* < 0.0001) and the corner and corridor (*p-value* = 0.012). We fail to reject the null hypothesis for comparisons between the

Table 3.3 Tests of proportions

Hypothesis	Test statistic
Overall proportions	rxc Chi square test of proportions
$P(X, Y, Z)_{core} = P(X, Y, Z)_{corridor} = P(X, Y, Z)_{corner}$ Rounds 1–10	$\chi^2_4 = 40.4; p - value < 0.0001$
$P(X, Y, Z)_{core} = P(X, Y, Z)_{corridor}$ Rounds 1-10	$\chi^2_2 = 15.4; p - value < 0.0001$
$P(X, Y, Z)_{core} = P(X, Y, Z)_{corner}$ Rounds 1-10	$\chi^2_2 = 19.1; p - value < 0.0001$
$P(X, Y, Z)_{corridor} = P(X, Y, Z)_{corner}$ Rounds 1-10	$\chi^2_2 = 31.2; p - value < 0.0001$
Probability of playing payoff-dominant strategy	Fisher's exact test
$P(X)_{core} = P(X)_{corridor}$ Rounds 1–10	*p-value* = 0.4321
$P(X)_{core} = P(X)_{corner}$ Rounds 1–10	*p-value* < 0.0001
$P(X)_{corridor} = P(X)_{corner}$ Rounds 1–10	*p-value* = 0.0120
ABA design	Fisher's exact test
$P(X)_{core} = P(X)_{corridor}$ Rounds 1–30, sessions 1, 2, 3, 4	*p-value* < 0.0001
$P(X)_{core} = P(X)_{corridor}$ Rounds 1–10, sessions 1, 2, 3, 4	*p-value* = 0.1751
$P(X)_{core} = P(X)_{corridor}$ Rounds 21–30, sessions 1, 2, 3, 4	*p-value* = 0.2476
Type of previous experience	Fisher's exact test
$P(X)_{corridor-core} = P(X)_{corner-core}$ Rounds 11–30	*p-value* = 0.3039
$P(X)_{corridor-core} = P(X)_{corner-core}$ Rounds 11–20	*p-value* = 0.2243
$P(X)_{corridor-core} = P(X)_{corner-core}$ Rounds 21–30	*p-value* < 0.0001
$P(Z)_{corridor-core} = P(Z)_{corner-core}$ Rounds 11–30	*p-value* < 0.0001
$P(Z)_{corridor-core} = P(Z)_{corner-core}$ Rounds 11–20	*p-value* < 0.0001
$P(Z)_{corridor-core} = P(Z)_{corner-core}$ Rounds 21–30	*p-value* < 0.0001

core and corridor (*p-value* = 0.432). The probability of playing the payoff-dominant strategy, X, in rounds 1–10, is statistically greater in the corner as opposed to the core or corridor, but is not statistically different in the core relative to the corridor. This is not surprising given the corner conservation objective has but one Nash equilibrium and, as such, one dominant strategy. Both the core and the corridor objectives result in Pareto ranked coordination game with numerous Nash equilibria and resulting strategy choices.

Turning to Result 1(b), the affects of coordination complexity on strategy choice are examined by turning to the results from the core, corridor, ABA, BAB design: sessions 1, 2, 3, and 4. Here we classify coordination complexity as a measure of the number of individuals that must coordinate their strategies to achieve maximum payoffs. In the corridor treatment, maximum earnings are achieved if the subject coordinates with his row counterpart. For the core, coordination is required directly with the row and column players and indirectly with the adjacent player to earn maximum payoffs.[11] Based on this definition of coordination complexity, the core treatment has greater coordination complexity than the corridor treatment. The null hypothesis is the probability of playing the payoff-dominant strategy is equal across treatments. We reject the null hypothesis over all 30 rounds (*p-value* < 0.001), but fail to reject the null hypothesis for rounds 1–10 (*p-value* = 0.175) and rounds 21–30 (*p-value* = 0.248). These results indicate that play of the payoff-dominant strategy was significantly less for the core treatment in rounds 11–20 relative to the corridor treatment. One explanation is that it is harder to overcome the focal strategy created in the initial 10 rounds of play when starting in a less complex coordination problem and moving to a more complex coordination problem than when you move from a more complex to less complex coordination problem.

Result 1c examines the influence of the prior 10 rounds of exposure, cooperating conservation objectives (corridor) verses non-cooperating conservation objectives (corners), on strategy choice for the core conservation objective in rounds 11–30. A Fisher's exact test is used to test the null hypothesis: play of fragmented strategies in the core treatment following prior exposure to the corridor treatment is equal to the play of fragmented strategies in the core treatment following prior exposure to the corner treatment. We reject the null hypothesis for rounds 11–30 (*p-value* < 0.001), rounds 11–20 (*p-value* < 0.001), and in rounds 21–30 (*p-value* < 0.001). Fragmented strategies were played more frequently following exposure to the corners treatment than to the corridor treatment. Increased play of fragmented strategies occurred for inexperienced and experienced players.[12]

5 BEHAVIOR IN THE STEADY STATE

We now examine whether our results persist in the steady state. We establish a steady state strategy vector using a Markov process to examine the data (see Taylor and Karlin, 1984).[13] We use three state spaces, X, Y, and Z, that are consistent with the previous definitions for the corridor, core, corner, and cross treatments. The transition matrix, B_{KS}, is a 3×3 matrix in which the sum of entries in each column sum to one and all entries are nonnegative. Let K represent the type of conservation objective (corridor, $K = 1$; core, $K = 2$; corner, $K = 3$; and cross, $K = 4$), and let S represent the subsample of observations within K (all observations $= 1$; rounds 11–30 observations $= 2$; cooperating outcome experienced observations (rounds 11–20) $= 3$; and non-cooperating outcome experienced observations (rounds 11–20) $= 4$).

Each entry, b_{ij} ($i, j = X, Y, Z$) represents the probability that a subject playing an action in group i in round t will play an action in group j in round $t + 1$ ($i, j = X, Y, Z$). We calculate the probability, b_{ij} by summing ($t_i, t + 1_j$) across all transition periods and dividing by the total number of times group i was played in the preceding time period, t. The matrix B_{KS} and the equation for b_{ij} are

$$B_{KS} = \begin{bmatrix} b_{XX} & b_{YX} & b_{ZX} \\ b_{XY} & b_{YY} & b_{ZY} \\ b_{XZ} & b_{YZ} & b_{ZZ} \end{bmatrix}, \begin{array}{l} K = \text{type} = 1, 2, 3, 4, \text{ and} \\ S = \text{sample} = 1, 2, 3, 4 \end{array}$$

(3.1)

and

$$b_{ij} = \frac{\sum_{2}^{N}((t + 1)_j | t_i)}{\sum_{1}^{N-1} t_i}, \, i, j = X, Y, Z.$$

(3.2)

A transition matrix with all nonzero entries for B_{KS}^W, where W is the W-period transition matrix, such that the two-period transition matrix is $B_{KS}^2 = B_{KS}B_{KS}$, is said to be 'regular'. Over time the probabilities across groups of a regular transition matrix will approach a 'steady-state distribution vector', v_{KS}. v_{KS} is the only vector in which the components sum to one and also satisfy the equality: $B_{KS}v_{KS} = v_{KS}$, $K = 1, 2, 3, 4$ and $S = 1, 2, 3, 4$.

To solve for v_{KS} increase W until the resulting matrix, $B_{KS}^W =$ $[v_{KS} \ v_{KS} \ v_{KS}]$ The elements in each column are eqiual across rows, so the probability of playing state i in round $t+1$ is the same regardless of a subject's round t state. For each treatment and for each subsample within each treatment, we use MATLAB to calculate the 'steady-state distribution vector' that results from raising the transition matrix to the power W. Result 2 summarizes the findings from the steady state dynamic analysis.

Result 2

(a) From the estimated 'steady state distribution vectors', individuals in rounds 11–30 play first- and second-best outcomes more frequently than the aggregate group play. For the core and corridor treatments, individuals shift their strategy choices from the worst strategies to the payoff-dominant strategy with additional play. (b) The payoff-dominant strategy is played most frequently in the corridor and corners treatment, 90 percent and 93 percent, where payoff-dominant strategies require subjects to cooperate with only one other subject. For the cross and core treatments in which the coordination problem increases in complexity, optimal outcomes require a subject to cooperate with two other subjects, the payoff-dominant strategy is played 84 percent and 72 percent in the steady state. (c) Further, evidence from the core analysis indicates subjects' previous coordination exposure, or lack thereof, also influences the type of strategies that subjects play: subjects with exposure to cooperating outcomes (corridor treatment) result in less play of fragmented habitat strategies as opposed to subjects experienced in non-cooperating outcomes (corner treatment), 22 percent compared to 57 percent.

Corridor Table 3.4 summarizes the results for all observations and for rounds 11–30. For all observations, we see in the steady state 90 percent play the payoff-dominant corridor strategy; 2 percent second best habitat strategies, and about 8 percent fragmented strategies. For individuals' strategy choices in rounds 11–30, we see play of the payoff-dominant corridor strategy increased to 95 percent, second best habitat strategies fell to 1 percent, and fragmented strategies fell to 4 percent.

Core For all observations, we see in the steady state 72 percent payoff-dominant core strategy; 15 percent second best habitat strategies, and about 13 percent fragmented habitat strategies. For strategy choices in rounds 11–30 for the core treatment, we see the payoff-dominant core strategy increased to 77 percent, second best habitat strategies fell to 12 percent, and fragmentation fell to 11 percent. For corner-experienced subjects, play in rounds 11–20 resulted in more fragmentation in the steady state: 17 percent payoff dominant core strategy, 26 percent second best habitat, and about

Table 3.4   Steady-state distribution vector

Incentive design / Participant action	X: payoff-dominant strategy	Y: second best contiguous habitat strategies	Z: fragmented habitat strategies
Corridor			
All observations	0.8979	0.0230	0.0792
Rounds 11–30	0.9447	0.0132	0.0421
Core			
All observations	0.7217	0.1455	0.1327
Rounds 11–30	0.7725	0.1182	0.1093
Corridor–core Rounds 11–20	0.0417	0.7361	0.2222
Corner–core Rounds 11–20	0.1672	0.2596	0.5732
Cross			
Rounds 11–20	0.8412	0.1264	0.0324
	X: dominant strategy	Y: second best strategies	Z: strategies that result in more or less than four habitat reserves
Corners			
All observations	0.9296	0.0254	0.0450
Rounds 11–30	0.9226	0.0000	0.0774

57 percent fragmented strategies. Over half of the subjects played the safe bet and created fragmented habitat. For corridor-experienced subjects, in rounds 11–20 we see more second best outcomes: 4 percent payoff-dominant core strategy, 74 percent second best habitat strategies, and about 22 percent fragmented strategies.

Cross   84 percent payoff-dominant cross strategy, 13 percent second best habitat strategies, and about 3 percent strategies resulting in fragmentation.

Corner   For all subjects, we observe 93 percent dominant corner strategy, 3 percent second best isolated habitat strategies, and about 5 percent strategies resulting in more-or-less-than four habitat reserves. In latter rounds, 11–30, we see 92 percent dominant corner strategy, 0 percent second best isolated habitat, and about 8 percent strategies resulting in more-or-less-than four habitat reserves.

6   ECONOMETRIC ANALYSIS OF COMPLEXITY AND EXPERIENCE

Now we test the significance of these results using a conditional probit analysis with random effects that corrects for individual specific heteroscedasticity and serial correlation (Brosetta, 2000; Crawford, 1995). We consider how experience, coordination exposure, and the complexity of the coordination problem affect the probability of achieving the payoff-dominant strategy when cooperation between landowners is necessary; that is, the core, corridor, and cross treatments.[14] Here *complexity* is the number of other subjects whose conservation decisions impact a subject's maximum payoffs: either one other subject (corridor treatment), or three other subjects (core or cross treatments). We expect play of the payoff-dominant strategy to decrease as complexity increases. We define *experience* to be prior play of the same treatment in rounds 1–10. The expectation here is for play of the payoff-dominant strategy to increase with experience. Lastly, we define *coordination exposure* as prior exposure in rounds 1–10 or 11–20 to other treatments that require coordination to earn maximum payoffs: core, corridor, or cross. We expect subjects who have been exposed to coordination in prior rounds to play strategies that result in coordinated outcomes: payoff-dominant or second best strategies, more frequently than subjects whose prior exposure was to the non-coordinated corners treatment. We test four hypotheses: H1: play of the payoff-dominant strategy is unaffected by the complexity of the coordination problem; H2: play of the payoff-dominant strategy is unaffected by experience; H3: play of the payoff-dominant strategy is invariant to coordination exposure; and H4: play of fragmented habitat strategies is unaffected by coordination exposure.

In the probit model, we code play of the payoff-dominant strategy as $X = 1$. The log-likelihood function for the probit model and the first order conditions for maximization follow the standard binomial probit form. The marginal effects or slope coefficients are computed at the means of the variables (for explicit equations, see Greene, 1993). We test the influence of coordination exposure on the play of fragmented strategies (Z) in H4 by substituting Z into the probit equation for X. Consider each hypothesis in turn.

We first test complexity (H1), experience (H2), and coordination exposure (H3) by limiting the sample to observations from the core, corridor, and cross treatments. Following Parkhurst *et al.* (2004), the exponential equation to examine how complexity, coordination exposure, and experience affect coordination is:

$$\beta' X_{i,t} = \alpha + \beta_1 LEFF_{i,t-1} + \beta_2 S2 + \beta_3 coord + \beta_4 xp + \sum_{t=3}^{30} \lambda_t D_t + u_i + \varepsilon_{i,t},$$

(3.3)

where u_i is an individual specific random effect with zero mean and ε_{it} is normally distributed with mean zero and unit variance. Equation (3.3) accounts for the influence of the payoffs, complexity, coordination exposure, and experience. $LEFF_{i,t-1}$ is the percentage of the maximum rent that player i obtained in round $t - 1$. If $LEFF_{i,t-1} = 1$ player i earned the maximum possible payoff in round $t - 1$, and is only possible when player i plays the payoff-dominant strategy. If $LEFF_{i,t-1} < 1$, a coordination failure occurred in round $t - 1$.[15] We expect β_1 to be positive: higher payoffs in previous rounds increase the probability of playing the same strategy in future rounds (Erev and Roth, 1998). $S2$ is a dummy variable equaling 1 for the most complex coordination problem; 0 otherwise. *Coord* is a dummy variable that equals 1 when coordination exposure occurred in prior rounds 1–10 or 11–20; 0 otherwise. *xp* is a dummy variable equaling 1 if prior experience to the identical treatment occurred in rounds 1–10; 0 otherwise. D_t are dummy variables that represent round-specific effects, including learning.

We then test how coordination exposure, or lack thereof, affects the frequency of choosing fragmented habitat strategies (H4) by limiting the sample to the core observations from rounds 12–20. We exclude complexity dummy variable, $S2$, and experience dummy variable, *XP*. The second exponential equation is

$$\beta' X_{i,t} = \alpha + \beta_1 LEFF_{i,t-1} + \beta_3 coord + \sum_{t=13}^{20} \lambda_t D_t + u_i + \varepsilon_{i,t}.$$

(3.4)

All other variables are the same as in equation (3.3).

Tables 3.5–7 present the results. Both the coefficient and marginal effects are reported for the explanatory variables. We focus on the marginal effects because they directly measure the effect of the explanatory variables on the probability of playing the payoff-dominant strategy. First, we consider complexity (H1) by testing $H_0 : \beta_2 = 0$, or $H_A : \beta_2 \neq 0$. For experienced subjects, we reject the H1 null hypothesis. The coefficient on $S2$ is negative and significantly different from zero at the 1 percent level, with a marginal effect equal to -0.39. With more complexity, the probability of playing the payoff-dominant strategy decreases by 39 percent. As expected, the marginal effect for *LEFF* is positive and significantly different from zero.

Table 3.5   Descriptive statistics by sample

Variables	All Core	Rounds 12–20
X	0.63	0.06
	(0.48)	(0.24)
Y	0.18	0.50
	(0.38)	(0.50)
Z	0.19	0.43
	(0.40)	(0.50)
LEFF	0.95	0.92
	(0.08)	(0.06)
S2	0.70	
	(0.46)	
COORD	0.50	0.50
	(0.50)	(0.50)
XP	0.30	
	(0.46)	
N	1440	288

Note: Standard deviations in parentheses.

Result 3

As expected and observed in the unconditional results, play of the payoff-dominant strategy decreases as the complexity of the coordination problem increases.

We next consider H2, the influence of experience on the play of the payoff-dominant strategy, by testing $H_0: \beta_4 = 0$, or $H_A: \beta_4 \neq 0$, Table 3.6 shows the estimated coefficient on experience, β_4, is positive and significantly different from zero at the 1 percent level with a marginal effect equal to 0.74. The probability of playing the payoff-dominant strategy increases by 74 percent for individuals with prior experience in the conservation objective.

Result 4

As expected and observed in the unconditional results, play of the payoff-dominant strategy increases as subjects gain experience in a conservation objective.

Consider next coordination exposure and frequency (H3) by testing $H_0: \beta_3 = 0$, or $H_A: \beta_3 \neq 0$. We observe in Table 3.6 the estimated coefficient on coordination exposure, β_3, is negative but not significantly different from zero; we fail to reject the null hypothesis. Exposure to other coordinating outcomes has no statistical influence on the probability of playing the

Table 3.6   Probit model with random effects

Variable	Dependent Variable: X LRI = 0.54 Predicted correctly = 76%	
	Coefficient	Slope
CONSTANT	−4.63*	
	(0.70)	
LEFF	6.58*	1.25*
	(0.61)	(0.23)
S2	−2.08*	−0.39*
	(0.46)	(0.10)
COORD	−0.57	−0.11
	(0.41)	(0.09)
XP	3.91*	0.74*
	(0.60)	(0.09)
RHO	0.67*	
	(0.06)	
LR TEST FOR RE MODEL	$\chi_1^2 = 283.78*$	
N	1440	

Note: Denotes significance level at 1%, ** 5% significance level; standard errors are in parentheses.

payoff-dominant strategy. However, Result 1 indicates the type of exposure, corridor or corner, had differing affects on strategy choice in the core treatment suggesting this coefficient should be negative and significant. One explanation for the insignificant variable is that, although prior exposure to other configurations created focal points that were difficult to overcome when moving from less complex to more complex treatments, focal points were easily overcome when moving from more complex to less complex treatments; thus the effects were negated.

Turning to the observations on the core treatment for rounds 11–20, Table 3.5 shows play of strategies other than the payoff-dominant strategy, X, to be split about 50–50 between second best strategies, Y, and fragmented strategies, Z. Result 1 indicates the type of exposure, corridor or corner, had differing affects on strategy choice. We now test the effect of coordination exposure on play of fragmented strategies (H4) formally by replacing X with Z and limiting the sample to core observations in rounds 11–20.

The testable hypothesis is $H_0:\beta_3 = 0$, or $H_A:\beta_3 \neq 0$, Table 3.7 shows the coefficient on *coord* is negative, and different from zero at the 1 percent

Table 3.7   Probit model with random effects, CORE: rounds 12–20

Variable	Dependent Variable: Z LRI = 0.24 Predicted correctly = 68%	
	Coefficient	Slope
CONSTANT	0.46	
	(1.62)	
LEFF	−0.07	−0.02
	(1.65)	(0.47)
EXPCO	−1.30*	−0.37*
	(0.42)	(0.12)
RHO	0.47*	
	(0.10)	
TEST FOR RE MODEL	$\chi_1^2 = 49.15$*	
N	288	

Notes: *Denotes significance level at 1%; standard errors are in parentheses.

significance level, with a marginal effect equal to −0.37. We reject the null hypothesis: subjects exposed to coordination in earlier rounds tend to choose strategies resulting in second best outcomes as opposed to fragmented strategies. Alternatively, individuals with prior exposure to non-coordinated objectives play fragmented habitat strategies more frequently.

Result 5
The frequency with which the payoff-dominant strategy is played is not affected by exposure to other coordinated outcomes. However, the alternative choice of strategies depends on the type of exposure. As observed in the unconditional results, subjects with exposure to cooperating outcomes are more likely to play second best strategies compared to subjects with exposure in non-cooperating outcomes.

7   CONCLUSION

Compensating landowners for their stewardship can help align their land use decisions with social goals of species protection. The challenge is to provide a compensation mechanism that is both voluntary and can create spatially contiguous habitats across several private landowners. The agglomeration bonus is one potential incentive mechanism that could work toward meeting this challenge. By making participation voluntary, the agglomeration bonus creates a setting that aligns landowners' incentives and species protection goals into contiguous habitat preserves.

In this chapter we explore individual behavior to coordinate conservation efforts given we design the agglomeration bonus to induce specific habitat targets, such as a corridor, core, cross and isolated corners. We design an experimental grid game, in which four landowners have thousands of potential strategy choices about which acres to retire. Our results at the individual level suggest the agglomeration bonus remains relatively robust within a relatively complex coordination game environment. Subjects played the payoff-dominant strategy 83 percent of the time in the corridor treatment. Subjects also found the first- and second-best isolated four corners conservation objective 89 percent of the time.

People, however, found it more challenging to find the first-best outcome for the core and cross objectives: 52 and 39 percent payoff-dominant strategy. We see 27 percent played fragmented strategies in the core, and 21 percent for the cross. The poorer results arose here because the complexity of the grid coordination game increased: now one had to coordinate with three other landowners, not just one, as in the corridor or none in the corner objectives. We observed greater complexity increased the probability of coordination failure by 39 percent. Alternatively, prior experience with the treatment increased play of the payoff-dominant strategy by 74 percent. In addition, play of fragmented habitat strategies was more likely (37 percent) if players first had an incentive to go to the corners; isolation incentives made it more difficult to convince them to use the core even when it was more profitable.

NOTES

1. See Parkhurst *et al.* (2002).
2. The Appendix, which can be obtained by request from the authors, provides the complete experimental instructions.
3. These AB sessions were run in part to test whether initial experience with non-coordination on the fence line (corner) affected a group's ability to coordinate on the fence line (core or cross).
4. In contrast, Parkhurst *et al.*'s (2002) two-player study of the agglomeration bonus had eight strategy choices, which created a 64-cell payoff matrix, with four Nash equilibria.
5. For the corridor, core, and cross treatments X, Y, and Z are defined as follows: X is the payoff-dominant strategy that results in the optimal conservation configuration when played by all subjects; Y is the set of strategies that when played by all subjects result in a non-optimal conterminous habitat reserve; and Z is any strategy that results in fragmented habitat. For the corners treatment X, Y, and Z are defined as follows: X is the dominant strategy that results in the Nash equilibrium four isolated habitat reserve outcome; Y is any strategy that if played by all subjects results in four non-optimal

isolated habitat reserves; and Z is any strategy that if played by all subjects results in more or less than four habitat reserves.

6. The experimental design limits us to the following comparisons: (1) corridor and core in sessions 1, 2, 3, and 4, for all observations, rounds 1–10, and rounds 21–30; (2) corridor, core, and corners in rounds 1–10; (3) corridor–core and corner–core in rounds 11–20 for sessions 1, 2 and 7, 8; and (4) core–corridor–core and core–corner-core in rounds 21–30 for sessions 3, 4 and 5, 6.

7. 'Experienced' means the subjects have encountered this identical conservation objective in rounds 1–10.

8. 'Corridor (corner) experienced' means subjects faced the corridor (corner) objective in the 10 rounds preceding play of the core objective. This could be corridor (corner) in rounds 1–10 and the core in rounds 11–20 or the corridor (corner) in rounds 11–20 and the core in rounds 21–30.

9. See Table 3.3 for a description of the hypotheses and test statistics. A Fisher's exact test is used to test all the null hypotheses for Result 1(a), (b), and (c).

10. We establish differences in proportion of play of strategy groups X, Y, and Z by using an rxc chi square test of proportions (see Table 3.3).

11. Another difference exists between the two treatments: payoffs are flatter in the core relative to the corridor treatment. Successfully coordinating with the row player in the corridor treatment increased payoffs from $191 to the dominant Nash earnings of $227, which is an increase of $36 (16 percent) of maximum earnings. For the core treatment, coordination with both the row and column player yielded an increase from $262 to $282, or $20, which is 7 percent of maximum earnings. The potential losses associated with playing the payoff-dominant strategy are smaller for the core treatment, $50, relative to $80 in the corridor treatment. A comparison of the gains-to-losses ratio across the two treatments shows they are within a reasonable range: 0.40 for the core and 0.45 for the corridor.

12. The probability of playing a fragmented strategy in the core treatment in rounds 1–10 in sessions 1 and 2 was not statistically different from playing a fragmented strategy in the first 10 rounds of the core treatment for sessions 5 and 6; *p-value* $= 0.374$.

13. A Markov process is a finite state space stochastic process independent of time in which a subject's future action depends only on his current state. This implies that subjects base this period's conservation strategy decision only on the conservation strategy choice in the previous period. For expediency, we bunch the millions of possible conservation strategies into three groups constructing a three-state space transition matrix. The Markov process is characterized as a discrete time Markov chain with stationary–transition probabilities, which means the Markov process has a finite number of periods, and that equal weight is assigned to each transition probability regardless of when it occurs (that is, the weight from period 1 to 2 equals the weight from period 29 to 30).

14. The corner treatment is excluded from this analysis because it is not a coordination game. The corner treatment has only one Nash equilibrium and therefore one dominant strategy and theory dictates there is no uncertainty regarding which strategy should be played.

15. When player i plays the payoff-dominant strategy but the others do not, $LEFF_{i,t-1}$ can be as low as 0.68. The minimum value for $LEFF_{i,t-1}$ is 0.49, which results when coordination failure occurs.

REFERENCES

Bean, M.J. (1998), 'The Endangered Species Act and private land: four lessons learned from the past quarter century', *Environmental Law Reporter News and Analysis*, 10701–10.

Bean, M.J. (1999), 'Lessons from Leopold in assessing the ESA', *Endangered Species Bulletin*, **24**, 18–19.

Beier, P. and R.F. Noss (1998), 'Do habitat corridors provide connectivity?', *Conservation Biology*, **12**, 1241–52.

Black-footed Ferret Recovery Implementation Team (BFFRIT) (2002), 'Black-footed ferret: ferret facts', http://www.blackfootedferret.org/ (cited 5\20\02).

Brosetta, B. (2000), 'Adaptive learning and equilibrium selection in experimental coordination games: an ARCH(1) approach', *Games and Economic Behavior*, **32**, 25–50.

Brown, G. and J. Shogren (1998), 'Economics of the Endangered Species Act', *Journal of Economic Perspectives*, **12**, 3–18.

Crawford, V.P. (1995), 'Adaptive dynamics in coordination games', *Econometrica*, **63**, 103–43.

Erev, I. and A.E. Roth (1998), 'Predicting how people play games: reinforcement learning in experimental games, with unique mixed strategy equilibria', *The American Economic Review*, **88**, 848–81.

Greene, W.H. (1993), *Econometric Analysis*, 3rd edn, Englewood Cliffs, NJ: Prentice-Hall.

Harsanyi, J.C. and R. Selten (1988), *General Theory of Equilibrium Selections in Games*, Cambridge, MA: The MIT Press, pp. xi–378.

Hof, J. and M. Bevers (1998), *Spatial Optimization for Managed Ecosystems*, New York: Columbia University Press.

Idaho Department of Fish and Game (IDFG) (2002), 'Habitat improvement program (HIP): key to the future for Idaho's game birds' (cited 1 March), www.state.id.us/fishgame/hip.html.

Innes, R., S. Polasky and J. Tschirhart (1998), 'Takings, compensation and endangered species protection on private lands', *Journal of Economic Perspectives*, **12**, 35–52.

McKenzie, E. (2003), 'Important criteria and parameters of wildlife movement corridors – a partial literature review', http://www.silvafor.org/library/docs (cited 5/13/2003).

Milgrom, P. and J. Roberts (1990), 'Rationalizability and learning in games with strategic complementarities', *Econometrica*, **58**, 1255–77.

Noss, R. (1993), 'The Wildlands Project land conservation strategy', *GreenDisk Paperless Environmental Journal*, February–March, http://www.connix.com/~harry/nosswild.txt.

Parkhurst, G. and J. Shogren (2004), 'Spatial habitat design by agglomeration bonus', working paper, University of Wyoming.

Parkhurst, G. and J. Shogren (2005), 'An economic review of incentive mechanisms to protect species on private land', in J. Shogren (ed.), *Species at Risk: Economic Incentives to Protect Endangered Species on Private Property*, Austin, TX: University of Texas Press.

Parkhurst, G., J. Shogren and C. Bastian (2004), 'Repetition, communication, and coordination failure', *Experimental Economics*, **7**, 141–52.

Parkhurst, G., J. Shogren, C. Bastian, P. Kivi, J. Donner and R.B.W. Smith (2002), 'Agglomeration bonus: an incentive mechanism to reunite fragmented habitat for biodiversity conservation', *Ecological Economics*, **41**, 305–28.

Saunders, D.A., R.J. Hobbs and C.R. Margules (1991), 'Biological consequences of ecosystem fragmentation: a review', *Conservation Biology*, **5**, 18–32.

Schelling, T.C. (1960), *The Strategy of Conflict*, Cambridge, MA: Harvard University Press, pp. 3–303.

Simberloff, D., J.A. Farr, J. Cox and D.W. Mehlman (1992), 'Movement corridors: conservation bargains or poor investments?', *Conservation Biology*, **6**, 4.

Smith, R.B.W. and J.F. Shogren (2002), 'Voluntary incentive design for endangered species protection', *Journal of Environmental Economics and Management*, **43**, 169–87.

Taylor, H.M. and S. Karlin (1984), *An Introduction to Stochastic Modeling*, Orlando, FL: Academic Press.

4. Forest management under the Endangered Species Act

Dean Lueck and Jeffrey A. Michael

1 INTRODUCTION

In 1973, the Endangered Species Act (ESA) was passed with the near unanimous approval of Congress.[1] Within a few years the ESA had become perhaps the most contentious of all the various pieces of federal environmental legislation passed during the early 1970s. Battles over landuse and development between landowners and the Fish and Wildlife Service (FWS)[2] became hostile and costly.

Within this context, some of the important battles have centered on the management of forestlands. Though there are many forest species involved, most of the US debate regarding the ESA and forest management has revolved around two species – the red-cockaded woodpecker (RCW) and the northern spotted owl[3] – because these species have impacted millions of acres of productive timberland. In this chapter, we focus on these two species, examining the extent to which private forest owners have acted to preemptively harvest timber in order to avoid ESA regulations and environmental groups have altered landuse on public forestlands by using ESA regulations to limit timber harvests.

Economists have noted that, under the ESA, the incentives of both private and public forest managers are altered (Brown and Shogren, 1998). On private land, the ESA effectively limits the property rights a forest owner has to timber value and thus can create incentives for the owner to alter the habitat (Epstein, 1997; Polasky and Doremus, 1998; Stroup, 1997). In some cases, landowners have been known to secretly kill endangered species, behavior now known as 'shoot, shovel, and shut up' (Dolan, 1992; Lambert and Smith, 1994). In other cases, landowners take action to destroy habitat that may prove suitable to endangered species. In these ways, landowners can avoid costly regulations that can severely limit their ability to earn income on their forest assets. Environmentalists have also recognized that ESA regulations intended to protect endangered species habitat may actually provide incentives for private landowners to reduce the available habitat (Wilcove *et al.*, 1996). On public forests, the situation is different because bureaucratic land managers do not have the control over forest uses or incentives of a private landowner. Similarly, commercial lumber companies who use these forests for their source of raw timber do not have direct control of landuse. In this chapter we examine the economic incentives for forest management that are created by the ESA (Brown and Shogren, 1998) and then examine some of the implications for actual forest practices. We also present some evidence of the impacts of the ESA on forest management in the United States on both private and public lands.

2   ECONOMICS OF FOREST MANAGEMENT UNDER THE ESA

A   Management of Private Forests under the ESA

Consider the economics of forest use under private ownership of a forest, by first assuming that the forest is valued only for timber production and that the forest owner starts with a plot of bare land. In this model, the owner of a private forest must choose the optimal rotation period for each successive stand of timber. We assume that the forest is an even-aged stand, that the forest site only has value for its harvested timber, and that there are no costs of replanting once the forest is harvested.

To begin, assume there are no ESA regulations and hence no uncertainty about the ability to harvest. Assuming the value of the forest grows over time and is given by $V(t)$, where $V'(t) > 0$ and $V''(t) < 0$, the problem for the forest owner is to maximize the present value of the forest, or

$$\max_t \left[\frac{V(t)e^{-rt}}{1 - e^{-rt}} \right]. \tag{4.1}$$

The optimal rotation age, $t^*(r)$, solves the following first-order necessary condition:

$$V'(t^*(r)) \equiv rV(t^*(r)) + \left(\frac{rV(t^*(r))}{e^{rt^*(r)} - 1} \right). \tag{4.2}$$

This well-known formulation has a simple interpretation. The left-hand side is simply the marginal benefit of allowing the forest to grow another period; the right-hand side is the total marginal cost of such growth and comprises two parts. The first term is the marginal cost of the current forest stand and the second term is the marginal cost of all future stands (or the forest's 'site value').

1 The ESA and forest management incentives

Although many of the high-profile conflicts over the ESA have involved public land management, such as of the snail darter in Tennessee and the northern spotted owl, the majority of endangered and candidate species reside on private land (General Accounting Office, 1994). For private land, sections 9 and 3 of the ESA are the most important. Section 9 made it unlawful to take any endangered species[4] within the jurisdiction of the United States, and section 3 defined 'take' to mean 'harass, harm, pursue, hunt, shoot, wound, kill, trap, capture, or collect'. In 1975, the Secretary of Interior went on to define 'harm' as follows:

> An act or omission which actually injures or kills wildlife, including acts which annoy it to such an extent as to significantly disrupt essential behavioral patterns, which include, but are not limited to, breeding, feeding, or sheltering; significant environmental modification or degradation which has such effects is included within the meaning of 'harm'.[5]

By the mid-1980s, a combination of administrative and court rulings combined to make habitat modification a violation of the ESA's section 9.[6] This policy was further solidified in 1995 in *Babbitt* v. *Sweet Home*, where the Supreme Court overturned a lower court's decision and upheld the broad definition of 'take' that includes habitat alteration.[7] Thus, under section 9 of the ESA, it is not only illegal to destroy an endangered species, but it is also illegal to damage their habitat.

The legal linkage from take to harm to habitat modification, clearly settled in *Babbitt*, is only the first of two steps in understanding how the ESA can generate private landuse restrictions. The second step is an explicit definition of habitat for each listed species. In practice, the FWS develops habitat protection guidelines as part of 'recovery plans' for all listed species.[8] Recovery plans typically discuss the species' distribution and history, target recovery populations, and outline actions necessary to promote species recovery, including habitat requirements. Most important, a recovery plan will define 'critical habitat' – specific habitat requirements (for example, grass of a certain height, water of a certain quality, or trees of a certain age) – that limits the range of compatible landuses.[9]

By linking take to harm and by linking harm to specific habitat recovery plans, the ESA becomes a landuse regulation.[10] Even so, the ESA is not like a typical zoning statute because its application is contingent on the presence of a listed species, rather than an explicit geographical zone. If a listed species inhabits a plot of land the landowner is clearly subject to the habitat recovery plan and its guidelines so that habitat modification would violate the ESA under section 9.[11] Still, if a landowner has habitat suitable for the species – perhaps even identical to land inhabited by the species – but presently the species does not inhabit his land, he is not subject to the habitat modification restriction of the recovery plan. Such habitat could potentially attract individuals from a mobile, nearby population of the endangered species and thus may ultimately be subject to landuse restrictions intended to prohibit harm. Because of this possibility of landuse restrictions, landowners with potential endangered species habitat may have the incentive to 'preempt' the ESA by destroying those characteristics of the land that would attract the species. Such preemptive activity would be a completely legal landuse decision spurred by the potential for costly regulations.

2 Optimal forest rotation under the ESA

The possibility of endangered species inhabitation and attendant ESA landuse regulation can be examined by considering potential ESA regulations as a possible 'catastrophe' that destroys the value of current and future timber stands.[12] Under ESA habitat guidelines for forest species (for example, red cockaded woodpeckers, spotted owls) the existing timber stand must often be preserved thus preventing future stands from being established. Because forests are long-lived, this prohibition sufficiently rules out future rotations after the endangered species leave the area. Let $\lambda \in (0,1)$ be a constant probability (each period) that the ESA will be invoked (because of inhabitance by an endangered species and detection by FWS), thus eliminating all current and future timber value. To simplify we assume that λ does not depend on the age of the forest so that the probability of no ESA regulation during the first period is $(1-\lambda)$ and the probability of no ESA regulation after t periods is $(1-\lambda)^t$. Because of the permanent nature of ESA regulation, a second timber rotation will only occur with probability $(1-\lambda)^t$, the chance that endangered species were not discovered during the first rotation. Thus the probability of no ESA regulation after the initial rotation and the first period of the second rotation is $(1-\lambda)^t(1-\lambda) = (1-\lambda)^{t+1}$, and the probability of no ESA regulation at the end of two rotation periods is $(1-\lambda)^{2t}$, and so on.

Because the ESA only allows the entire stand to be harvested if there are no endangered species present, the expected market value of the timber at the end of the first rotation is $V(t)e^{-\lambda t}$, and the expected value of the nth rotation is $V(t)e^{-\lambda nt}$.

The forest owner will now maximize the expected present value of the forest, which is given by

$$\max_t \left[\frac{V(t)e^{-(r+\lambda)t}}{1 - e^{-(r+\lambda)t}} \right]. \tag{4.3}$$

The optimal time to harvest the forest, $t^{ESA}(\lambda, r)$, must satisfy the following first-order necessary condition:

$$V'(t^{ESA}(\lambda, r)) \equiv (r + \lambda) V(t^{ESA}(\lambda, r)) + \left(\frac{(r + \lambda) V(t^{ESA}(\lambda, r))}{e^{(r+\lambda)t^{ESA}(\lambda,r)} - 1} \right). \tag{4.4}$$

The optimality condition in (4.4) has a simple interpretation that is best seen when it is compared to equation (4.2) and is different only because of the addition of the ESA regulation probability, λ, essentially as an additional discounting term. This effectively increases the marginal cost of letting a stand grow in terms of forgone value derived from both current and future stands. It is clear from inspection of (4.2) and (4.4) that optimal rotation decreases with the potential for endangered species inhabitation; that is, $t^{ESA} < t^*$. More important, however, is the result that, as the probability of endangered species colonization increases, the shorter will be the optimal forest rotation; that is, $\partial t^{ESA}/\partial \lambda < 0.$[13]

It is a straightforward extension to incorporate a species' proclivity for older trees (for example, both red cockaded woodpeckers and spotted owls prefer old growth forests) by assuming that the probability of the regulatory 'catastrophe' is increasing with the age of the stand (that is, $\lambda = \lambda(t)$, $\lambda'(t) > 0$). Thus, as stand age increases, the probability of endangered species inhabitation and ESA regulation increases, causing a decrease in the optimal rotation period.

B   Management of Public Forests under the ESA

On public land such as national or state forests, the ESA creates different incentives because land managers and land users do not have effective control over landuse like a private landowner (Deacon and Johnson, 1985; Nelson, 1995). Property rights to public lands can take the form of long-term leases (for example, cabins, ski areas), shorter-term use permits (for example, timber harvest contracts) or simply long-term historical practice. For example, in the Pacific Northwest timber companies have been purchasing and cutting public timber for nearly a century and likely had (prior to the ESA) the expectation that this practice would continue. So, while property rights to public lands do exist, they are much less clearly defined compared to private forests and subject to changes through political and administrative processes.

On public forests the ESA creates a mechanism by which rights can be claimed for species preservation without compensation to the prior users of the land. The presence or the possibility of an endangered species on public land weakens and possibly dissolves other property claims to public lands such as timber harvest rights or other actions that might alter the habitat for the listed species (for example, road development, mineral extraction, grazing). If, for example, an endangered species is found in an area where public timber is harvested, the ESA may be used to place a moratorium on timber harvest and essentially transferring property rights over this land to the FWS or environmental groups pushing for the implementation of the ESA. Claiming public land can also occur when a known species becomes listed under the ESA as a 'threatened' or 'endangered' species and invokes ESA protections.[14] Because the ESA allows third parties to nominate species for protection and because the ESA allows third parties to sue the FWS (and other federal agencies) for improperly administering the ESA, environmentalists can use the ESA to claim forest habitat and limit timber harvest. Because the precise incentives are difficult to determine in public forest management it is accordingly difficult to develop a precise economic model with clear predictions, yet the following outcomes are plausible predictions about public forest management under the ESA. First, we expect that timber harvest rates will decline in the presence of ESA regulations. Second, we expect the public forest agencies will divert their budgets and employees from timber management (and other extractive landuses) toward wildlife management and recreational uses that do not adversely impact wildlife.

3   THE RED-COCKADED WOODPECKER AND THE SOUTHEAST PINE FOREST

The red-cockaded woodpecker (*Piocoides borealis*) was one of the original species listed under the ESA, having been listed in 1970 under the ESA's precursor, the Endangered Species Conservation Act of 1969. The RCW is a non-migratory, territorial woodpecker that resides primarily in southern pine ecosystems ranging from Texas, to Florida, to Virginia. RCWs live in social units called clans or colonies, which consist of a single breeding pair, the current year's offspring and a several 'helpers'. Costa and Walker (1995) estimate that there were 4582 surviving RCW colonies, 3639 clans on public lands and 893 clans on privately owned lands.

The North Carolina Sandhills region (part of our study area) is home to the second largest RCW population with 371 colonies and is the only large population with a significant amount of habitat on private land. From the early 1980s to 1990 the estimated number of colonies in the Sandhills declined by over a third. Declining RCW populations are directly related to the loss of suitable habitat, from timbering, the encroachment of hardwoods into mature pine stands, and the demographic isolation of individual groups.[15] Timber harvesting directly reduces RCW habitat by eliminating the pine trees necessary for nesting and foraging habitat.

For our purposes, the most important ecological characteristics of RCWs are their dependence on mature forests for nesting and foraging habitat and their limited mobility. Although RCWs are considered 'non-migratory', they are known to travel up to 15 miles to find new habitat or a mate.[16] RCWs typically excavate nesting cavities in pines greater than 70 years old, but have been known to nest in 40–70-year-old trees when older trees are not readily available (Jackson *et al.*, 1979; Lennartz *et al.*, 1983; Hooper, 1988). While older pines are preferred for nesting cavities, trees as young as 30 years can provide RCW foraging habitat. Depending on the age structure and density of the trees, between 60 and 200 acres of pine forest are required for the nesting and foraging habitat of a single colony of RCWs.

A The History of RCW Policy

Changes in FWS habitat guidelines, and the events that led to these changes, are the most important aspect of RCW management for our study (Environmental Defense Fund, 1995; McFarlane, 1992; Michael, 1999; U.S. Fish and Wildlife Service, 2003). Throughout most of the 1970s, there was no formal recovery plan in place for the RCW. U.S. Forest Service policy was to leave an undisturbed 200-foot buffer around cavity trees, while the forest industry standard was simply to not harvest RCW cavity trees. In 1979, the FWS finally approved the first RCW Recovery Plan. The primary habitat requirements were a 200-foot buffer protecting cavity trees and providing 100–250 acres of adjacent foraging habitat consisting of trees at least 20 years old.

Disappointed in the recovery plan and its implementation on public lands, the National Wildlife Federation filed a notice of violation of the Endangered Species Act with the FWS and the Forest Service in 1983.[17] In response, the two agencies agreed to resolve their differences and develop a revised recovery plan that was issued in 1985. The 1985 RCW Recovery Plan significantly strengthened the habitat requirements of its predecessor (Lennartz and Henry, 1985). The new plan increased the minimum age for foraging habitat from 20 to 30 years, and required that 40 percent of foraging habitat be maintained in trees of at least 60 years of age. An alternative specification allowed owners of particularly well-stocked foraging habitat to meet their requirements on somewhat less land than the previously required 125 acres, perhaps as little as 60 acres.[18] Increasing the required age of foraging habitat increases the cost of providing habitat and reduces the management flexibility of rotating the available foraging habitat between different forest stands. Bonnie (1995) uses the 1985 guidelines to estimate the cost of forgone timber harvests from providing habitat for a single RCW colony at $196 107 ($981 per acre) of forgone timber revenue. If the forest owner is able to harvest pine straw (needles) while maintaining the old growth pine forest these costs fall to $101 694 ($508 per acre). These estimates indicate that, under the 1985 guidelines, there was a large financial incentive for landowners to preemptively harvest timber if there is a chance that RCWs may locate on their land.[19]

In addition to the stricter guidelines, there appeared to be an increase in ESA enforcement following 1985, perhaps because of the threat of third party lawsuits such as the complaint filed by the National Wildlife Federation. For example, in 1987, a development company was found guilty of killing two RCWs and cutting and burying 200 cavity trees to prepare a site for a 4500-home residential development near Ocala, Florida.[20] In 1989, the FWS issued the 'Blue Book Guidelines'[21] to clear up some confusing areas of the 1985 Recovery Plan. The Blue Book specifically stated that, if a landowner took action that reduced habitat below the levels specified in the guidelines, and colony abandonment followed, there would be 'strong evidence' of a taking violation. In 1991, the regulation of private landowners for RCW habitat made national headlines with the case of North Carolina landowner Ben Cone. To protect 12 colonies of RCWs, the FWS restricted Cone from harvesting timber on 1500 of his 7200 acres. After a consultant estimated the timber value of the regulated acres at $2 million, Cone became an outspoken critic of the ESA and proceeded to clearcut potential RCW habitat on his unregulated acres. Cone's behavior clearly demonstrates how the incentives of the ESA can drive some landowners to destroy more habitat than they protect (Stroup, 1997).

Since the Cone case in 1991, FWS enforcement has been characterized by greater flexibility (Environmental Defense Fund, 1995). In 1992, the FWS prepared a draft private lands manual that effectively cut in half the required acreage of old growth pine per RCW colony. Habitat Conservation Plans (HCPs) with private landowners became more common in the mid-to-late 1990s.[22] In 1995, the FWS implemented the first 'Safe Harbor' program in the North Carolina Sandhills region, which allows a landowner with RCWs to establish and protect a base population in return for no future landuse restrictions. By 2001, the FWS had authorized 12 'incidental takes' of RCW habitat by private landowners in return for some mitigation actions, and had implemented statewide Safe Harbor programs in South Carolina, Texas and Georgia. The most recent revision of the RCW recovery plan, approved in January 2003, emphasizes voluntary participation of landowners in RCW management, and places HCPs,

Safe Harbor and mitigation for incidental takes at the center of its private lands strategy. Clearly, the FWS has changed the regulations and enforcement of RCW habitat several times over the past 30 years. Enforcement was strongest between 1985 and 1992, but has become increasingly cooperative and flexible since that time. Thus we expect the probability of preemptive forest harvest to be greatest during from late 1980s and early 1990s.

B Evidence of Preemptive Habitat Destruction

The anecdotal stories of habitat destruction in the previous section are informative, but are insufficient to determine whether the ESA has induced habitat destruction on a larger, more significant scale. To test explicitly for the presence of preemptive timber harvesting requires examination of a large sample of landowners that face varying possibilities of being regulated under the ESA. We use two different data sets covering different time periods to explore preemptive timber harvest in North Carolina. First, we use the US Forest Service's Forest Inventory and Analysis (FIA) data to examine timber harvesting between 1984 and 1990, a period of strict FWS enforcement of RCW regulations. Second, we use a survey of forest landowners conducted by North Carolina State University (NCSU) to examine timber harvesting in the mid-1990s, a period of increasing flexibility and cooperation by the FWS when regulating private landowners with RCWs.

Our theoretical analysis predicts an increase in the probability that inhabitation of endangered RCWs and subsequent timber harvest restrictions will decrease the age at which forest stands are harvested.[23] To test this prediction, we combine data on timber harvest and other characteristics of randomly selected forest plots with the location of RCW colonies. The forest plot characteristics in each data set are different, and are described separately in the following sections. In both data sets, we measure the RCW inhabitation probability with data on the density of known populations of woodpeckers in the proximity of a particular forest plot.

Our measures of RCW density use GIS to map the location of forest plots and RCW colonies and then calculate the number of RCW colonies within a given radius of each forest plot. The data on RCW colonies are from the North Carolina Natural Heritage Foundation which maintains the most comprehensive database on the location of known RCW colonies. There are 1194 colonies in their database, which is consistent with the biological literature indicating the North Carolina population to be around 1000 colonies. Since RCWs may travel up to 15 miles, we calculate the number of RCW colonies within a five, 10 and 15-mile radius of each forest plot. The descriptive and summary statistics are shown in Tables 4.1 and 4.2.

Table 4.1 *Descriptive and summary statistics, FIA data, 1984–90*

Variable name	Definition	Minimum	Maximum	Mean	Standard deviation	Observations
Dependent variables						
HARVESTAGE	Age of forest at the time of harvest	7	136	47.9	19.8	385
Exogenous variables						
Timber market variables						
NMB	Net marginal benefit of additional year of growth	−196.91	581.43	−6.43	38.47	1199
TIMBERVALUE	Value of timber on plot in 1984	1.05	5513.43	676.76	801.43	1199
ESA variables						
RCW-10	Number of RCW colonies within 10 miles of a plot	0	326	12.5	40.2	1199
RCW-15	Number of RCW colonies within 15 miles of a plot	0	526	28.0	77.6	1199
Timber stand variables						
INDUSTRY	= 1 if landowner is industrial firm; = 0 if a non-industrial private firm	0	1	0.29	0.46	1199
SITEINDEX	Timber site productivity (height of a 50-year-old stand, in feet)	30	120	70.1	13.3	1199
STANDAGE	Age of forest stand in 1984	1	130	31.5	20.2	1199
LONGLEAF	= 1 if longleaf pine is the dominant species; = 0 if not	0	1	0.04	0.20	1199
LOBLOLLY	= 1 if loblolly pine is the dominant species; = 0 if not	0	1	0.55	0.50	1199
PONDPINE	= 1 if pond pine is the dominant species; = 0 if not	0	1	0.13	0.33	1199
OAKPINE	= 1 if pine with oak under-story is the dominant forest; = 0 if not	0	1	0.23	0.42	1199
SLASH	= 1 if slash pine is the dominant species; = 0 if not	0	1	0.043	0.20	1199

1 The FIA data: 1984–90

The FIA data are a detailed inventory of timber and other forest characteristics for approximately 5000 randomly selected forest plots in North Carolina. The forest plots were surveyed first in 1984–5 and again in 1989–90, providing information on timber harvest, forest characteristics, and forest growth for each plot during the period between the surveys that coincides with the period when FWS policy for RCW protection was most onerous to private landowners. Because we limit our analysis to privately owned plots of southern pine within the RCW's historical range, our data consist of 1199 forest plots.

Table 4.1 shows the descriptive and summary statistics for the FIA data. It shows, for example, that the average age at harvest (*HARVESTAGE*) was 47.9 years. The age of the stands at the beginning of our study period (*STANDAGE*) has a mean value of 31.5 years but ranges from 1 year to 130 years. The data contain information on the dominant species and distinguish between four species of southern pine (longleaf, loblolly, pond, and slash) and a mixed pine–oak forest. Loblolly pine is the most common species, found on 55 percent of the plots, and longleaf is the least common, found on just 4 percent of the plots.[24] The data also include a measure of timber site productivity (*SITEINDEX*), which measures the height (in feet) of a fifty-year-old stand of pine grown on a specific plot. The data also identify plots by ownership type (private forest industry and private nonindustrial) using the dummy variable *INDUSTRY* which shows 29 percent of the plots are owned by industrial firms.

We use timber prices and FIA data on timber volume and growth for each plot to create variables controlling for timber market considerations in the harvest decision. Our data allow us to create two such variables: the total value of the timber at the beginning of the survey period (*TIMBERVALUE*) and a measure of the net marginal benefit of an additional year of forest growth (*NMB*). From the harvest age model the marginal benefit (*MB*) is $V'(t)$ and the marginal cost (*MC*) is $rV(t) + rV(t)/(e^{rt} - 1)$. By combining information on timber volume with information on prices we are able to calculate *MB* and *MC* for each plot by computing the market value of the sampled timber stands at the time of each survey. Each tree is valued for different products as it grows, and each of these products has a different price per unit (for example, board foot) of timber. As a result, the value of a timber stand is not directly proportional to the total timber volume, but is increasing in volume (and age), and typically increases with the age and size of the trees.[25] Thus the stand's value must be calculated by classifying each tree in the sample plot into one of five product classes,[26] each with a different price.

Table 4.2 Descriptive and summary statistics, NCSU data 1993–97

Variable name	Definition	Minimum	Maximum	Mean	Standard deviation	Observations
Dependent variables						
HARVESTAGE	Age of forest at the time of harvest, in years	12	200	43.97	22.44	204
Exogenous variables						
Timber market variables						
TIMBER IMPORTANCE	Index of timber versus recreation importance to landowner*	–6	6	1.68	2.55	379
ESA variables						
RCW-10	Number of RCW colonies within 10 miles of a plot	0	330	34.95	65.43	520
RCW-15	Number of RCW colonies within 15 miles of a plot	0	530	86.31	130.49	520
Timber stand variables						
ACRES	= number of acres of softwood (pine) forest owned	26	12 000	183.59	606.84	530
RESIDE	= 1 if owner resides on the tract; = 0 if not	0	1	0.27	0.44	517
QUAIL	= 1 if owner hunts quail on the tract; = 0 if not	0	1	0.27	0.44	520
STRAW	= 1 owner generates income from pine straw; = 0 if not	0	1	0.06	0.24	530

Note: * Respondents were asked to rate the importance of timber production and recreation on a 7-point scale where 1 represents 'low priority' and 7 represents 'high priority'; this variable is the difference between the rating for timber production and recreation. For example, the maximum value of 6 means a landowner rated timber production as 7, and recreation as 1.

2   The NCSU data: 1993–7

Data from North Carolina forest landowners was collected from a Fall 1997 survey conducted by the School of Forestry and the College of Agriculture and Life Sciences at North Carolina State University. The survey generated a sample of 530 non-industrial forest landowners. Compared to the FIA data, these data contain less information on such variables as species composition and timber value,[27] but do contain information on non-timber landuses such as quail hunting, residential sites, and pine straw collection, which are often important for non-industrial forest owners in this region. The presence of these landuse characteristics adds value to standing timber and is likely to increase the optimal rotation age, and possibly decrease or mitigate the incentive to preemptively destroy potential RCW habitat.[28]

Table 4.2 shows the descriptive and summary statistics for the NCSU data. It shows, for example, that the average age at harvest (*HARVESTAGE*) was 44 years and that the average size of forest holding (*ACRES*) was 184 acres. *RESIDE, QUAIL*, and *STRAW* are dummy variables that indicate whether the landowner has their principal residence, hunts quail or gathers pine straw[29] for income on the forest tract. The table shows that 27 percent of the owners used the forest as a residence, that 27 percent hunted quail on the forest property, and that 6 percent collected pine straw for revenue.[30] The survey did not have enough detail on timber volume to allow a calculation of FIA variables like *NMB* or *TIMBER VALUE*, but we did construct an index (*TIMBER IMPORTANCE*) based on self-reported information on the value of timber compared to recreational uses. The index is positive if landowners place a higher priority on timber production than recreation, and negative if recreation is a higher priority. The mean value of 1.68 for *TIMBER IMPORTANCE* shows that timber production is more important than recreation for most survey respondents.

3   Harvest age and preemption estimates

To test the prediction that increases in the probability of ESA regulations will reduce the age of harvest we estimate the age of a forest stand at the time of harvest. For both the FIA from the 1980s and the NCSU data from the 1990s we use both OLS and censored regression estimation methods. For both data sets, only a fraction of the forest plots are harvested: 385 out of 1199 for the FIA data and 204 out of 530 for the NCSU data). This means the information on the age at harvest is thus censored and OLS estimation of age using this censored data would yield inconsistent parameter estimates. Thus, in addition to OLS estimation, we also use the following empirical specification:

$$A_i^* = X_i\beta + ESA_i\theta + \varepsilon_i \qquad \varepsilon_i | X_i, A_i^0 \sim Normal(0, \sigma^2) \qquad (4.5)$$

$$A_i = \min\{A_i^*, A_i^0\}. \tag{4.6}$$

In this specification i indicates a specific plot; X_i is a row vector of exogenous timber market and timber stand variables plus a constant; β is a column vector of unknown coefficients; ESA_i is the measured probability that the ESA will be enforced for plot i; θ is an unknown coefficient; and ε_i is a plot specific error term. A_i is the observable age of the stand but, as implied by (4.6), it takes on different values because of data censoring. A_i^* is the age of a stand that is harvested and A_i^0 is the age of the unharvested plots at the end of the study period (1990 for FIA data, 1997 for the NCSU survey data).[31] Our prediction is that the age of a forest at harvest will be lower as nearby RCW populations become more dense; that is, $\theta < 0$. We use censored normal regression to generate maximum likelihood estimates of the model given by (4.5) and (4.6). For comparison we also estimate A_i^* using OLS. Our dependent variable, *HARVESTAGE*, equals the age at harvest for uncensored observations and the age of the unharvested stand for censored observations.

Table 4.3 presents the parameter estimates from eight (four OLS and four censored regressions) different specifications using the 1980s FIA data. For both OLS and censored regressions, two equations include *NMB* and two include *TIMBERVALUE*.[32] All equations include timber stand variables that control for the ownership category, site productivity, and species composition. All of the coefficient estimates for the *RCW* variables have a negative sign as predicted. The estimates are not statistically significant in the OLS specifications but are in the censored regression specifications. These estimates indicate that proximity to larger populations of a listed endangered species decreases the age at which a forest stand will be harvested. As predicted the estimated coefficients from *NMB* are negative, and statistically significant, in all three equations. The specifications that use *TIMBERVALUE* as a timber market variable (instead of *NMB*) show, as predicted, positive estimated coefficients.

The estimated coefficients can be directly interpreted. For example, using the coefficient in specification (4.6) – *RCW-15* – an additional colony of RCWs will reduce the harvest age by 0.012 years, or 4.4 days. Using the 10-mile RCW density (specification 4.5) the age reduction is 0.039 years, or 14.2 days. A more relevant measure of these effects is seen by examining a movement from low to high-density RCW areas. For the 10-mile density, this means a change from three colonies to 66 colonies, or a reduction in harvest age of 2.5 years. For the 15-mile density, this means a change from seven colonies to 171 colonies, or a reduction in harvest age of 2.0 years. These effects should probably not be interpreted as inducing every forest owner to make a small adjustment in harvest age. A more plausible

Table 4.3   OLS and censored regression estimates of the age at harvest, 1984–90 (Dependent variable = HARVESTAGE)

Exogenous variables	OLS regression				Censored regression			
	(1)	(2)	(3)	(4)	(5)	(6)	(7)	(8)
Constant	36.46*** (5.67)	36.46*** (5.67)	53.10*** (5.59)	53.01*** (5.58)	66.109 (5.458)***	66.156 (5.460)***	79.379 (5.253)***	79.339 (5.253)***
Timber market variables								
NMB	−0.174*** (0.024)	−0.174*** (0.024)			−0.046 (0.183)**	−0.460 (0.0183)**		
TIMBER VALUE			0.013*** (0.0011)	0.013*** (0.0012)			0.0094 (0.0011)***	0.0094 (0.0011)***
ESA variables								
RCW-10	−0.021 (0.021)		−0.0084 (0.019)		−0.039 (0.0204)**		−0.029 (0.182)*	
RCW-15		−0.011 (0.011)		−0.0032 (0.010)		−0.0120 (0.0107)**		−0.0140 (0.0096)*
Timber stand variables								
INDUSTRY	−5.218*** (2.308)	−5.27*** (2.315)	−2.921 (2.15)	−2.906 (2.16)	−5.634 (2.074)***	−5.711 (2.078)***	−2.544 (1.878)	−2.591 (1.803)
SITEINDEX	1.79*** (0.750)	1.80*** (0.749)	−1.63*** (0.797)	−1.62*** (0.796)	−0.718 (0.7103)	−0.713 (0.7100)	−3.651 (0.0745)***	−3.638 (0.0745)***
LOBLOLLY PINE	−7.66*** (2.11)	−7.65*** (2.11)	−12.17*** (2.00)	−12.17*** (2.00)	−0.522 (2.091)	−0.505 (2.090)	−4.199 (1.899)**	−4.182 (1.899)**
LONGLEAF PINE	9.67** (4.94)	9.38** (4.85)	5.22 (4.60)	4.95 (4.51)	14.042 (4.663)***	13.721 (4.612)***	8.824 (4.218)**	8.499 (4.177)*
PONDPINE	−0.340 (3.07)	−0.326 (3.06)	−3.914 (2.87)	−3.901 (2.87)	3.129 (2.964)	3.108 (2.964)	−0.551 (2.690)	−0.554 (2.690)

Table 4.3 (continued)

Exogenous variables	OLS regression				Censored regression			
	(1)	(2)	(3)	(4)	(5)	(6)	(7)	(8)
SLASH PINE	−14.322***	−14.368***	−15.816***	−15.94***	−4.914	−4.884	−6.127	−6.164
	(6.283)	(6.278)	(5.80)	(5.79)	(5.143)	(5.144)	(4.601)	(4.603)
Observations	385	385	385	385	1199	1199	1199	1199
R^2	0.2399	0.2399	0.3509	0.3507				
Log-likelihood					−1963.08	−1963.17	−1936.51	−1936.71

Note: Standard errors in parentheses. ***, **, * statistically significant at the 1%, 5%, and 10% levels, respectively; 1-tailed test for predicted coefficients (ESA variables). Lueck and Michael (2003) is the source for the censored regression estimates.

78

interpretation is that a small number of owners make large adjustments in optimal harvest age. A switch from 70 to 40-year rotations by just 10 percent of the landowners would be consistent with a three-year decrease in average harvest age. Ben Cone, who shortened his timber rotations from 80 years to 40 years to protect himself from increases in his RCW population, is such an example.

The estimated coefficients for site productivity (*SITEINDEX*) are always negative in the censored regressions, but only statistically significant in those specifications that include *TIMBERVALUE*. These findings are intuitive; more productive timberland will be harvested at a younger age. The estimated effect of ownership (*INDUSTRY*) shows that industry timber tends to be harvested at a younger age (from two-and-a-half to six years) than non-industrial private forests. The effects of species mix vary among the species. Again, the pine species dummies are used and the oak–pine mix is the left out category. The estimates consistently show that longleaf pine forests are harvested at an older age. Loblolly pine is harvested at a younger age but these estimates are only statistically significant when *TIMBER-VALUE* is included. The estimated effects for pond and slash pine are never statistically significant.

Table 4.4 presents the parameter estimates from eight (four OLS and four censored regressions) different specifications using the 1990s NCSU data. All equations include variables that control for pine straw production, residential home use, the size of the forest tract, and the relative importance of timber production to the landowner.[33] For some models, we also included an interaction variable between the *RCW* variables and *STRAW*. Pine straw production is one income-producing use of land that is compatible with the presence of RCWs; in fact the open understory forests preferred by RCWs are ideal for pine straw raking because there are fewer contaminants (such as leaves) and obstacles (such as brush) to interfere with collecting pine straw from the forest floor. We expect a positive coefficient for *RCW*STRAW* variables, because landowners who produce pine straw have lower costs from RCW regulation and are therefore less like to preemptively harvest timber.

The estimated coefficients for the timber stand variables do not give as clear a picture as with the FIA data. The *RESIDE* variable has the expected positive coefficient and is statistically significant in all specifications, indicating that landowners who live on the forest tract harvest their timber about nine years later than landowners who do not reside on the tract. The *STRAW* variable is consistently positive when the interaction term is not present, and is statistically significant in the censored regressions. In the specifications with *STRAW*RCW*, the coefficient on *STRAW* is not statistically significant, indicating that pine straw raking does not lead to longer

Table 4.4 OLS and censored regression estimates of the age at harvest, 1993–97 (Dependent variable = HARVESTAGE)

Exogenous variables	OLS regression				Censored regression			
	(1)	(2)	(3)	(4)	(5)	(6)	(7)	(8)
Constant	51.62*** (5.80)	50.269*** (5.925)	54.030*** (5.632)	53.421*** (5.757)	78.974*** (4.963)	77.889*** (5.022)	78.834*** (4.748)	78.514*** (4.832)
Timber market variables								
TIMBER	-2.211* (1.688)	-1.841 (1.695)	-2.732** (1.629)	-2.331* (1.624)	-3.730*** (1.161)	-3.752*** (1.158)	-3.974*** (1.109)	-3.966*** (1.103)
IMPORTANCE								
ESA variables								
RCW-10	-0.101** (0.0535)		-0.105** (0.0513)		0.0107 (0.0408)		-0.0190 (0.0389)	
RCW-15		-0.0337 (0.0277)		-0.0451** (0.0267)		0.0167 (0.0208)		-0.00438 (0.0201)
RCW-10*STRAW			4.616*** (1.766)				2.714* (1.742)	
RCW-15*STRAW				0.438*** (0.158)				0.297** (0.130)
Timber stand variables								
ACRES	0.000124 (0.00218)	-0.000035 (0.00222)	0.000204 (0.00209)	0.0000512 (0.00211)	-0.00359* (0.00240)	-0.00346* (0.00240)	-0.00275 (0.00225)	-0.00267 (0.00225)
RESIDE	19.221*** (6.944)	19.049*** (7.081)	15.510** (6.802)	15.314** (6.878)	9.411* (5.956)	9.245* (5.938)	9.481** (5.693)	9.120* (5.645)

STRAW	7.414	9.733	−23.345	−16.678	24.003**	23.168**	−3.754	−3.412
	(13.777)	(13.902)	(17.684)	(16.327)	(10.749)	(10.796)	(13.368)	(12.461)
Observations	71	71	71	71	320	320	320	320
R^2	0.153	0.127	0.235	0.220				
Log-likelihood					−394.169	−393.875	−388.471	−388.215

Note: Standard errors in parentheses. ***, **, * statistically significant at the 1%, 5%, and 10% levels respectively; 1-tailed test for predicted coefficients.

forest rotations in areas with few RCWs. The negative coefficient on
ACRES indicates that forest rotations are slightly shorter for larger tracts,
but the magnitude of this effect is very small.

The estimated coefficients for the *RCW* variables have the expected negative effect and are statistically significant in the OLS specifications, but are
of varying sign and insignificant in the censored regressions. When the
interaction term is included, the point estimates on the RCW variables are
smaller than with the FIA data. For example, using *RCW-15*, a move from
an area of low RCW density to high density would decrease harvest age by
0.72 years compared to two years for the FIA data. The coefficient on the
*RCW*STRAW* variables is of the expected positive sign and statistically
significant for both the OLS and censored regressions. This indicates that
pine straw producers do not preemptively harvest their timber and may
actually increase their forest rotation age near RCWs.

Compared to the 1984–90 FIA data, the *RCW* coefficient estimates for
the 1993–97 NCSU data do not strongly support the prediction that the
possibility of ESA regulations leads to preemptive timber harvesting. At
least two reasons for this finding are plausible. First, the 1990 NCSU data
contain less information on stand composition and timber value than do
the FIA data, and thus may suffer from omitted variable bias. Second, as
we noted in section 2, the FWS's enforcement policy change for habitat
modification changed substantially from the late 1980s until the mid-1990s,
so that the incentive to preemptively harvest timber may simply have largely
diminished for the RCW.[34]

C RCWs on Public Land

In section 2 we argued that the incentive for preemptive harvest will be
absent from public lands because public land managers will have little
incentive to push for earlier harvests since they do not gain directly from
the timber revenues. For public lands with prospective RCW habitat, then,
the ESA is expected to alter landuse from timber harvest to non-timber
management compatible with RCW conservation. Though we have not
done a comprehensive survey of public land management in the RCW's
southeastern pine forest, there is some case study evidence that indicates
this has been the case.

In the South, the most important public landuse conflict over the RCW
has been on military bases. In particular, Eglin Air Force Base in Florida
and Fort Bragg Army Base in North Carolina are both home to over 200
active RCW colonies. Approximately 22 percent of the 3500 remaining
active colonies are on Army installations. Large expanses of these bases are
now off limits to many training exercises. Training realism and scope has

been reduced, as infantry cannot train all of its wartime missions on base because of the restrictions on the use of armor and aviation near protected RCW habitat. In addition, training costs have increased substantially as units must be relocated to other bases for many exercises. For example, required gunnery qualifications cost an additional $42 000 to conduct because it is necessary to transport an attack helicopter battalion from Fort Bragg, NC to Fort Stewart, GA owing to restrictions on training near RCW habitat on Fort Bragg (Sneddon, 1995). Military administrative resources have also been diverted into RCW management developing management guidelines, conducting research, and ensuring compliance with the ESA.[35]

Our prediction that preemption is not likely to occur on public lands ultimately depends on the political and bureaucratic constraints faced by the public land managers. It is possible that, if the agency were sufficiently captured by a commercial timber interest group, the public land managers might pursue a policy of preemption. Indeed, something like this may have happened on the national forests in east Texas in the late 1980s. In 1988, a federal court explicitly ruled that timber harvest could be a taking of RCWs under section 9 of the ESA. The decision, in *Sierra Club* v. *Lyng*,[36] came after a group of environmental groups led by the Sierra Club and Wilderness Society filed suit against the Forest Service, charging that the agency was failing to obey and enforce federal laws regarding the RCW in Texas. The court concluded that Forest Service timber management, by adversely modifying RCW habitat, constituted a taking of RCWs, and ordered the Forest Service to immediately change its practices in Texas. The Forest Service responded by developing a new management policy throughout the southeast that included halting all active timber sales within three-quarters of a mile of RCW colonies.[37]

4   THE SPOTTED OWL AND THE ANCIENT NORTHWEST FORESTS

Although the red-cockaded woodpecker has led to considerable conflict over forestland use, the conflict over the northern spotted owl has been even more contentious and perhaps more costly. The northern spotted owl (*Strix occidentalis caurina*), named for the white spots on its head and nape and its mottled belly, is a medium-size owl that inhabits the old-growth conifers of the Pacific Northwest (including British Columbia) and California (Forsman and Meslow, 1986).[38] Its numbers have been dwindling as old growth is harvested and converted into managed second growth forests. Although it is not clear why the owls prefer old growth the likely reasons are that the old growth forests provide desirable prey, suitable perches, or protection from extreme weather. Adult owls tend to mate for life and occupy the same territory year after year; in the northwest they nest in cavities or platforms in trees. The home range for adult owls can vary from 1000 acres to 8000 but because a mating pair does not always travel together the combined home range for such a pair is much larger.

A   The History of Spotted Owl Policy

Though interest in spotted owl conservation actually began in the 1970s with a graduate student's thesis at Oregon State University (Forsman and Meslow, 1986), it was not until the early 1980s that environmentalists became concerned and began to pressure federal forest managers (U.S. Forest Service, or USFS, and the Bureau of Land Management, or BLM) to limit harvest of old growth forests. The owl was not even listed under the ESA as a threatened species until 1990. During the 1980s there were several spotted owl management plans designed to protect certain areas from logging but new information about declining owl numbers and their rather large home ranges ultimately spurred litigation against federal land managers (Chase, 1995; Yaffee, 1994). In two lawsuits filed during the late 1980s, environmentalists challenged both the BLM and the USFS under a variety of federal environmental laws for failing to consider how proposed timber sales would affect the spotted owl.[39] The first bite from this litigation took place in May 1988 when the 9th U.S. Circuit Court of Appeals, in *Portland Audubon Society* v. *Hodel*, temporarily enjoined the BLM from selling old growth timber. Although this particular case was temporarily overturned upon appeal, the general trend of the litigation had been established. Federal land managers would have to prohibit the harvest of old growth timber in order to provide habitat for the spotted owl (Chase, 1995; Yaffee, 1994). Once the spotted owl was listed as a threatened species throughout its range in 1990, litigation focused on the ESA rather than other, more general, environmental laws.

B   Changing Landuse in the Northwest Forests

As a result of these lawsuits and the settlements that followed, millions of acres of public lands in California, Oregon and Washington were set aside as critical habitat for spotted owls and thus removed from the stock of potentially harvestable timber.[40] By 1996, nearly 11 million acres of federal land in California, Oregon and Washington were considered as critical habitat and off limits for timbering operations.[41] This acreage represents a substantial fraction of public forests in these three states, as much as 50 percent in Oregon and Washington.[42] These data do not include millions of acres of public land in national parks and wilderness areas where logging is already prohibited and therefore already committed to preserving old growth forests. Although the data are highly aggregated and do not show how owl lands differ from other forest lands, the evidence is clear that, by invoking the ESA (and related environmental legislation), environmentalists have substantially altered landuses on public forest land in the Pacific Coast states.

Given that a substantial proportion of public forests has been designated as spotted owl habitat under the ESA, it is not surprising that timber harvests from public lands dramatically declined in the 1990s.[43] Table 4.5 shows mean annual timber harvest in the Pacific Northwest from 1965 to 1996. The decline in harvest begins around 1988, when *Portland Audubon Society* v. *Hodel* was decided in a federal court. Table 4.5 shows the mean annual harvest for two periods by various forest ownership classes. We use 1978–88 as our pre-ESA period and 1989–96 as our post-ESA period and find that annual harvest rates decline substantially on public forests but do not change appreciably on private industrial forests.[44]

Our examination of the effects of the ESA on forests of the Pacific northwest is limited by the highly aggregated nature of the data and our inability to control for other economic forces such as timber prices. At the same time, the data on spotted owl habitat preservation acreage and the time series for regional timber harvest suggest a relatively large impact on landuse allocation after the ESA. These effects are roughly consistent with our idea that environmentalists can gain control over public forest management by invoking the ESA. Of course, there are many other possible issues to examine to more fully understand the effect of spotted owl protection on landuse and timber markets in the Pacific northwest.[45] Simple supply and demand analysis suggests that timber prices should have increased as owl acreage increased. This analysis also suggests that forest owners with few old growth stocks may have benefited substantially from the reduction in the supply of old growth timber. Indeed, the apparent lack of change in timber harvest in industrial forests (see Table 4.5) suggests that private forest owners (likely to have less old growth) may have been such beneficiaries, as also might be the case for forest owners in other parts of the country.[46]

5   OTHER FOREST MANAGEMENT ISSUES

The red-cockaded woodpecker and the northern spotted owl are the most important (in terms of acreage and timber values) involved endangered

Table 4.5   *Mean annual timber harvest in the Pacific Northwest before and after spotted owl preservation*

Place/period	Industry	USFS	BIA	BLM	State	Other public	Total
OREGON							
1978–88	3259	2982	112	889	228	30	7500
1989–96	3393	1426	91	448	129	33	5519
% change	+3.9	−52.2	−18.8	−50.4	−43.4	+10.0	−26.4
WASHINGTON							
1978–88	3865	1175	276	22	811	27	6176
1989–96	3716	485	212	10	549	25	4996
% change	−3.9	−58.7	−23.2	−54.5	−32.3	−7.4	−19.1
NORTHWEST							
1978–88	7124	4157	389	910	1038	57	13675
1989–96	7109	1911	302	457	678	58	10515
% change	−0.01	−54.0	−22.4	−49.8	−34.7	+1.8	−23.1

Note: *All timber harvest numbers are mean annual harvest rates by owner class, in millions of (Scribner) board feet. For Washington, BLM means 'other federal' lands besides USFS.

species inhabiting forests, yet there are many other endangered species on forestland. Some species like the spruce fir moss spider are found in extremely limited locations and their protection under the ESA appears to have had little impact. Other species, such as the golden-cheeked warbler and the marbled murrelet, have had significant impacts. The marbled murrelet is a small seabird, a bit larger than a robin, which lives along the Pacific Coast, from Alaska to central California. Even though its natural history is much different, its recent economic history is tied closely to that of the spotted owl. Like the owl it inhabits old growth forest, including the giant redwoods of northern California. Along with the spotted owl, the marbled murrelet was enlisted in the litigation effort to preserve old growth (spruce–fir) forest along the Pacific Coast, ultimately leading, among other things, to the acquisition of 44 000 acres for Redwood National Park.[47]

The golden-cheeked warbler is a small songbird (four or five inches long) that inhabits the central Texas woodlands during the spring and the summer, returning to Mexico and Central America for the remainder of the year.[48] It was listed as an endangered species in 1990, although the FWS had listed it as a 'Category 2' species in 1982, indicating that it might need attention in the near future. Not only does the warbler inhabit a relatively small region of Texas but also this area has been the site of rapid development around the city of Austin.[49]

In the late 1980s, the city of Austin and Travis County were already in the process of addressing the protection of the black-capped vireo, another small and endangered bird (listed under the ESA in 1986) that also inhabits the Hill Country around Austin. The city of Austin formed a committee to study the issue and develop a plan (the Balcones Canyonlands Conservation Plan, or BCCP) in order to be prepared for what seemed to be the inevitable listing of the golden-cheeked warbler. The idea was to develop the BCCP and get the approval of FWS so that development in the area could proceed according to some predetermined ground rules for species preservation.

The plan never came to fruition, however. In 1989, a biological study indicated that 123 000 acres in the Austin area, where land prices hovered at roughly $1000 per acre, would be required to protect a viable population of warblers. It was clear that the stakes were much higher than anyone had imagined. Shortly thereafter, the FWS announced its decision to list the warbler as 'endangered' and the decisions of landowners reverted to those discussed in our preemptive harvest model. As Mann and Plummer (1995) note, landowners began destroying ash juniper forests in order to thwart ESA regulations.[50] Hundreds of landowners had their lands surveyed for warblers and warbler habitat; if a parcel was clean a landowner could receive a 'bird letter' from the FWS indicating the land was not suitable for the warbler preserve and thus not subject to ESA regulations that might limit development. Mann and Plummer report that the value of such a letter was as much as a 25 percent increase in the value of a parcel. The complex and contentious negotiations between locals (developers, environmentalists and voters) and the FWS broke down and the BCCP, at least in it grandest form, was never enacted. While politicians and bureaucrats negotiated, individual developers began cutting deals (via habitat conservation plans and incidental take permits) with the FWS, which jeopardized the grand BCCP. Travis County voters rejected the plan trumpeted by Interior Secretary Bruce Babbitt in 1993. Ultimately, a preserve – the Balcones Canyonlands National Wildlife Refuge – was established well beyond the city limits and scattered parcels are protected under individual habitat conservation plans. Meanwhile, landowners near the new refuge 'mismanage' their land in order to limit the possibility of settlement by warblers and regulation by the ESA.[51] The lesson of the golden-cheeked warbler is that the ESA can have significant impacts on forest land even when timber considerations are not important.

6   SUMMARY AND CONCLUSIONS

The enactment of the 1973 ESA was a major shift in wildlife law in the United States (Lueck, 1998). Prior to the 1973 Act, preservation of endangered populations was limited to season closures or explicit compensation to those providing habitat (by either lease or purchase). The 1973 Act also extensively broadened the scope of federal action at the expense of state authority. By introducing strict landuse controls on both public and private landowners the ESA has altered the property rights to habitat that sustains endangered species. In this chapter we have focused on how the ESA has impacted the use of forests in the United States.

Our framework indicates that the effects of the ESA will be different on private and public lands. On private land, there are incentives for landowners to kill species and preemptively destroy habitat in order to avoid costly regulation.[52] Our evidence for the red-cockaded woodpecker indicates that this has, indeed, occurred in some southeastern pine forests, at least during the 1980s when FWS enforcement was strongest and before the Safe Harbor policy was implemented. On public land, there is an incentive for environmentalists and others supporting wildlife preservation to use political and legal methods under the ESA to get species listed and put habitat conservation plans in place in order to effectively claim control over landuse. Because these groups do not face the opportunity costs of these actions and because they cannot easily compensate previous landusers, battles can be contentious and costly. Aggregate evidence from the Pacific Northwest indicated that since the late 1980s environmentalists have been successful in claiming public forest from commercial timber users by using the ESA's protection of the northern spotted owl.[53]

The current dissatisfaction with the ESA, among both environmentalists and property owners, suggests that the relevant interest groups recognize some of the incentive problems with the current ESA examined in this chapter. While property owners tend to be uniformly opposed to the ESA (unless they can be sure they will avoid its force), the ESA has been a double-edged sword for environmental groups. On the one hand, the ESA has allowed environmentalists to hold great sway in the use and management of public lands. On the other hand, habitat is being destroyed and species are losing ground on private land, because of the ESA. These combined forces seem to be generating pressure to change the ESA, especially as it affects private landowners. Indeed, the rapidly increasing use of HCPs, Safe Harbor, and some landowner assistance grants shows movement in this direction, although it appears to be change within the framework of the existing ESA rather than taking on the more difficult challenge of changing the law.

NOTES

1. The vote was 92–0 in the Senate and 390–12 in the House (Yaffee, 1982).
2. The FWS is the prime federal agency charged with administering the ESA, although on federal lands other agencies can also be involved and marine endangered species administered by the National Marine Fisheries Service.
3. See Chase (1995) for a detailed study of forest management in the face of the ESA with a focus on the Pacific Northwest.
4. The lesser category of 'threatened' species are not strictly protected by section 9 but the FWS typically regulates its take so that in practice they are treated the same as 'endangered' (Bean and Rowland, 1997).
5. 40 Fed. Reg. 44412, 44416 (1975). Initially, however, the ESA gave no protection against taking for listed plants. The 1988 amendments did apply section 9 to plants on federal land (Rohlf, 1989).
6. This began to change with several federal decisions, starting with *Palila I* in 1979, where the court sided with the Sierra Club and other environmental groups who charged the state of Hawaii was 'taking' an endangered bird (the palila) by maintaining populations of feral sheep and goats (for sport hunting) that adversely impacted the palila's nesting sites. The court ordered the state to remove the animals after considering the ESA's definition of take and harm. In the *Palila II* decision in 1986, the court held that harm applies to a species not just individual animals, strengthening the connection between habitat modification and 'harm'. See 1986 *Palila* v. *Hawaii Department of Land and Natural Resources* 471 F. Supp 985 (D. Hawaii 1979) *aff'd* 639 F2d 495 (1981) and *Palila* v. *Hawaii Department of Land and Natural Resources* 649 F. Supp 1070 (D. Hawaii 1986) *aff'd* 852 F2d 1106 (9th cir.1988).
7. *Babbitt* v. *Sweet Home Communities for a Greater Oregon* 515 U.S. 687 (1995). The exact boundaries of 'harm' and 'take' are unknown (Bean and Rowland, 1997, pp. 213–25).

For example, while timber harvesting constitutes a take, bulldozing and livestock grazing may or may not. This ambiguity stems from such unresolved issues as causation, intent, knowledge, and omission.

8. Although section 4 of the 1978 ESA amendments requires plans (Rohlf, 1989, p. 87), many listed species do not have them.

9. For federal land critical habitat must be designated under section 4 and it is protected under section 7 (Rohlf, 1989, pp. 48–52).

10. This aspect of the ESA makes it unique among species conservation law. No other country has such landuse restrictions. See 'Issues in International Conservation', ed. Justina Ray, *Conservation Biology*, 13 (1999), 956–69. States also tend not to have ESA-like landuse restrictions in their species protection legislation. Rohlf (1989, p. 67) also agrees with our claim that Congress did not intend for the ESA to generate 'sweeping controls on non-federal landuse'.

11. Landowners, of course, might still choose to damage habitat and face the expected penalties. Section 11 provides for fines up to $50 000 and one year in prison for each violation, civil damages up to $25 000 for each violation and litigation costs, and forfeiture of property used in a violation (Rohlf, 1989; Bean and Rowland, 1997). Under the 1982 Amendments to the ESA, a landowner may acquire an incidental take permit (where the taking of species or habitat is incidental to and not the primary purpose of the activity) provided they develop a habitat conservation plan designed to mitigate the taking through appropriate conservation measures and habitat enhancement. Landowners also may simply ignore the law and eliminate any endangered species currently residing on their land before government officials can react.

12. Our model is an adaptation of Reed's (1984) fire model. Preemption can also be studied in a framework similar to industrial organization models of preemption and entry deterrence (for example, Lueck and Michael, 2003).

13. This simply extends the well-known result of the effect of the discount rate on optimal rotation (Bowes and Krutilla, 1989; Hartman, 1976).

14. Claiming could and does take place through arguing over the definition of what is the minimum required habitat.

15. Cely and Ferral (1995) study declining RCW populations in South Carolina between 1977 and 1989, finding hardwood encroachment (32.6 percent), Hurricane Hugo (27.4 percent), and timbering (21.0 percent) were important causes of loss. Hugo did not affect North Carolina forests and is not relevant for this study. Development is not always harmful; golf courses are often compatible with RCWs.

16. Costa and Walker (1995) estimate movement of five to 10 miles, while Winkler, Christie and Nurney (1995) estimate up to 15 miles for males.

17. The intense lobbying over the details of FWS guidelines are consistent with Ando's (1999) study of listing politics.

18. The plan also allowed a timber volume-based habitat requirement in which a colony could be provided with 6350 pine stems greater than 10 inches in diameter (at breast height) and 8490 square feet of basal area within a half mile of colony sites.

19. A typical one-acre stand of 70-year-old pine holds around 12–13 thousand board feet of saw timber, valued at roughly $200 per thousand board feet. This generates a timber value approximating $2500 per acre. For other similar estimates see Cleaves *et al.* [1994] and Lancia *et al.* (1989). Some selective cutting of trees is allowed under FWS guidelines as long as a minimum standards are met, and foraging habitat does not have to be totally provided by old growth stands, only nesting habitat. Thus the cost estimates of about $1000 per acre are less than the total old growth timber value assuming landowners manage their property as efficiently as possible.

20. The two top officials of the company were fined a total of $400 000 and each received two-year probationary sentences for this violation of the ESA (McFarlane, 1992). For a summary, see Bryanna Latoof, 'Two Accused of Killing Rare Birds: Indictment Charges Woodpeckers Shot, Nesting Trees Removed', *St. Petersburg Times*, August 3, 1987, p. 3B, and 'Men Fined for Killing Woodpeckers', *St. Petersburg Times*, September 16,

1987, p. 1B. In total the company incurred over one million dollars in penalties including court costs and habitat mitigation expenses.

21. The publication was officially titled, 'Guidelines for Preparation of Biological Assessments and Evaluations for the Red-Cockaded Woodpecker'. Because the Guidelines were distributed in a blue binder, this became commonly known as the 'Bluebook Guidelines'.

22. Ben Cone dropped his lawsuit against the FWS in 1996 after signing an HCP that released him from any future responsibilities under the ESA in return for paying approximately $40 000 to relocate the 12 RCW colonies from his property to a nearby National Forest.

23. Lueck and Michael (2003) use probit models to estimate the impact of potential ESA regulations on the probability of timber harvest.

24. Loblolly is the fastest growing species and is thus preferred for the establishment of timber plantations. Accordingly, loblolly stands tend to be younger than stands comprising other pine species.

25. Let $V(t) = p(t)f(t)$ where $f(t)$ is the volume of timber at time t with $f'(t) > 0$ and $f''(t) < 0$; and $p(t)$ is the competitive price per unit of harvested timber, which depends on the age of the timber, so that $p'(t) > 0$.

26. Three of these classes are the ones noted above and two are for hardwoods that are occasionally present in southern pine forests.

27. Because of the collaborate agreement that guided the survey, there were constraints on the survey questionnaire that prevented us from obtaining more detailed information.

28. Models with valuable standing timber do not generate clear predictions about optimal rotation age.

29. Pine straw is a popular mulch for landscaping in this region.

30. The correlation coefficient for *QUAIL* and *RESIDE* is just 0.055 despite the nearly identical means.

31. This is right censoring or what is sometimes called 'top coding' (Wooldridge, 2002, p. 571).

32. Lueck and Michael (2003) find this evidence to be robust to various specifications and methods.

33. We also used *QUAIL* in other specifications, but the coefficient estimates were always statistically insignificant, of inconsistent sign and very close to zero.

34. In fact, the high RCW density area for the landowner survey is the five-county Sandhills region where the FWS launched the first Safe Harbor program in 1995.

35. Since the war in Iraq, however, the Department of Defense has put pressure on FWS and Congress to relax these restrictions.

36. *Sierra Club* v. *Lyng*, 694 F. Supp 1260 (E.D. Tex. 1988) *aff'd* in part, vacated in part; *Sierra Club* v. *Yuetter*, 926 F. 2d. 429, 439 (5th Cir. 1991). Also see *Friends of Endangered Species* v. *Jantzen*, 760 F. 2d 976 (9th Cir. 1985).

37. This exceeds 1000 acres, more than the standard guidelines.

38. The northern spotted owl is one of three subspecies of the spotted owl. The other two are the California spotted owl and the Mexican spotted owl (Forsman and Meslow, 1986).

39. The two key cases are *Portland Audubon Society* v. *Hodel* (the BLM case) and *Seattle Audubon Society* v. *Robertson* (the USFS case). The key laws are the Federal Land Policy and Management Act, the National Forest Management Act of 1976, and the National Environmental Policy Act.

40. This dispute culminated in the 'forest summit' held in Portland by President Clinton in April 1993 which led to the policy recommend by the Forest Ecosystem Management Team (FEMAT). See Chase (1995) and Yaffee (1994).

41. These acreages are designated as either 'congressionally withdrawn' or 'administratively withdrawn', depending on the origin of the action and indicate areas for which timber harvest is prohibited (Forest Ecosystem Management, 1993).

42. This fraction depends on how one defines federal forest lands. If only USFS and forested BLM lands are included (so that national park lands are excluded) the fraction is about one-half for Oregon and Washington combined.

43. Chase (1995, pp. 374–8, 396–9) examines other economic impacts, including timber price increases and regional mill closures.
44. 1988 is, of course, not the only possible date to use but this seems to be the beginning of major policy changes for spotted owl management. Murray and Wear (1998) also find that 1988 is a useful cut-off in their study of timber market integration.
45. Montgomery and Brown (1992) and Montgomery *et al.* (1994) examine the costs of spotted owl conservation policies.
46. This is consistent with Murray and Wear (1998) who find that, after the ESA-based owl restrictions were in place, the US timber market became more integrated, indicating that southern timber producers entered the northwest timber market. Montgomery *et al.* (1994) estimate the cost of increasing the probability of spotted owl survival.
47. Chase (1995) documents the highly contentious, and sometimes dangerous, battles between loggers and environmentalists in the northern California redwood forests.
48. See Mann and Plummer (1995, pp. 190–210) for a detailed discussion of the conflicts surrounding the golden-cheeked warbler in central Texas.
49. Warblers make their nests from strips of ash juniper (native to central Texas), the bark from which cannot be stripped until the tree is at least 20 years old.
50. The evidence, though not systematic, is fairly clear here because some landowners were caught and because members of the environmental group Earth First! began collecting information by trespassing on private land (Mann and Plummer, 1995).
51. In 1992, Austin voters approved a $22 million bond to fund its share of the preserve designed in the BCCP.
52. The economic theory of crime suggests that to eliminate this behavior penalties for violating the ESA will have to be quite high because of the high costs of detecting violations.
53. We should emphasize that without a detailed study it is hard to determine the net economic effects of this change in landuse. In some cases, using the ESA to alter landuse could limit 'pork barrel' projects, thus leading to a net gain.

REFERENCES

Ando, Amy Whritenour (1999), 'Waiting to be protected under the Endangered Species Act: the political economy of regulatory delay', *Journal of Law and Economics*, **42**, 29–60.
Bean, Michael J. and Melanie J. Rowland (1997), *The Evolution of National Wildlife Law*, 2nd edn, Westport, CT: Praeger.
Bonnie, Robert (1995), 'An analysis to determine opportunity costs of red-cockaded woodpecker habitat protection on private lands in the Sandhills of North Carolina', *Incentives for Endangered Species Conservation: Opportunities in the Sandhills of North Carolina*, New York: Environmental Defense Fund.
Bowes, M. and J. Krutilla (1989), 'Multiple-use management: the economics of public forestlands', Resources for the Future, Washington, DC.
Cely, J.E. and D.P. Ferral (1995), 'Status and distribution of the red-cockaded woodpecker in South Carolina', in D.L Kulhavy, R.G. Hooper and R. Costa. (eds), *Red-cockaded Woodpecker Recovery, Ecology and Management*, Stephen Austin State University, Center for Applied Studies in Forestry, School of Forestry, Nacogdoches, TX.
Chase, Alston (1995), *In a Dark Wood*, New York: Houghton Mifflin.
Cleaves, D., R. Busby, B. Doherty and J. Martel (1994), 'Costs of protecting red-cockaded woodpecker habitat: interaction of parcel and cluster size', unpublished manuscript, USDA Forest Service, Southern Region, New Orleans.

Costa, R. and J. Walker (1995), 'Red-cockaded woodpecker', in Edward T. Laroe et al. (eds), *Our Living Resources: A Report to the Nation on the Distribution, Abundance and, Health of U.S. Plants, Animals and Ecosystems*, Washington, DC: US Department of Interior, National Biological Service.

Deacon, Robert T. and M. Bruce Johnson (eds) (1985), *Forestlands: Public and Private*, San Francisco: Pacific Institute.

Environmental Defense Fund (1995), *Incentives for Endangered Species Conservation: Opportunities in the Sandhills of North Carolina*, Report to the Bernice Barbour, Beneficia, Underhill, and National Fish and Wildlife Foundations.

Forest Ecosystem Management: An Ecological, Economic and Social Assessment; Report of the Forest Ecosystem Management Assessment Team (1993), Forest Service, National Marine Fisheries Service, BLM, Fish and Wildlife Service, National Park Service, Environmental Protection Agency.

Forsman, Eric and E. Charles Meslow (1986), 'The spotted owl', *Audubon Wildlife Report*.

General Accounting Office (1994), *Endangered Species Act: Information on Species Protection on Nonfederal Land*, Publication no. GAO/RCED 95-16, Washington DC: US Government Printing Office.

Hartman, R. (1976), 'The harvesting decision when a standing forest has value', *Economic Inquiry*, **16**, 52–8.

Hooper, R. (1988), 'Longleaf pines used for cavities by red-cockaded woodpeckers', *Journal of Wildlife Management*, **52**, 392–8.

Jackson, J.A., M.R. Lennartz and R.G. Hooper (1979), 'Tree age and cavity initiation by red-cockaded woodpeckers', *Journal of Forestry*, **77**, 102–3.

Lancia, R.A., J.P. Roise, D.A. Adams and M.R. Lennartz (1989), 'Opportunity costs of red-cockaded woodpecker foraging habitat', *Southern Journal of Applied Forestry*, **13**, 81–5.

Lennartz, M. and V. Henry (1985), *Red-Cockaded Woodpecker Recovery Plan*, Atlanta, GA: US Fish and Wildlife Service.

Lennartz, M., H.A. Knight, J.P. McClure and V.A. Rudis (1983), 'Status of red-cockaded woodpecker nesting habitat in the South', in Don Wood (ed.), *Red-cockaded Woodpecker Symposium II: Proceedings*, State of Florida Game and Fresh Water Fish Commission.

Lueck, D. (1998), 'Wildlife Law', *The New Palgrave Dictionary of Economics and the Law*, New York: Palgrave/Macmillan.

Lueck, D. and J.A. Michael (2003), 'Preemptive habitat destruction under the Endangered Species Act', *Journal of Law and Economics*, **46**, 27–60.

Mann, Charles C. and Mark L. Plummer (1995), *Noah's Choice: The Future of Endangered Species*, New York: Alfred A. Knopf.

McFarlane, Robert W. (1992), *A Stillness in the Pines: The Ecology of the Red-Cockaded Woodpecker*, New York: W.W. Norton.

Michael, Jeffrey A. (1999), 'The Endangered Species Act and Private Landowner Incentives', unpublished PhD dissertation, NC State University.

Montgomery, Claire A. and Gardner M. Brown, Jr (1992), 'Economics of species preservation: the spotted owl case', *Contemporary Policy Issues*, **10**, 1–12.

Montgomery, Claire A., Gardner M. Brown, Jr. and Darius Adams (1994), 'The marginal cost of species preservation: the northern spotted owl', *Journal of Environmental Economics and Management*, **26**, 111–28.

Murray, Brian C. and David N. Wear (1998), 'Federal timber restrictions and inter-regional arbitrage in U.S. lumber', *Land Economics*, **74** (1), 76–91.

Nelson, Robert H. (1995), *Public Lands and Private Rights*, Lanham, MD: Rowman and Littlefield.

Reed, William J. (1984), 'The effects of the risk of fire on the optimal rotation of a forest', *Journal of Environmental Economics and Management*, **11**, 180–90.

Rohlf, Daniel J. (1989), *The Endangered Species Act: A Guide to Its Protections and Implementation*, Stanford, California: Stanford Environmental Law Society.

Sneddon, B.A. (1995), 'Trained and ready while protecting our environment', in D.L Kulhavy, R.G. Hooper and R. Costa (eds), *Red-cockaded Woodpecker Recovery, Ecology and Management*, Stephen Austin State University, Center for Applied Studies in Forestry, School of Forestry, Nacogdoches, TX, pp. 36–41.

Stroup, Richard L. (1997), 'The economics of compensating property owners', *Contemporary Economic Policy*, **15**, 55–65.

U.S. Fish and Wildlife Service (2003), 'Recovery plan for the red-cockaded woodpecker, 2nd revision', Southeast Region, Atlanta, GA.

Winkler, H., D. Christie and D. Nurney (1995), *Woodpeckers: A Guide to the Woodpeckers of the World*, New York: Houghton Mifflin.

Wooldridge, Jeffrey M. (2002), *Econometrics of Cross Section and Panel Data*, Cambridge, MA: MIT Press.

Yaffee, Steven Lewis (1982), *Prohibitive Policy: Implementing the Federal Endangered Species Act*, Cambridge, MA: MIT Press.

Yaffee, Steven Lewis (1994), *The Wisdom of the Owl: Policy Lessons for a New Century*, Washington, DC: Island Press.

PART II

Resource modeling, growth and environmental quality

5. Is the environmental Kuznets curve an empirical regularity?

Robert T. Deacon and Catherine S. Norman

1 INTRODUCTION

The environmental Kuznets curve (EKC) hypothesis describes the time path of pollution a country will follow as economic development proceeds. When growth occurs in an extremely poor country, pollution initially grows because the increased production generates pollution emissions and because the country, given its poverty, places a low priority on pollution control. Once a country gains a sufficient degree of affluence, however, its priorities shift to protecting air quality. If this income effect is strong enough, it will cause pollution to decline. To some, this reasoning suggests that environmental improvement cannot come without economic growth. The World Bank, in its 1992 World Development Report (World Bank, 1992), reported that 'economic growth is essential for environmental stewardship' and GATT (1992) offered a similarly positive policy message from the EKC literature. The EKC hypothesis is intuitively appealing. Moreover, it seems in general agreement with the experiences and casual empiricism of those who lived through the last half of the 20th century in North America and Western Europe. To date, however, no carefully documented examples of specific countries following the EKC path as economic growth proceeds have been offered.

In what follows we examine data on air pollution and GDP growth for individual nations to see if clear examples of the EKC phenomenon can be found. We make use of a recently available extension and revision of the GEMS database on air pollution around the world. This update was compiled by the EPA's Aerometric Information Retrieval System (AIRS) and in what follows we refer to this data set as GEMS/AIRS. Harbaugh, Levinson and Wilson (2002) (HLW) studied these data thoroughly to check the robustness of results in the EKC literature. HLW also explain differences between the GEMS/AIRS data and the earlier GEMS data set. They point out that many observations that were missing in the original data set have been filled in, duplicate entries have been eliminated, and some original entries have been amended.[1] Overall, the new series contains many more observations and is more accurate than the original GEMS data.

Our main reason for relying on the GEMS/AIRS data is their extensive temporal coverage. Data are available as early as 1971 for some countries and the last observations are for 1992. This is a long enough period to observe significant economic growth and it includes the time span when nations around the world initiated substantive environmental policy. If the EKC phenomenon is an important empirical regularity, we should see it operating in data from individual nations over this period. A second advantage is that its country coverage (46 individual nations) is extensive. Finally, the primary factual basis for the now-famous inverted-U is the GEMS data set. To have the best chance of success, it makes sense to base our search for EKC behavior on this vehicle.

Our approach is simple: we plot air pollution against income in as many countries as possible, to see whether or not the EKC hypothesis is an empirical regularity. Looking only within countries permits simple tests of the EKC hypothesis: we literally look at plots of pollution against income. Looking only within countries also mitigates observable and unobservable cross-country heterogeneity in economic, political, and climatic factors. Assuming we can measure air pollution and income accurately, the only attributes that might be of concern are those that clearly changed within countries during the sample period.

While this simplifies the empirical approach somewhat, it highlights the importance of measuring air pollution and income accurately. Surprisingly, this is less straightforward than it might first seem. Consider measurement of the dependent variable in an EKC model, air pollution. The GEMS/AIRS data are annual observations from hundreds of individual monitoring sites around the world. Many sites opened and closed sporadically, while others operated more or less continuously. Contemporaneous readings from different monitoring sites in the same city clearly show that some sites were located in dirtier neighborhoods than others. Simply averaging across sites within a city or country, given that sites come and go, will introduce measurement errors.[2] Our approach is to compile within-country air pollution series from a consistent set of monitoring sites, which necessitates dropping observations from sites that do not report consistently.

Accurately measuring income, the most important *independent* variable in an EKC model, is arguably even more crucial because measurement error here will lead to biased estimates. The most common income measure in the empirical literature is national level per capita GDP, used apparently for reasons of data availability.[3] On theoretical grounds, however, a local income measure is arguably more appropriate. The main driving force in the upward-sloping portion of the hypothesized EKC is the pollution generation that accompanies an increase in production. Because air pollution is generally experienced near the source, the appropriate measure of the production driving it is local GDP. The downward-sloping portion of the EKC is expected to occur because higher incomes may lead to more stringent pollution controls.[4] National-level GDP would be the right income measure for this pollution control effect if air pollution policies were set only by national governments. Subnational governments also control air quality through landuse controls and environmental permitting, however.[5] Accordingly, local income, that is, income near the monitoring site, should be a determining factor in an EKC model. Summarizing, a failure to include local income, either in addition to or instead of national income, will lead to biased income coefficients. This is particularly unfortunate because the key point of the EKC exercise is accurate estimation of the income coefficient(s) and the turning point.[6]

Our approach to this problem is to take care to use income and air pollution data that are matched to one another. The starting point is the income data available to us and to other researchers: national-level GDP per capita. The air pollution measures we seek are, accordingly, series that indicate the time pattern of national level air pollution in each country. We construct these by averaging readings from a consistent set of monitoring sites in each country. Readings at individual sites within a country generally differ from one another, perhaps owing to variations in community income or climatic conditions. If these differences were stable over time they would not pose a problem. In that case readings from any of the individual monitoring sites would serve as a national air pollution series. Of course they are not stable over time, because of the effect of transitory idiosyncratic factors. We average the yearly readings across a stable set of sites in each country, with the thought that positive and negative idiosyncrasies will tend to cancel out in the process, reducing measurement error.

2   LITERATURE REVIEW

The EKC literature began with two papers in the early 1990s. Shafik and Bandyopadhyay (1992) examined the empirical relationship between per capita income and ambient concentrations of air pollution, rates of deforestation, access to clean water and production of solid wastes. Grossman and Krueger (1993, 1995) used a similar empirical approach to estimate the likely effects of increased income, attributed to NAFTA, on air pollution. In both studies, the authors found that airborne sulfur dioxide and smoke concentrations rose with per capita income, up to $3000–$4000 in the former study and $4000–$6000 in the latter, beyond which they declined.

Although these authors cautioned that their results did not necessarily imply an automatic reduction in pollution as income rose, some observers drew this interpretation.[7]

The intriguing idea that greening might follow automatically from economic growth led to a large empirical literature on the subject. Other researchers attempted to control for the influence on pollution of determining factors that might be correlated with income. Panayotou (1997) considered the industrial and institutional structure of countries and used GDP per unit area to separate the effect of production on pollution generation from the effect of income on pollution control. Torras and Boyce (1998) examined the effects of literacy, inequality, and civil freedoms on the turning point and significance of the EKC coefficients. Barrett and Graddy (2000) re-estimated the Grossman and Krueger equations after adding measures of political and civil liberties. Significantly, all of these papers relied on the GEMS air pollution data, and all found the inverted-U relationship.[8]

Some authors questioned the methodology of estimating a single regression model with panel data from many different countries, that is, trying to identify a 'global' EKC. Stern *et al.* (1996) advised against including countries at different stages of development in a single equation, arguing that factors other than differences in income might affect the relationship between pollution and income. Coondoo and Dinda (2002) cautioned that the pattern of causality between pollution and income might differ from one group of countries to another. De Bruyn (1997) estimated the pollution–income relationship for emissions in four OECD nations separately, highlighting the importance of structural changes within countries.[9]

Interpretation of early empirical findings on the EKC was clouded by the absence of a clear theoretical model (Thompson and Strohm, 1996; Stern, 1998). More emphasis on theory was needed to inform the methodology and to allow empirical tests to distinguish the relationships behind the observed inverted-U. Antweiler, Copeland and Taylor (2001) developed a theoretical model of pollution generation and abatement to study the pollution effects of opening trade. As with many others before, they used the GEMS air pollution data as a vehicle for estimation.[10]

An important feature of this empirical literature is its heavy reliance on the GEMS air pollution data. As noted earlier, Harbaugh, Levinson and Wilson (2002) examined the properties of an expanded and corrected air pollution data set. Using these revised data, they compared pollution –income relationships between the old and new data sets and studied the sensitivity of EKC findings to functional forms, samples, and estimation methods. They found that the original GEMS data set contained significant inaccuracies. They also found that results from the new data set are not robust to rather slight changes in the sample, empirical specification, and estimation technique. Overall, they found little support for the inverted-U, the icon of the EKC hypothesis.

This review leads to three generalizations that are important for our purposes. First, the air pollution data reported in the GEMS and subsequent GEMS/AIRS data sets form the primary foundation for the now familiar EKC generalization, the inverted-U. Second, despite a decade of concerted empirical work, there is still significant skepticism in the profession that the inverted-U is an empirical regularity.[11]

Third, and most important for our purposes, the empirical support offered for the EKC story, which purports to show how a country's pollution will change as its income increases, is drawn from cross-country panel data on pollution and income. Most of the variation in pollution in these data is across countries or monitoring sites, rather than over time. In the GEMS/AIRS data for SO_2 and particulates, the within-site (across years) standard deviation in air pollution is less than one-third as great as the across-sites (within years) standard deviation. For smoke the within-site standard deviation is about half as large as the across-sites standard deviation. The EKC hypothesis is a story about how a country's pollution will change as that country's economy grows. Support for that story has come mainly from variations in income and pollution across countries, however, rather than direct examination of how pollution within a country changes as its income increases.[12]

3   DATA

We use the GEMS/AIRS data set on air quality because of its extensive coverage and its prominence in the EKC literature. The measures used are median ambient air concentrations of sulfur dioxide, suspended particulates (TSP), and smoke (fine particulates). The income measure used is per capita real GDP in 1985 dollars from the 1991 Penn World Tables.[13]

For non-parametric, within-country estimation, we need to observe one concentration per country per year for each pollutant. The GEMS/AIRS data set generally includes observations from several cities in a country and often from multiple sites within a particular city. If a country adds a monitoring site in a relatively dirty region toward the end of the sample period, the average pollution readings for that country may indicate declining air quality simply due to the addition of the new site. Even within a city there can be considerable variation in pollution concentrations across sites.[14]

To avoid composition bias in the final series, we collect data only from monitoring sites that operated throughout all or most years covered by the GEMS/AIRS data. Observations from sites that report only sporadically are dropped. In most countries the selection of which sites to include and which to drop is a straightforward matter of choosing the longest-active site and all the other sites that are active over the same time period. Observations tend to be confined to a few major cities in each country. In a few cases where the longest-active site had n observations and there were quite a few sites with $n-1$ observations, we dropped the extra year in the interests of having a broader data base for annual pollution readings in the country. In the sulfur dioxide data set, the largest of the three, some cases were less clear-cut. The US data include at least some observations for 23 locations. There were a few sites with 20 observations, but the available years were often different and confining the sample to these cities would have excluded some of the largest US cities. By including a consistent set of 15 years we were able to include 10 US cities, with multiple observation sites for a few of the largest.[15]

We excluded any country that did not have at least 10 years of data after processing for consistent composition over time. The average number of monitoring sites in each country-year observation is 2.3 for smoke, 2.6 for TSP, and 3.1 for sulfur dioxide. For some larger countries, a significant share of the available data is from sites that report only sporadically. Eliminating data from sporadically reporting sites and from sites that fail to report data for at least 10 years reduces the overall sample of site observations from 687 to 409 for smoke, from 1085 to 484 for particulates, and from 2381 to 1113 for sulfur dioxide.[16]

4   WITHIN-COUNTRY RELATIONSHIPS BETWEEN POLLUTION AND GDP

We examine the relationship between income and pollution within countries to see if the overall pattern accords with predictions from the EKC theory. We use a simple, non-parametric approach. For each country, observations on pollution and per capita GDP are ordered by per capita GDP and tritiles are formed. The tritiles are three subsets of observations that contain, respectively, the lowest one-third of income observations, the middle one-third, and the highest one-third. We then compute mean pollution and mean per capita GDP for each tritile and plot the results: mean pollution against mean GDP for each country. We perform this analysis twice for each country and pollutant, once using current per capita GDP as the income measure and once using a three-year average of lagged per capita GDP.

Our intent is to see whether these plots of pollution against income, each with three data points, are consistent or inconsistent with the EKC hypothesis. With only three data points, there are only four possible ways the data could be ordered: monotone increasing, monotone decreasing, a single peak (inverted-U,) and a single trough (U-shaped). We regard the following patterns as *consistent* with the EKC story: monotone increasing for a 'poor' country, monotone decreasing for a 'rich' country, and single peaked for a country of any income. We regard the following patterns as *inconsistent* with EKC behavior: monotone decreasing for a 'poor' country, monotone increasing for a 'rich' country, and a single trough (U-shaped) for any country. The criteria used for identifying 'rich' and 'poor' countries are explained later.

We begin by simply identifying countries displaying each pattern, counting their numbers, and giving summary information on their income levels. Later we examine the consistency of these results with the EKC hypothesis more formally. Using lagged income is consistent with previous EKC analysis and seems a more appropriate measure because it allows the policy response to be gradual. For this reason we place more emphasis on these estimates in discussions.

Tables 5.1 and 5.2 show results for sulfur dioxide using lagged and current per capita GDP, respectively. There are 23 countries in the sample overall. When *lagged* GDP is used as an income measure, six countries exhibit a trough while only four display a single peak. On the positive side, the average income of countries for which SO_2 decreases as income increases exceeds average income for countries with a monotone increasing relationship. Japan is present in the former group and Brazil and Iran are in the latter, however, which does not accord well with the EKC hypothesis.

For the estimates based on *current* GDP per capita, seven exhibit the

Table 5.1   The shape of the pollution–GDP relationship: SO_2 vs. lagged real per capita GDP

SO_2	N	Countries
Single peak	4	China, Ireland, Hong Kong,
Mean lagged GDP at peak	4 240	Thailand
Single trough	6	Chile, India, Israel, Poland,
Mean lagged GDP at trough	5 905	Yugoslavia, Canada
Increasing	2	Japan, Venezuela
Mean center of lagged GDP range	8 977	
Decreasing	11	Australia, Belgium, Brazil, Finland,
Mean center of lagged GDP range	9 861	W. Germany, Iran, Netherlands,
		New Zealand, Spain, UK, US

Table 5.2   The shape of the pollution–GDP relationship: SO_2 vs. current real per capita GDP

SO_2	N	Countries
Single peak	7	China, Chile, Ireland, Poland, HK,
Mean GDP at peak	4 804	Thailand, Venezuela
Single trough	4	Brazil, India, Israel, Netherlands
Mean GDP at trough	5 904	
Increasing	1	Japan
Mean center of GDP range	11 562	
Decreasing	11	Australia, Belgium, Canada, Finland
Mean center of GDP range	10 686	W. Germany, Iran, NZ, Spain, UK, USA,
		Yugoslavia

classic inverted-U associated with the EKC hypothesis while four exhibit a trough. Again, the increasing relationship between income and SO_2 in relatively rich Japan and the decreasing relationships in relatively poor Brazil and Iran do not support the EKC paradigm. Neither does the fact that the midrange of GDP for the one country showing an increasing relationship between pollution and income exceeds the midrange of GDP for countries showing a decreasing relationship.

European Union policies on pollution control affected the behavior of some countries in our sample and this fact bears on the interpretation of results. EU regulation of ambient air quality began in 1980 with Directive 80/779/EEC, requiring member nations to harmonize standards for SO_2 and suspended particulates. EU members and prospective members were required to adhere to the 'environmental acquis', the EU's body of environmental standards and laws. The deadline for compliance was 1983, which is right in the middle of the sample period. Adherence to this directive is an environmental policy response, of course, and policy responses are part of the EKC story. A single policy response was required of all EU members, however, rich and poor alike, which is not in keeping with the EKC hypothesis. Furthermore, Portugal and Spain entered the EU after this environmental legislation went into force, so their pollution control efforts may have represented a preference for admission to the Union rather than clean air, per se. It is also significant that the EU heavily subsidized the pollution control costs of four relatively poor EU members, Ireland, Spain, Greece, and Portugal. The EU Structural Fund and Cohesion Fund provided assistance so that these countries 'could build the public sector infrastructure needed to comply with the environmental acquis' (Hansen and Rasmussen, 2001) when they were unable to meet EU pollution targets.

Table 5.3 The shape of the pollution–GDP relationship: particulates vs. lagged real per capita GDP

Total suspended particles	N	Countries
Single peak	4	China, Finland, Japan, Thailand
Mean lagged GDP at peak	6 674	
Single trough	6	W. Germany, India, Iran, Malaysia
Mean lagged GDP at trough	6 005	Yugoslavia, Belgium
Increasing	0	
Mean center of lagged GDP range	—	
Decreasing	3	Australia, Brazil, Canada
Mean center of lagged GDP range	10 242	

Table 5.4 The shape of the pollution–GDP relationship: particulates vs. current real per capita GDP

Total suspended particles	N	Countries
Single peak	5	China, India, Thailand, Finland, Japan
Mean GDP at peak	8 045	
Single trough	4	Belgium, Brazil, W. Germany, Malaysia
Mean GDP at trough	7 759	
Increasing	1	Iran
Mean center of GDP range	4 853	
Decreasing	3	Australia, Canada, Yugoslavia
Mean center of GDP range	10 793	

To summarize, all four of these poorer EU members may have pursued relatively vigorous pollution control simply owing to EU policy. These considerations may account for certain results in Tables 5.1 and 5.2. Spain experienced decreasing SO_2 as income rose, while Ireland's pollution decreased with income at relatively high income levels, that is, on the right-hand side of the peak.

Tables 5.3 and 5.4 give results for suspended particulates. Overall, the number of cases displaying a trough, 10, slightly exceeds the number displaying a peak, nine. Judging from these cases alone, the predictive power of the EKC hypothesis is poor for particulates. Among the seven cases of monotone behavior, two are anomalous (Brazil in Table 5.3 and Yugoslavia in Table 5.4). Ignoring countries exhibiting a single trough, which are clearly inconsistent with EKC, the ordering of mean income for groups in Tables 5.3 and 5.4 broadly agrees with the EKC hypothesis.[17]

Our results for smoke, shown in Tables 5.5 and 5.6, are the most problematic for the EKC hypothesis. Looking across results for lagged and current GDP, more countries exhibit a U-shaped relationship (six), than an inverted-U shape (four). The cases of monotone relationships also contain contrary evidence. The countries for which pollution increases as income increases are relatively rich, Denmark and Ireland. The group for which pollution decreases as income increases includes such relatively impoverished nations as Brazil, Chile, Egypt, Poland, and Venezuela. Overall, the smoke data are the least consistent with the EKC hypothesis.

Table 5.5   The shape of the pollution–GDP relationship: smoke vs. lagged real per capita GDP

Smoke	N	Countries
Single peak	3	Egypt, Venezuela
Mean lagged GDP at peak	6 549	New Zealand
Single trough	3	Belgium, Chile, Iran
Mean lagged GDP at trough	5 798	
Increasing	2	Denmark, Ireland
Mean center of lagged GDP range	9 069	
Decreasing	5	Brazil, HK, Poland,
Mean center of lagged GDP range	6 634	Spain, UK

Table 5.6   The shape of the pollution–GDP relationship: smoke vs. current real per capita GDP

Smoke	N	Countries
Single peak	1	Poland
Mean GDP at peak	4 218	
Single trough	3	Belgium, Iran, UK
Mean GDP at trough	8 092	
Increasing	2	Denmark, Ireland
Mean center of GDP range	9 826	
Decreasing	7	Brazil, Chile, Egypt, HK,
Mean center of GDP range	6 203	NZ, Spain, Venezuela

When considered across all three pollutants, are the pollution–income relationships in Tables 5.1–5.6 generally consistent with the EKC prediction? Figure 5.1 shows the four possible shapes for relationships among three data points, our tritiles. Each cell, corresponding to a given income level and pollution–income relationship, is labeled consistent, inconsistent, or inconclusive to indicate whether or not it agrees or disagrees with the EKC hypothesis. We count a single peak as consistent with the hypothesis regardless of the country's income level, and regard this as a generous interpretation of the EKC prediction. A trough is considered inconsistent with EKC behavior for any level of income. An increasing relationship between pollution and GDP is consistent for a poor country but not a rich country, and vice versa for a decreasing relationship. We characterize the EKC's prediction for the remaining two cases as inconclusive.

Countries were divided into low, middle and high income groups according to their 1983 per capita GDP. Cutoff points for each income category were set to be consistent with the estimated turning points in the EKC literature. For example, the income range for countries classified as poor was set purposely to correspond to the left side of the EKC peak for air

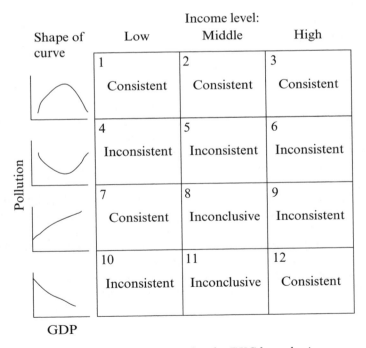

Figure 5.1   Expected relationships under the EKC hypothesis

pollutants, as reported in the empirical EKC literature. Specifically, a country was classified as low-income if its 1983 income (GDP per capita) was below $3500 (1986 dollars), as middle income if its income was between $3500 and $7000, and as high income if its income exceeded $7000. To judge what fraction of observations would be expected to fall into each cell in Figure 5.1 under random assignment, we start by observing the fraction of countries that fall into each of the three income ranges. For a given income category, we then assume (under random assignment) that each of the four income–pollution relationships is equally likely. This is the pattern expected under random assignment, and a simple X^2 test can be used to determine if the observed pattern is significantly different.

The test was performed for three pollutants (SO_2, smoke, and suspended particles) and two income measures (current and lagged GDP per capita), so six tests were performed in all. The $X^2(11)$ statistics and significance levels for these tests are as follows:

Pollutant:	Income measure:	X^2	(signif.)
SO_2	lagged GDP	18.40	(7.28%)
SO_2	current GDP	23.10	(1.71%)
Particulates	lagged GDP	8.50	(66.79%)
Particulates	current GDP	14.33	(21.53%)
Smoke	lagged GDP	4.60	(94.9%)
Smoke	current GDP	9.93	(53.67%)

Only one of the six cases, for SO_2 and current GDP, beats random assignment with 95 per cent confidence.[18] The SO_2 with lagged GDP case beats random assignment with a bit more than 90 per cent confidence. The income–pollution relationships for particulates and smoke are not significantly different from what one would get by throwing (poorly aimed) darts at Figure 5.1.

We replicated this analysis with the original, smaller GEMS data set used by Grossman and Krueger (1995), Shafik and Bandyopadhyay (1992), Torras and Boyce (1998), Antweiler, Copeland and Taylor (2001) and others. The intent was to see if this earlier data set, which consistently yielded a single peaked EKC in cross-country analysis, would also produce within-country patterns that agree with the EKC hypothesis. We used all countries for which we had at least nine years of observations to construct country-year pollution data and tritiles and followed the procedure explained earlier.

Sulfur dioxide is the only pollutant for which the EKC outperforms random assignment; however, it does so with a high degree of confidence.

Only four of 20 nations in the SO_2 sample exhibit the inverted-U within the sample period, however. Three of these nations (Ireland, Greece, and Spain) were being brought into compliance with European Union environmental standards during the sample period, as discussed earlier. Thus it would be unwise to place much emphasis on an SO_2 'turning point' estimate from these data.

For particulates, within-country results from the original GEMS data set show little if any correspondence with the EKC hypothesis. Contrary to the EKC story, countries exhibiting a negative relationship between pollution and income tend to be poor (for example, Greece and Thailand) and those with a positive relationship between pollution and income tend to be rich (for example, Germany and Denmark). Two countries exhibit a trough-shaped relationship. The level of agreement is even worse for smoke. For this pollutant the troughs outnumber the peaks, three to two, countries with increasing pollution–income relationships tend to be rich (for example, Denmark and Ireland), and countries with decreasing pollution–income relationships tend to be poor (for example, Chile and Egypt).

To summarize results from the GEMS/AIRS data, we observe significant agreement with EKC predictions for SO_2 when current GDP is used as an income measure, and near significant agreement when the preferred income measure, lagged GDP, is used. Overall, however, the famous inverted-U is not prominent in any of these results. Scanning across all three pollutants and two income measures, the reverse of the inverted-U, a trough, is actually more common. For the best behaved pollutant, SO_2, peaks beat troughs by only 11 to 10. It is worth reiterating that most of the evidence we count as supporting the EKC prediction for SO_2 is simply observations on rich countries exhibiting a negative relationship between pollution and GDP. For smoke and particulates, the EKC hypothesis does no better at predicting pollution–income patterns than random assignment.

5   ARE IMPLIED INCOME ELASTICITIES OF POLLUTION PLAUSIBLE?

Average GDP in nations covered by the GEMS/AIRS data grew by 45 percent between the early 1970s and late 1980s, clearly creating a *potential* for increased pollution. Actual pollution levels fell over this period, however. Average SO_2 concentrations in the GEMS/AIRS data set used to construct our tritiles dropped by 22 percent.[19] Average concentrations of smoke and suspended particulates also fell, but less dramatically. The EKC hypothesis attributes declining pollution in the face of growing income to an increase in the demand for pollution control.[20] In what follows, we

examine whether or not such an income effect could plausibly account
for the observed combination of reductions in air pollution and increases
in income.

Figure 5.2 illustrates our approach. For a given country, S denotes pollution (SO_2, smoke, suspended particulates), X denotes output (real
national GDP), and the subscripts L and H indicate years of low and high
GDP in our sample.[21] Thus, S_L and X_L are the country's observed pollution and GDP in the low output year. Absent a change in pollution control
policy, technology, or the composition of output, the pollution generated
per unit output will be constant. Hence, 'pollution generation' in the high
output year, S_E, is calculated as:

$$S_E = (S_L/X_L) \cdot X_H, \qquad (5.1)$$

where X_H is GDP in the high output year.

If observed pollution in the high output year falls short of the pollution
generated, S_E, we regard the difference as pollution control. In keeping with
the EKC hypothesis, we attribute this reduction in pollution to an increase
in income and compute an implied income elasticity of demand. To do this
we simply calculate the percentage difference between S_E and S_H and then
divide it by the corresponding percentage change in per capita GDP.[22] The

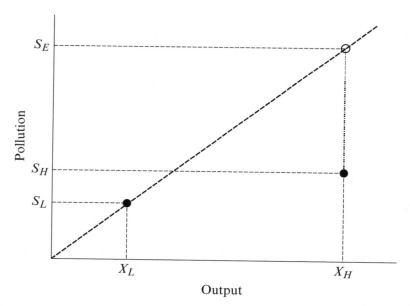

Figure 5.2   Income growth, pollution generation and abatement

result is an income elasticity of demand for pollution and is expected to be negative because pollution is a 'bad'. Per capita income is used because a policy response seems most likely to follow from a change in individual income. We also compute income elasticities with respect to the percentage change in total GDP, however, to see how sensitive the results are to this choice.

Table 5.7 reports implied income elasticities for SO_2, smoke, and suspended particulates for countries in the sample.[23] Results for SO_2 are highlighted in the following discussion since the country coverage is most extensive for this pollutant. The elasticities computed from percentage changes in per capita GDP, which seems the more appropriate definition, average -3.71 over the entire sample. If one regards income growth as the driving force behind the reductions in observed SO_2 pollution (relative to levels that would be expected based on growth in output), then a 10 percent increase in per capita income will induce a 37 percent reduction in pollution in the average country. Average elasticities for smoke and particulates are smaller, but still large relative to our expectations. They imply that a 10 percent increase in per capita income will reduce smoke and particulate pollution by 20 percent and 24 percent, respectively.

In some cases a country experienced a drop in output late in the sample period, causing the years of maximum and minimum GDP per capita to be close to one another. In some cases minimum GDP actually occurred after maximum GDP, as in Iran and Poland. Because the pollution experienced in these cases may be atypical, we recomputed the averages for countries in which the minimum and maximum GDP were separated by more than 10 years and more than 15 years. These results are in the last two rows. Restricting the sample in this way typically increases the elasticity in absolute value.

Elasticities computed from the percentage change in total GDP, shown in the last three columns, are smaller in absolute value because most countries experienced population growth. Thus total GDP increased at a faster rate than per capita GDP and the resulting income elasticities are smaller. Even these elasticities are large in absolute value, particularly for SO_2.[24]

The implied elasticities in Table 5.7 relate to the response of *environmental quality levels* to changes in income, which corresponds to a conventional income elasticity of demand for a market commodity.[25] Valuation studies generally estimate the determinants of *willingness-to-pay* for environmental improvement, rather than determinants of 'demand', and this renders comparisons somewhat ambiguous. Flores and Carson (1997) point out that the income elasticity of willingness-to-pay for a quantity-constrained good is less than the ordinary income elasticity of demand under plausible circumstances, though there are exceptions.

Table 5.7   Implied income elasticities of demand for pollution

Pollutant GDP measure	SO_2 Per cap.	Smoke Per cap.	Partic. Per cap.	SO_2 Total	Smoke Total	Partic. Total
Australia	−7.92		−4.15	−4.52		−2.37
Belgium	−5.47	−4.52	−3.59	−5.15	−4.24	−3.45
Brazil	−8.98	−10.80	−4.68	−2.75	−3.31	−2.43
Canada	−1.84		−3.44	−1.30		−2.42
China	−1.06		−1.99	−0.76		−1.43
Chile	−1.00	0.94		−0.82	0.77	
Denmark		0.94			0.77	
Egypt		−2.79			−1.45	
Ireland	−2.89	0.22		−2.36	0.18	
Finland	−2.42		−0.86	−2.20		−0.78
W. Germany	−3.93		−1.62	−3.46		−1.43
Hong Kong	−2.27	−1.51		−1.75	−1.16	
India	−2.47		−3.20	−1.26		−1.63
Iran	−1.45	0.11	0.41	−1.87	0.14	0.54
Israel	−3.26			−1.49		
Japan	−0.13		−0.56	−0.15		−0.50
Malaysia			−3.12			−1.65
Netherlands	−6.30			−4.36		
New Zealand	−10.31	−3.62		−7.34	−2.57	
Poland	−0.87	−1.14		−0.97	−1.27	
Spain	−4.45	−4.06		−3.44	−3.14	
Thailand	−1.56		−2.10	−1.15		−1.56
UK	−6.09	−3.97		−5.87	−3.83	
USA	−6.78			−3.58		
Venezuela	1.23	2.91		−0.82	−1.95	
Yugoslavia	−2.91		−2.99	−2.57		−2.64
Avg. elasticity	−3.71	−2.01	−2.45	−2.68	−1.52	−1.67
Avg. >10 years	−4.12	−3.23	−2.24	−2.84	−2.35	−1.56
Avg. >15 years	−3.58	−3.42	*	−2.95	−2.29	*

Notes: Excludes countries with fewer than 10 observations on pollution and GDP; avg.>10 years is an average elasticity for countries with more than 10 years between minimum and maximum GDP, etc.; *insufficient observations.

Regarding the income elasticity of willingness-to-pay, the valuation litera-ture generally concludes that it is no greater than unity. Kristrom and Riera (1996) survey a group of contingent valuation studies from Europe and conclude that the income elasticity is less than one in each case.[26] In a hedonic property value study, Harrison and Rubinfeld (1978) concluded that the income elasticity of willingness-to-pay for reductions in one type of air pollution is roughly 0.8 to 1.0. Nelson (1978) uses a hedonic approach to estimate a conventional income elasticity of *demand for air quality* in the Washington DC area, where air quality is measured as the reciprocal of particulate air pollution. His income elasticity is comparable to ours and he finds it is approximately unity. Khanna (2002) examined US census tract data on pollution and income, controlling for factors that should determine scale and composition effects, in order to identify the technique, or abatement, effect, and found a significant income elasticity only for particulates, its absolute value being less than unity. Overall, the valuation literature gives some evidence (Nelson, 1978; Khanna, 2002) that the demand for clean air is approximately unity, and no clear evidence that the income elasticity of demand for clean air or other environmental amenities exceeds unity.

For purposes of comparison, focus on the first three columns and last two rows of Table 5.7. These are implied elasticities that use per capita GDP as an income measure, which we regard as more appropriate, and exclude countries for which minimum and maximum GDP are separated by less than 10 years. These implied income elasticities of demand are between 3.5 and 4.1 (in absolute value) for SO_2, between 3.2 and 3.4 for smoke, and 2.2 for particulates. We are unaware of *any* valuation-based income elasticity estimates in this range; indeed, income elasticities for market goods are seldom if ever this large. Accordingly, it appears implausible to us that the pollution control observed in these countries could be due to an income effect operating through the demand for clean air.

6   DOWNWARD TRENDS IN SO_2: DOES EKC THEORY ADD ANY INSIGHT?

The preceding income elasticity estimates attribute *all* shifts in the demand for clean air to changes in income. They also assume that pollution control costs remained constant over the period. It seems clear, however, that increased knowledge of the health effects of air pollution and the general increase in public support for environmental protection caused the desired level of air quality to rise independent of income effects, certainly in the USA and other wealthy nations. In addition, pollution control technology almost surely improved during the sample period. Both factors should account for some of the pollution reduction observed in the data, reductions that, in keeping with the EKC hypothesis, we attributed to an income effect. In what follows we examine this possibility.

Although pollution control regulations clearly were on the books earlier, air quality became a prominent public policy issue in the late 1960s and the 1970s, particularly in wealthy countries.[27] The close correlation in time with events such as Earth Day, highly publicized oil spills, initiatives to protect endangered species, and efforts to eliminate pesticides suggests that more stringent air quality regulations arose partly from a broad shift in public attitudes toward better environmental protection. An alternative to the EKC income effect is to view these events as signals of a shift in the equilibrium level of pollution, particularly in wealthier nations, brought about by education and by better information on environmental problems. Such a shift cannot be achieved instantly, however, but only gradually as more stringent regulations are adopted, as enforcement strategies are devised, and as old heavily polluting capital wears out and is replaced.

This is a story about a shift in the desired level of pollution control from an old 1960s equilibrium, where environmental health risks are not widely publicized, environmental education is largely non-existent, and pollution control technologies are primitive, to a new 1990s equilibrium where each of these gaps has been filled to some degree. It does not highlight income growth as a factor that drives environmental protection. Of course, income may well be an important factor in this process; wealthy nations may have made the transition from the old to the new equilibrium more quickly than poorer nations, and they may have adopted more ambitious pollution control targets. This does not imply that an inverted-U should describe the relationship between income and pollution over this period, however, either in cross-country or in time series data.

In what follows we examine the explanatory power of this alternative 'trend model' for SO_2. Sulfur dioxide is emphasized because the available data are most extensive for this pollutant. Also, SO_2 is the only pollutant for which our within-country analysis found any support for the EKC hypothesis. First, we estimate individual, within-country time trends for SO_2. Next, to see if rates of pollution reduction were more rapid in richer countries, we compute the correlation between the country-specific pollution trends and country income. Finally, we add income and income squared to the simple trend model for each country, test the significance of the income terms, and see whether or not they correspond to EKC behavior.

Results are presented in Table 5.8. The dependent variable is the country-specific average SO_2 concentration in a given year, in micrograms per cubic meter. Column (1) shows the trend coefficients and their significance levels. Fifteen of the 23 are significant, and all but one of these is negative. Only Japan experienced a significant, positive trend in sulfur dioxide over the sample period. The simple correlation between the within-country

Table 5.8   *Country–specific trends in SO_2 and shapes of country-specific EKCs (GDP refers to real per capita GDP)*

Country	Trend	Lagged GDP:		Current GDP:		GDP
		Peak or trough?	Turning point ($)	Peak or trough?	Turning point ($)	in 1980 ($)
	(1)	(2)	(3)	(4)	(5)	(6)
Australia	−3.69***	—		—		12 520
Belgium	−6.75***	T**	11 347	T***	10 102	11 109
Brazil	−5.23***	P**	4 139	—		4 303
Canada	−0.79***	T*	8 450	—		14 133
China	−0.01	P**	983	P*	1 096	966
Chile	1.73	—		—		3 892
Ireland	−1.17*	—		—		6 823
Finland	−1.36***	—		P*	13 641	10 851
W. Germany	−4.60***	—		—		11 920
Hong Kong	−0.18***	P**	10 578	—		8 719
India	1.32	—		—		882
Iran	1.46	P**	1 913	T**	5 572	3 434
Israel	−0.71	—		—		7 895
Japan	2.86***	P**	9 593	P*	14 749	10 072
Netherlands	−3.00***	T***	10 519	T***	10 980	11 284
New Zealand	−1.50***	T***	10 941	T***	12 445	10 362
Poland	−0.11	T***	4 500	—	4 319	4 419
Spain	−5.95***	T***	8 297	T**	8 431	7 390
Thailand	−0.13	—		—		2 178
UK	−9.77***	T***	10 010	—		10 167
US	−1.87***	T***	15 755	T***	14 795	15 295
Venezuela	−0.21	P***	7 952	—		7 401
Yugoslavia	−2.12**	T***	4 980	T***	5 459	5 565

Notes: *** 1% or better, ** 5% or better, * 10% or better; P indicates peak, T indicates trough, — indicates no significant relationship.

trends and country income, measured as per capita GDP in 1980, is indeed negative, −0.36, and significant at 10 percent. We carried out the same procedure with exponential trends, that is, trends from regressing the log of SO_2 pollution against time. The results were generally similar; 13 of the 23 countries had significant trends, all of which were negative. The correlation between the exponential trends and per capita GDP was also negative, and stronger: −0.56, which is significant at 0.5 percent.[28] Using either linear or exponential trends, higher income countries reduced SO_2 pollution at a more rapid rate than poorer countries.[29]

Can the EKC hypothesis enhance our understanding of the within-country behavior of pollution over the period 1970–92, beyond what the trends show? This was checked by adding lagged per capita GDP and its square to the trend model. Column (2) reports whether the income terms describe a peak (P) or trough (T) and their significance levels.[30] Cases where the income terms are not jointly significant at 10 percent or better, eight of the 23, are not reported. Of the 15 significant income terms, troughs out-number peaks by nine to six. Column (4) provides summary information for models that use current per capita GDP as the income measure. Here, the income terms are jointly significant in 10 of the 23 cases. Of these 10 significant cases, seven are troughs and only three are peaks.

An estimated trough need not be inconsistent with the EKC hypothesis. If the country involved is wealthy and if the trough bottoms out at an income level above the income range of the sample, the country might just be on the downward-sloping portion of an EKC. According to the data in columns (3), (5), and (6), however, this is not the case. Some of the countries exhibiting troughs are poor (Iran, Poland, and Yugoslavia) and, where troughs do occur, they tend to hit bottom at an income level close to the country's sample mean.

On balance, the EKC hypothesis adds little if any insight over a simple 'trend model' for SO_2, one that posits that countries generally tried to reduce pollution during the 1970–92 period and rich countries cleaned up faster than poor ones.

7   CONCLUSIONS

The preceding analysis of trends is clearly not intended as a serious model of pollution control, or as a thorough econometric analysis of the available time series data. We view it mainly as a vehicle for questioning whether the EKC hypothesis can add to our understanding of pollution control world-wide, beyond what is obvious. The vast majority of countries experienced growth in per capita GDP during the 1970–92 period, and average world-wide pollution levels fell during this same period. The EKC hypothesis attributes the pollution decline to the increase in income. Our intent was simply to point out that any other determining factor that is trended over time, for example, better information and education on the benefits of environmental protection, would have the same effect. Most of the data points from Tables 5.1 and 5.2 that we classified as supporting the EKC hypothesis for SO_2 are simply within-country observations of increasing income and decreasing pollution. Once we allow for the effects of trended variables, as in Table 5.8, income remains a significant determining factor in some countries, but the way it affects pollution generally does not agree with the EKC hypothesis. Indeed, the oddly shaped pollution–income relationships summarized in Table 5.8 have no ready explanation.

We have not attempted to formulate a model of what causes the pollution level to be what it is in a given country at a given time, so our empirical results may be open to several interpretations. This is a valid criticism, especially with respect to the income elasticity estimates, though it is one we share with most of the empirical literature on the EKC. In defense, it was not our aim to develop a framework for understanding why pollution behaves as it does in individual countries. Rather, our aim was to see if the inverted-U is a useful stylized fact about the way pollution and income are related within individual countries. On balance, and given the data presently available, we are not convinced that it is.

NOTES

1. Thanks are due to Arik Levinson for making these data available to us. As Harbaugh, Levinson and Wilson (2002, p. 542) point out, the simple correlation between average pollution observations in the original GEMS data set and observations in the revised AIRS data set is disturbingly low for SO_2 and for smoke, 0.75 and 0.77, respectively.
2. It is common in panel data EKC studies to include site-specific fixed effects. This clearly is a sensible approach if baseline pollution differences across sites are additive and constant. It is not if they are proportional or if the individual effects should be interacted with other variables.
3. Two studies on income–pollution relationships within US jurisdictions have used pollution and income data at the county and census tract level. See, respectively, Carson *et al.* (1997) and Khanna (2002).
4. Antweiler, Copeland, and Taylor (2001) call this the 'technique effect'. They also point out that air quality will be affected if the composition of output changes.
5. This is evident in the common observation that affluent communities tend to have better air quality than poor communities.
6. Including fixed effects for communities or monitoring sites, along with national level income, will not fix this problem. Consider the seemingly advantageous case where income in each community differs from national income by a fixed proportion. The confounding problem is that the proportionality factors should be different for each community, which necessitates community-specific coefficients for the national income term. That is, one would need to interact the fixed effects with national-level income.
7. Bartlett (1994) argued that this implied a perverse effect of environmental regulation – that it might inhibit growth and thereby stall environmental improvement.
8. Subsequent work examined emissions rather than concentrations. Hilton and Levinson (1998) separated emissions of lead from leaded gasoline into lead intensity per gallon, which reflects pollution control policy, and total gasoline consumption, which reflects the scale of activity. Selden and Song (1994) looked at emissions data for mostly OECD nations and found a turning point between $8000 and $10 000 of per capita income for sulfur dioxide and suspended particulate matter. Holtz-Eakin and Selden (1995) found no turning point at all for carbon dioxide. Stern and Common's (2001) EKC for sulfur

dioxide did not begin to slope down until per capita income reached $100 000, a level that is irrelevant to any actual economy.

9.   De Bruyn (1997) pointed out that only 13 percent of the variation in SO_2 emission targets could be explained by variations in income; hence the emphasis on income as a determining factor seemed misplaced. Carson *et al.* (1997), estimated EKCs for air quality within the United States, using state-level panel data.

10. Andreoni and Levinson (2001) showed that sufficiently strong increasing returns to scale in abatement can generate a theoretical EKC. Copeland and Taylor (2003) present four theoretical mechanisms that could yield an EKC. In their treatment, the source of economic growth and the nature of abatement costs are key factors determining the resulting relationship between pollution and income.

11. See, for example, HLW. Vincent (1997) tested some of the cross-country panel predictions on data from Malaysian states. Not only did the parameters fail to predict the pattern of changes in Malaysian air and water pollution, but none of the measures of environmental quality exhibited an EKC.

12. Researchers have generally been careful to use empirical methods that allow for unobserved additive heterogeneity across countries or monitoring sites. Apart from country- or site-specific constant terms, however, a single empirical model is assumed to apply to all countries.

13. Later in this section we compare results obtained from the GEMS/AIRS data set with results from the unmodified GEMS data set used in earlier studies.

14. For example, the data we use for Brussels, Belgium are from a monitoring site that collected TSP observations from 1976 to 1986. Also in the data set is TSP information from a different monitoring site in Brussels that collected observations only in 1985 and 1986. Observations from the second site are about 25 percent higher than readings from the first. To aggregate them would indicate an upward trend in pollution in Brussels that may not exist in reality. For estimation of a parametric model with panel data, a sensible way to deal with this composition problem is to include fixed effects for sites.

15. We tested the sensitivity of the results reported in the next section to the choice of monitoring sites by considering two alternative data sets for the USA, one for Japan, one for Australia, and one for New Zealand. The pattern of the relationship between income (or lagged income) and pollution did not change in any of the alternate cases.

16. Details about the procedure for eliminating observations and the final data set actually used are available on request.

17. The average income for cases exhibiting a single peak is higher than average income for those with an increasing relationship between pollution and GDP and lower than those with a declining relationship between pollution and GDP.

18. If we test the number of observations falling into *any* of the EKC-consistent vs. EKC-inconsistent or inconclusive categories, the resulting $X^2(2)$ statistic differed from random assignment only at the 90 percent confidence level.

19. The coverage of countries is somewhat different in our sample. The percentages in the text are only meant to indicate general trends.

20. Other causes would include the development of new technologies for controlling pollution and increased knowledge regarding the effects of air pollution on health. These causes do not figure prominently in the EKC literature, however. Another potential cause is the 'composition effect', which occurs if an economy's output shifts toward production of cleaner goods either over time or as income rises.

21. The estimate of pollution generation is based on total GDP rather than per capita GDP because total output is the pollution source.

22. For a 1 percent increase in GDP, the elasticity is the percentage difference between actual pollution and the pollution that would result from the higher output with no abatement. We compute arc elasticities, so the percentage change in pollution is calculated as: $(S_E - S_H)/(.5*(S_E + S_H))$. It is negative if actual pollution is lower than estimated pollution generation. Percentage changes in income are computed similarly.

23. The criterion for including countries in samples was explained earlier.

24. The elasticities with respect to per capita income for Venezuela are positive and relatively large, but are negative with respect to national GDP, which deserves explanation. Between its years of low and high total GDP, Venezuela's change in pollution indicated that some abatement took place. This implies a negative income elasticity of pollution with respect to national GDP. Venezuela's per capita GDP actually fell over the same period, however, resulting in a positive elasticity of pollution with respect to per capita income. Japan shows a small negative elasticity despite experiencing growth in SO_2 pollution, because Japan's income growth was more rapid. The positive elasticities for smoke in Denmark and other countries result from the fact that actual smoke pollution increased faster than national GDP, which our approach interprets as 'negative abatement'. Since this occurred while national and per capita GDP were rising, the result is a positive implied income elasticity of pollution.
25. The demand response comes about as a result of a political process in this case, which suggests interpreting the implied elasticities as pertaining to the median voter.
26. Unfortunately, these studies examine land use amenities rather than clean air.
27. Portney (1990, pp. 28–30) reviews pre-1970 air pollution policy in the USA Portney (ibid., p. 48) also presents data for the USA showing that emissions of particulates dropped rapidly after 1970 and sulfur dioxide emissions, which had peaked in 1970, fell steadily thereafter. He also cites EPA data from a limited number of monitoring sites, however, indicating that ambient concentrations of both pollutants had begun to decline during the 1960s (ibid., pp. 50–51).
28. These results are available on request.
29. It might be thought that high-income countries started with higher SO_2 concentrations in the early years, as a consequence of greater output, so they had more cleanup to undertake. This might, then, account for their more rapid rates of decrease. This possibility was checked by regressing SO_2 levels against per capita GDP for years prior to 1975. While the coefficient was positive, it was small and did not approach significance ($t=0.46$) so this hypothesis is not supported.
30. None of the estimates implied monotone relations between pollution and income.

REFERENCES

Andreoni, J. and A. Lavinson (2001), 'The simple analytics of the environmental Kuznets curve', *Journal of Public Economics*, **80** (2), May, 269–86 (18).

Antweiler, Werner, Brian R. Copeland and M. Scott Taylor (2001), 'Is free trade good for the environment?', *American Economic Review*, **91** (4), 877–908.

Barrett, Scott and Kathryn Graddy (2000), 'Freedom, growth, and the environment', *Environment and Development Economics*, **5** (4), 433–56.

Bartlett, Bruce (1994), 'The high cost of turning green', *The Wall Street Journal*, 14 September.

Carson, Richard T., Y. Jeon and D.R. McCubbin (1997), 'The relationship between air pollution and income: US data', *Environment and Development Economics*, **2**, 433–50.

Coondoo, D. and S. Dinda (2002), 'Causality between income and emissions: a country group-specific econometric analysis', *Ecological Economics*, **40** (3), 351–67.

Copeland, Brian R. and M. Scott Taylor (2003), *Trade and the Environment: Theory and Evidence*, Princeton: Princeton University Press.

de Bruyn, S.M. (1997), 'Explaining the environmental Kuznets curve: structural change and international agreements in reducing sulphur emissions', *Environment and Development Economics*, **2**, 485–503.

Flores, Nicholas E. and Richard T. Carson (1997), 'The relationship between the income elasticities of demand and willingness to pay', *Journal of Environmental Economics and Management*, **33** (3), 287–95.

General Agreement on Tariffs and Trade (1992), *International Trade 1990–1991*, vol. 1, Geneva.

Grossman, Gene and Alan B. Krueger (1993), 'Environmental impacts of a North American free trade agreement', in Peter Garber (ed.), *The Mexico–U.S. Free Trade Agreement*, Cambridge, MA: MIT Press.

Grossman, Gene M. and Alan B. Krueger (1995), 'Economic growth and the environment', *Quarterly Journal of Economics*, **112** (2), 353–78.

Hansen, Dinne and Michael Rasmussen (eds) (2001), *The Environmental Challenge of EU Enlargement in Central and Eastern Europe*, Ministry of the Environment, Danish Environmental Protection Agency.

Harbaugh, Willima T., Arik Levinson and David Molloy Wilson (2002), 'Reexamining the empirical evidence for an environmental Kuznets curve', *Review of Economics and Statistics*, **83** (3), 541–51.

Harrison, David and Daniel L. Rubinfeld (1978), 'Hedonic housing prices and the demand for clean air', *Journal of Environmental Economics and Management*, **5** (2), 81–102.

Hilton, F.G. Hank and Arik Levinson (1998), 'Factoring the environmental Kuznets curve: evidence from automotive lead emissions', *Journal of Environmental Economics and Management*, **35** (2), 126–41.

Holtz-Eakin, D. and T.M. Selden (1995), 'Stoking the fires? CO_2 emissions and economic growth', *Journal of Public Economics*, **57** (1), 85–101.

Khanna, Neha (2002), 'Is air quality income elastic? Revisiting the environmental Kuznets curve hypothesis', working paper WP0207, Department of Economics, Binghampton University, Binghampton NY.

Kristrom, Bengt and Pere Riera (1996), 'Is the income elasticity of environmental improvements less than one?', *Environmental and Resource Economics*, **7**, 45–55.

Nelson, Jon P. (1978), 'Residential choice, hedonic prices, and the demand for urban air quality', *Journal of Urban Economics*, **5**, 357–69.

Panayotou, T. (1997), 'Demystifying the environmental Kuznets curve: turning a black box into a policy tool', *Environment and Development Economics*, **2**, 383–99.

Portney, Paul R. (1990), 'Air pollution policy', in Paul R. Portney (ed.), *Public Policies for Environmental Protection*, Washington, DC: Resources for the Future.

Selden, T.M. and D. Song (1994), 'Environmental quality and development: is there a Kuznets curve for air pollution emissions?', *Journal of Environmental Economics and Management*, **27** (2), 147–62.

Shafik, N. and S. Bandyopadhyay (1992), 'Economic growth and environmental quality: time series and cross-country evidence', Policy Research working paper no. WPS 904, The World Bank, Washington, DC.

Stern, David I. (1998), 'Progress on the environmental Kuznets curve?', *Environment and Development Economics*, **3**, 173–96.

Stern, D.I. and M.S. Common (2001), 'Is there an environmental Kuznets curve far sulfur?', *Journal of Environmental Economics and Management*, **41**, 162–78.

Stern, David I., Michael S. Common and Edward B. Barbier (1996), 'Economic growth and environmental degradation: the environmental Kuznets curve and sustainable development', *World Development*, **24** (7), 1151–60.

Thompson, P. and L.A. Strohm (1996), 'Trade and environmental quality: a review of the evidence', *Journal of Environment and Development*, **5** (4), 363–89.

Torras, M. and James K. Boyce (1998), 'Income, inequality, and pollution: a reassessment of the environmental Kuznets curve', *Ecological Economics*, **25**, 147–60.

Vincent, Jeffrey (1997), 'Resource depletion and economic sustainability in Malaysia', *Environment and Development Economics*, **2** (1), 19–38.

World Bank (1992), *World Development Report: 1992*, New York: Oxford University Press.

6. Economic growth and natural resources: does the curse of natural resources extend to the 50 US states?

Ronald N. Johnson

1 INTRODUCTION

The search for the key determinants of economic growth has proved to be an elusive quest (Easterly, 2001). Because the standard production function approach, with its physical capital and human capital components, lacks empirical robustness, the door has been open to a myriad of causal arguments. Indeed, there seems no limit to the number of hypotheses concerning the sources of economic growth, with each having its moment of fame. Many of these arguments are supported, at least to some degree, by cross-country correlations. To this list can be added the notion that countries well endowed with natural resources have experienced relatively slow growth. Over the last 20 or 30 years, economic growth across countries has varied inversely with a variety of measures of natural resource abundance (for example, Auty, 2001a; Sachs and Warner 1997; Gylfason, 2001). This phenomenon, often referred to as 'the curse of natural resources', seems at odds with popular images of oil-rich nations and countries well endowed with nutrient-laden soils, abundant timber or fish stocks. While few authors go so far as to claim that discoveries of natural resource wealth leave countries poorer in the long run, the mechanics of relatively slow growth over the long run seem to suggest that as a possibility, and many of the studies abound with reference to stories of misspent natural wealth.

Like many of the statistical analyses of the determinants of economic growth, the correlations supporting the resource curse phenomenon appear fairly robust. Of course, the great disparity among countries in terms of their human capital, physical attributes, and institutions raises questions about whether this substantial variation can be adequately accounted for by a handful of right-hand-side variables. Supposedly, variation is less within a country. Accordingly, the key question addressed in this chapter is whether the resource curse phenomenon is evident in a cross-section sample of the 50 US states over the period 1977–2000 and, if so, whether any of the more popular explanations for the curse apply to the US experience.

Explanations for the resource curse abound, but the three channels of transmission from abundant natural resources to stunted economic development that have received the most attention are (a) the Dutch disease, (b) corruption or rent seeking, and (c) neglect of education. The evidence presented suggests the presence of a natural resource curse phenomenon for the USA, but little support for any of the popular explanations. Moreover, the finding that resource-abundant states grew at a slower rate over the period seems at odds with the earlier development of the USA when natural resource exploitation played a critical role in the historical development of certain states (for example, Irwin, 2000). There are, however, some basic arguments found in the natural resource literature that have received little more than cursory treatment in discussions of the so-called 'resource curse'. These arguments, which I was first introduced to in Gardner Brown's natural resource class, have to do with standard concepts of depletion, technological change, and the issue of growing resource scarcity, issues that are addressed in the concluding section of the chapter.

2 THE EVIDENCE

Casual observation is supportive of the hypothesized curse of natural resources. While there is no consensus on how to measure a country's stock and use of natural resources, few resource economists would consider Singapore, South Korea, and Hong Kong to be richly endowed with natural resources. In contrast, countries like Saudi Arabia, Kuwait, and the United Arab Emirates are richly endowed, at least with oil. Yet annual growth rates of real per capita GDP over the last 30 years are substantially greater for the former group of countries than for the latter. Moreover, the few cross-country measures of resource abundance that are available all seem to show a consistent and rather strong negative correlation between resources and economic growth. Gylfason (2001), for example, used 1994 World Bank estimates of the share of natural capital in total national wealth for 86 countries. The correlation between the World Bank's measure of resource abundance and annual growth of per capita GNP over the period 1965–98 was $\rho = -0.51$. Support for the hypothesized curse of natural resources has also been uncovered using such indicators as per capita land area and share of the labor force in the primary sector.[1] But the most-cited studies are by Sachs and Warner (1997, 2001) who use the ratio of primary product exports to GDP as their key indicator.

Sachs and Warner employ a basic growth model that has become the standard for investigating the determinants of growth across countries (see, for example, Barro, 1997),

$$(\mathrm{Log}GDP_T^i - \mathrm{Log}GDP_0^i)/T = \alpha + \beta_1 \mathrm{Log}GDP_0^i + \beta'X^i + e^i.$$

Here, the dependent variable is the annualized growth rate for country *i*. For Sachs and Warner's main data set *t*=0 is 1970 and *T*=1989. Included on the right-hand side is the initial level of per capita GDP. A negative coefficient on that variable implies economic convergences. The key variable in the Sachs and Warner model is the share of primary exports in GDP in 1970. While the simple correlation between growth in GDP and their measure of resource abundance is negative and statistically significant, Sachs and Warner investigate the sensitivity of this effect to the inclusion of variables accounting for the degree of openness of the economy, rule of law, changes in the terms of trade, and level of investment. The inclusion of these variables does not alter the finding that resource abundance has a negative and substantial impact on economic growth. Sachs and Warner also claim that distinguishing between agriculture and non-renewable resources such as oil in primary exports had little impact on their results. Accordingly, it appears that it is not just oil that is the problem, but natural resource-related products in general.[2]

The question posed in this chapter is whether a similar pattern holds for the US states. There are two measures of per capita income or product across the US states. The U.S. Department of Commerce, Bureau of Economic Analysis' estimates state personal income beginning in 1929; this is the longest series available. The Bureau of Economic Analysis also prepares Gross State Product (GSP) estimates for 63 industries, beginning in 1977.[3] The period 1970–77 was one of rapid expansion in the energy sector followed by a decline in the 1980s. Hence, 1977 is an excellent starting date for examining natural resource booms and subsequent impacts on growth. For each industry, GSP is composed of three components: compensation of employees, indirect business tax and nontax liability, and property-type income. Importantly, GSP attributes capital income to the state in which the business activity occurs, whereas personal income attributes it to the state of residence of the asset holder. Since the net benefits of natural resources can accrue largely in the form of economic rents, GSP is the better choice.[4] However, the results reported in this chapter are largely invariant to the use of real per capita personal income or real per capita GSP.[5]

Table 6.1, first data column, provides annualized percentage rates of growth in GSP for the 50 US states for the period 1977–2000. The data are listed in descending order. To those familiar with the 50 states, even casual observation of the table suggests a negative correlation between resource abundance and economic growth. Massachusetts and Connecticut were two of the fastest growing states, but it is difficult to consider these two eastern states as being relatively well endowed with natural resources. On the other hand, Montana and Alaska were the two slowest growing states. While one could argue that Alaska is unique, and it is, the exclusion of that state from the sample does not have any significant affect on the empirical results. Indeed, GSP in 1977 for states such as Wyoming were even more heavily weighted by oil and gas extraction than was Alaska.

Following Sachs and Warner, natural resource abundance is measured at the beginning of the sample growth period. In this case, the beginning period is 1977 and resource abundance is measured as the share of natural resource-related industries in GSP. Because they are likely influenced by different political factors and circumstances, two different resource sector shares are utilized. The first is the share of GSP accounted for by oil and gas extraction, coal, metal and nonmetallic mining (SHAREMINING). The second is the share of GSP accounted for by agriculture, forestry and fishing (SHAREAG). While the latter variable is dominated by commercial farms, the former is dominated by oil extraction and coal mining. Table 6.1 also shows the share data and rankings for the two natural resource sectors. Although the mining and agricultural sectors accounted for only 5.5 percent of total US GDP in 1977, it is clear from the table that their importance varied substantially across the states.

Table 6.2, column 1, offers some preliminary regression results. The coefficient on the log of initial GSP has the interpretation of a conditional rate of convergence. The estimated coefficient of -1.48 (t-statistic -3.75) is highly significant and implies a convergence rate of about 1.5 percent per year. Although the implied rate of convergence is slow, it is consistent with estimates obtained by Barro and Sala-i-Martin (1992) using data on state personal income since 1840. The coefficients on both the SHAREAG and SHAREMINING variables are negative and highly significant, implying that states with high shares of GSP in agriculture or the resource extraction sectors in 1977 grew at significantly lower rates than other states. To better gauge the impact on annual growth, consider the effect of a one standard deviation change in either of these two variables. The coefficient on SHAREAG is -5.96 and its standard deviation is 0.036. Multiplying these two numbers yields a negative growth effect of 0.22 percent per annum. The coefficient on SHAREMINING is -4.44 and its standard deviation is 0.065 implying a negative growth effect of 0.29 percent per annum. These effects are somewhat smaller than those reported by Sachs and Warner (1977), but they are comparable. Of course, Sachs and Warner also included a number of controlling variables, but it is likely that variables such as the degree of openness of a state's economy, the rule of law, and

Table 6.1 Annual growth and shares of state gross product in natural resource sectors

State	Annual growth of per capita gross state product, 1977–2000		Share of oil and gas extraction, and coal, metal and nonmetallic mining in GSP, 1977		Share of agriculture, forestry and fishing in GSP, 1977	
	Percent	Rank	Share	Rank	Share	Rank
New Hampshire	3.77	1	0.001	44	0.010	44
Massachusetts	3.44	2	0.000	48	0.006	49
Connecticut	3.22	3	0.001	43	0.007	45
Georgia	3.10	4	0.005	33	0.021	33
New Jersey	3.07	5	0.001	46	0.006	50
North Carolina	2.98	6	0.002	36	0.033	20
Delaware	2.94	7	0.002	39	0.016	37
Vermont	2.91	8	0.005	32	0.040	13
Rhode Island	2.85	9	0.001	47	0.007	46
Virginia	2.81	10	0.020	18	0.014	39
Colorado	2.80	11	0.038	13	0.030	24
South Carolina	2.67	12	0.002	37	0.022	32
Florida	2.66	13	0.008	28	0.033	22
Arizona	2.63	14	0.030	14	0.035	18
Utah	2.62	15	0.055	10	0.019	35
Tennessee	2.62	16	0.009	27	0.025	30
Washington	2.61	17	0.002	42	0.035	17
Minnesota	2.54	18	0.013	22	0.074	7
Maine	2.52	19	0.000	49	0.036	16
Maryland	2.49	20	0.001	45	0.011	43
New York	2.47	21	0.002	41	0.007	47
South Dakota	2.47	22	0.012	24	0.022	32

California	2.41	23	0.013	23	0.029	27
Oregon	2.41	24	0.003	35	0.033	19
Nevada	2.30	25	0.018	19	0.012	42
Alabama	2.27	26	0.025	16	0.026	28
Arkansas	2.18	27	0.021	17	0.077	6
Pennsylvania	2.18	28	0.014	21	0.012	41
Texas	2.14	29	0.125	6	0.026	29
Idaho	2.12	30	0.014	21	0.095	5
Nebraska	2.09	31	0.004	34	0.115	4
Kentucky	2.05	32	0.080	8	0.044	12
Missouri	2.05	33	0.007	30	0.039	14
New Mexico	2.02	34	0.175	3	0.030	25
Mississippi	2.01	35	0.025	15	0.064	10
Illinois	2.00	36	0.010	26	0.030	26
Wisconsin	2.00	37	0.002	40	0.051	11
Kansas	1.95	38	0.039	12	0.069	9
Indiana	1.93	39	0.006	31	0.037	15
Ohio	1.87	40	0.011	25	0.017	36
Hawaii	1.84	41	0.000	50	0.023	31
North Dakota	1.77	42	0.045	11	0.142	2
Michigan	1.66	43	0.008	29	0.015	38
Iowa	1.60	44	0.002	38	0.117	3
Oklahoma	1.56	45	0.129	5	0.033	21
Louisiana	1.46	46	0.212	2	0.020	34
Wyoming	1.38	47	0.324	1	0.031	23
West Virginia	1.22	48	0.173	4	0.006	48
Montana	1.04	49	0.072	9	0.072	8
Alaska	0.06	50	0.111	7	0.013	40

127

Source: U.S. Department of Commerce (2002), Bureau of Economic Analysis.

Table 6.2   Regressions of annual per capita GSP growth (1977–2000) on natural resource intensity and other controlling variables

Variable	(1)	(2)	(3)	(4)
Log GSP per capita, 1977	−1.48	−2.09	−1.69	−2.66
	(−3.75)	(−5.16)	(−3.60)	(−5.88)
SHAREAG, 1977	−5.96	−4.79	−4.47	−3.00
	(−3.15)	(−2.73)	(−2.58)	(−2.00)
SHAREMINING, 1977	−4.44	−3.67	−3.74	−2.48
	(−4.12)	(−3.64)	(−3.76)	(−2.80)
Education		0.08	0.09	0.10
		(3.27)	(3.69)	(4.66)
Tax rate			−0.07	0.01
			(−1.60)	(0.10)
SHAREGOV				−30.38
				(−4.38)
Constant	7.10	7.57	6.91	11.48
	(5.99)	(6.97)	(6.03)	(8.08)
Adjusted R-squared	0.48	0.57	0.58	0.74

Note: *T*-statistics in parentheses.

changes in the terms of trade vary little across the 50 states, jokes about Arkansas and North Dakota notwithstanding.[6] Accordingly, the evidence is consistent with the notion that the resource curse exists. Discussion of the applicability of some of the more popular explanations follows.

3   EDUCATION

Initial levels of human capital, usually measured in terms of years of schooling, are generally considered as having a very positive effect on economic growth (Barro, 1997). Gylfason (2001) argues that countries well endowed with natural resources have often neglected the education of their populace. In support, he presents results showing that expenditures on education and school enrollment are negatively correlated with the World Bank's 1994 measure of share of natural capital in national wealth. There are, of course, exceptions to this pattern, such as Norway. But Gylfason (2001, p. 858) argues that, more commonly, 'resource-rich countries become overconfident and therefore tend to underrate or overlook the need for good economic policies as well as for good education'. The question is whether this pattern extends to the US states.

Consider the result in Table 6.2, column 2. The regression reported there includes an educational attainment variable, measured as the percentage of the state's population having completed four or more years of college in 1980.[7] The coefficient on the education variable is positive and is both statistically and economically significant. Although the simple correlation coefficients between the education variable and SHAREAG and SHARE-MINING are negative, inclusion of the education variable has little impact on the two share variables and both remain statistically significant. Thus, controlling for the educational level of a state's populace does not appear to negate the resource curse argument.

Nevertheless, the argument that an abundance of natural resources leads to neglect of education may still be valid if it leads to a reduction in expenditures on education. Agricultural states, however, have long been considered to be educational incubators, having a young mobile workforce that migrates to urban areas (Goldin and Katz, 2000). Importantly, it is not at all evident that states with high shares of GSP in natural resource-related industries typically spend less on education.[8] Indeed, by controlling for the income base the opposite appears to be the more likely scenario. Although statistically insignificant, the ratio of public school expenditures divided by state personal income is positively correlated with both SHAREAG and SHAREMINING. Thus, the evidence for the USA does not support the notion that having a large sector of the economy based on natural resources leads to the neglect of education.

4 CORRUPTION, RENT SEEKING AND THE SIZE OF GOVERNMENT

There is little question that natural resource extraction and corruption have been frequent companions, especially in developing countries.[9] Abundance of natural resources does not, however, by itself create opportunities for corruption. Rather, corruption is symptomatic of the absence of well-defined property rights to those resources, a condition that seems to be present in many developing and transitional countries. In the absence of property rights, or where rights are somehow defective, resource rents can be dissipated and the rate of growth of the economy slowed. Because the term 'corruption' is often taken to imply illegal acts, such as bribery, a focus on corruption alone could deflect attention away from completely legal activities that have the same root cause and can have similar consequences. These activities, which perhaps are more germane to the US political scene, involve rent seeking, the socially costly pursuit of wealth transfers. In particular, the focus here will be on rent-seeking activities that lead to the expansion of state and local government.

State governments often tax a portion of the value of natural resources extracted within their jurisdictions. The expansion of the energy sector in the early 1970s substantially increased state severance tax receipts, and some states became highly dependent on energy-related taxes. For example, 1985 severance taxes on oil and gas accounted for almost 70 percent of Alaska's state tax receipts, while Wyoming obtained 15 percent of its total tax receipts from coal and almost an equal amount from oil.[10] The bonanza that befell states richly endowed with energy resources presented opportunities to expand the state's infrastructure, but it also likely increased the amount of rent-seeking activities.

Consider first the impact of state taxes on economic growth. There is competition among states, and that limits the extent to which a state can increase taxes before flight occurs to other states with more favorable tax bases (Benson and Johnson, 1986). Nevertheless, states do get out of line with their competition, and the evidence favors the opinion that relatively high taxes have a negative impact on growth (Wasylenko, 1997). Much depends, however, on what governments spend the money on as well as the type of taxes imposed. While the type of taxes imposed matters, a commonly used single indicator of whether a state is a high or low tax state is the ratio of total state and local tax revenues to total state personal income. The results in Table 6.2, column 3 provide some evidence, albeit weak, that an increase in a state's comprehensive tax rate lowers economic growth.[11] But the simple correlation between this tax rate variable and SHAREMINING, although statistically insignificant, is negative, suggesting that states with a large share of GSP in extractive industries were not, in general, high tax states.

Although the ratio of tax revenues to state personal income is a rather broad measure, as states have other sources of income besides direct taxes, how they use their funds likely matters for long-term growth. If, for example, renting-seeking activities result in an expanded and cumbersome bureaucracy, economic growth can be retarded. A relative measure of the size of state and local government is that sector's share of GSP. A major component of the state and local government sector in GSP is employee compensation. Accordingly, that sector's share of GSP provides a relative measure of the size of government across states.

The variable SHAREGOV in Table 6.2, column 4 is the average share of state and local government in GSP over the period 1977 to 2000. The coefficient on SHAREGOV is negative and highly significant. To gauge the impact on annual growth, consider the effect of a one standard deviation change in that variable. The mean of the SHAREGOV variable is 0.089 and its standard deviation is 0.0088, suggesting there is not a great deal of variability across the states. Nevertheless, the impact of a one standard deviation change is rather large, a negative growth effect of 0.27 percent per annum. Although the inclusion of that variable in the regression reduced the impact of the variables SHAREAG and SHAREMINING on growth, both coefficients remain negative and statistically significant. Moreover, it is generally recognized that the per capita cost of providing government services is lower in urban areas, and states with high shares of GSP in natural resource-related industries are mainly rural states. The simple correlation between SHAREGOV and percentage of the state's population living in urban areas is $\rho = -0.34$. Thus, the impact on the coefficients of the variables SHAREAG and SHAREMINING is more likely due to the rural nature of those states and not reflective of any particular proclivity towards rent-seeking activities that promote the size of government.

It is also noteworthy that the coefficients on the variables SHARE-MINING and SHAREAG are both negative and similar in magnitude. Yet these two sectors have often been treated very differently in the US political arena. Nevertheless, both sectors experienced declines in their shares of GSP over the period 1977–2000. While it could be argued that high severance taxes lead to slower growth of the mining and extraction sectors and thus slower state growth, the agriculture sector followed a similar decline and that sector has generally been a beneficiary of tax revenues.

5   THE DUTCH DISEASE

One of the more popular explanations for the resource curse employs a crowding-out logic, generated by an export boom in the primary commodity-exporting country. Supposedly, these booms create distortions that are not simply transitory effects. Rather, the boom affects the structure of the economy and alters the types of synergies that occur over the longer run. The mechanism involves a positive wealth shock from the natural resource sector that generates excess demand for non-traded goods. In particular, the excess demand increases the prices of non-traded input costs and wages. As a consequence of this increase in input costs, profits are squeezed in traded activities, such as manufacturing, that bid for the same inputs as the natural resource sector. The natural resource export boom also alters exchange rates, increasing the price of traded goods. This squeeze not only results in a decline of the other traded-good sectors, but it is argued that, relative to activities in the natural resource sector, these other sectors are more prone to positive spillover effects generated by technological synergies and have higher returns to learning by doing. Thus, natural resource abundance renders the export of other traded goods less competitive, and resource-abundant countries fail to experience the same degree of export-led growth as countries with poor endowments of natural resources.

The above scenario, and variants of it, are referred to as the Dutch Disease (for example, Neary and Van Wijnbergen, 1986; Sachs and Warner, 1997). Its origin is the discovery of huge quantities of natural gas in the Netherlands in the late 1950s. The first 15 years brought a gas-fueled economy to the Netherlands and resulted in substantial growth and expansion of government services. But this initial phase was followed by a stagnation in overall production and accelerating unemployment. It has been amply noted that the Dutch Disease is not really a disease, and its characterization as such seems ungrateful in the sense that the Dutch did experience a substantial increase in wealth. Moreover, there is a lack of direct tests of the theory's general applicability. Sachs and Warner (2001), however, provide some indirect support by showing that countries with natural resource-intensive economies tend to have higher price levels.

Although the exchange rate is the same across US states and inputs are likely more mobile than across countries, the Dutch Disease phenomenon remains applicable to the USA. It is the real exchange rate that matters, and frictions in labor and other input markets remain (for example, booms can lead to increases in local land prices). The 1970s were a boom period for natural resource-extraction sectors of the economy, and to a lesser extent for agriculture. Agricultural commodity prices, especially those for grains, spiked in 1973 (U.S. Department of Agriculture, 1980, Table 596). The energy boom continued through 1980, and growth in state per capita personal income over the period 1970–77 is highly correlated with SHAREMINING, $\rho = 0.53$, while the correlation between income and SHAREAG is $\rho = 0.25$. After 1981, agriculture and energy prices continued their long-term decline. Thus, the stage for a Dutch Disease phenomenon was set.

Importantly, following a boom in the natural resource sector, the Dutch Disease phenomenon requires a crowding-out of the other sectors of the economy. Supposedly, the boom retards growth of non-resource sectors. Accordingly, consider the results in Table 6.3. The dependent variable is the annual rate of growth in per capital GSP after subtracting the contribution from the agricultural and natural resource extraction sectors. While the coefficients on SHAREAG and SHAREMINING remain negative, they are no longer statistically significant. The coefficients on the control variables are very close to those reported in Table 6.2, column 4. Thus, the evidence does not support the notion that resource abundance retards the growth of other sectors of a state's economy.

These results not only fail to support the Dutch Disease phenomenon for the USA, but there are parts of the theory that do not seem to fit the US experience, or experiences elsewhere for that matter. Why natural resource sectors would have fewer positive spillover effects than, say, manufacturing has not

Table 6.3 *Regression of annual per capita growth of GSP less the contribution of agriculture and resource extraction sectors (1977–2000) on natural resource intensity and other controlling variables*

Variable	(1)
Log GSP per capita, 1977	−2.97
	(−6.07)
SHAREAG, 1977	−0.07
	(−0.04)
SHAREMINING, 1977	−0.40
	(−0.42)
Education	0.10
	(4.37)
Tax rate	−0.02
	(−0.48)
SHAREGOV	−31.21
	(−4.15)
Constant	12.73
	(8.28)
Adjusted R-squared	0.69

Note: T-statistics in parentheses.

been established. Manufacturing has its rust bowls and old smoke stack components, and it is difficult to imagine what the positive spillover effects are from those activities. In contrast, there is the high-tech sector, which did exceptionally well in the 1990s. But agriculture has also experienced a series of revolutions in biotechnology, and the mining industry has seen numerous advances in exploration, drilling and extraction. It is difficult to imagine that these advances did not result in significant spillovers of knowledge to other sectors of the economy. Of course, it may well be that agricultural and mining sectors had substantial negative environmental impacts, but also the results in Table 6.3 do not indicate that these impacts resulted in major negative effects on the growth of the other sectors within those states.

6   DISCUSSION

The above results indicate that the Dutch disease, neglect of education, and rent seeking or corruption are not the likely vehicles through which natural resource abundance has negatively impacted economic growth among the

US states. These results do not, however, imply that these explanations have no merit. Clearly, one contribution of numerous cross-country studies of the determinants of economic growth has been the finding that institutions, the rules of the game, seem to matter. Institutional factors, especially on a country-by-country basis, are likely important for understanding how some countries managed to misspend their natural wealth. Although the institutional factors across the US states are relatively similar, the results suggest that the resource curse phenomenon is present. Conclusions as to cause and effect, however, appear premature.

There are a number of arguments found in the literature on natural resource economics that are largely absent from discussions of the resource curse. These arguments raise questions about our ability to interpret the empirical results supportive of the existence of the resource curse, including the results offered in this chapter. Moreover, a simple factor, related to the geography of natural resources, likely contributes to the negative correlation between resource abundance and economic growth.

Consider that not only did both SHAREMINING and SHAREAG experience a sharp general decline over the period 1977–2000, but in real dollars both sectors were essentially stagnant, a status they held in common with only a few other sectors, such as textiles. That time frame, especially after 1981, corresponds to a sharp decline in the real price of oil and coal, the two main components of SHAREMINING. Concomitantly, after a sharp jump in the 1970s, agricultural prices continued their long-term secular decline. It could be argued that these sectorial declines are simply a continuation of a long-term decline in resource scarcity, as suggested by the results of Barnett and Morse (1963). But, as Brown and Field (1978) have pointed out, most of the common measures of changing resource scarcity, such as raw material prices, can be misleading indicators. They suggest that a better measure is *in situ* values, the user cost or shadow price of the resource, commonly referred to as the rental value of the resource. While there are potential problems even with that measure (Krautkraemer, 1998), the concept of economic rents is important not only to discussions of growing resource scarcity, but for better understanding the type and quality of data used to examine the curse of natural resources.

An underlying premise in the literature on the resource curse is that natural resources provide a bounty, a windfall. In particular, natural resources are a source of economic rents. It is supposedly these rents that set the stage for the numerous stories of how natural resource wealth gets misspent on frivolous consumption and misguided government projects. But resources *in situ* vary in quality, implying that in some localities rental flows can be small relative to gross sales. Moreover, the initial capture of rents may never occur. The natural resource economics literature is replete with examples of how the rental value of a resource can be dissipated if property rights are either nonexistent or ill defined (Brown, 2000).

Consider, for example, the case of the fishery. Under open access conditions the value of harvested fish could approximate the cost of boats and crew, leaving little left in terms of rents that can be attributed to the fishery. Recall that the key variable in the Sachs and Warner (1997; 2001) model is the share of primary exports in GDP. A country that harvests large quantities of fish could, by their measure, be labeled as well endowed with natural resources. But if open access conditions prevail, the export value of the fish may merely reflect the opportunity cost of the crew and boat. In defense, it could be argued that open access conditions lead to rent seeking, and it does, but Sachs and Warner and others have controlled for that by including variables such as the rule-of-law index (see Barro, 1997). Many western countries, like the USA, rate high on the rule-of-law scale, yet their fishery policies often seem aimed at dissipating as much of the potential rent as possible. Moreover, even if rights to resources are well defined, the Sachs and Warner measure does not distinguish between products from marginal and inframarginal sites. That is, they do not have measures of resource rents. As a consequence, light crude oil production in Saudi Arabia gets treated the same as secondary recovery operations in Texas, and corn production in Iowa gets lumped with wheat production in Siberia.

Of course, similar complaints could be made about the GSP measures used in this chapter. Although rental payments are a component of GSP, there is no clean way to separate them from the other contributors to a sector's measure of value added. On the other hand, the World Bank's estimates of the natural wealth of nations supposedly measure the value of land, water, timber, and subsoil assets. But these are very indirect measures and do not correspond to the type of estimates resource economists claim is needed to study issues of resource scarcity (Halvorsen and Smith, 1984; Krautkraemer, 1998). While it could be argued that such a standard is too high, other issues remain.

It would seemingly matter whether resource stocks were newly discovered or were old stocks being rapidly depleted, as booms and busts have different effects on local growth rates, yet this author is unaware of any empirical exercises that include estimates of resource stocks and rates of depletion. Mining has always been associated with discoveries, booms and busts. In testimony to this sequence are the ghost towns of the western USA. Essentially, many of these places were geographically isolated and, once the stocks were depleted, few opportunities remained. Depletion would eventually lead to declining payrolls and rental flows. Labor would exit the area and the natural resource bounty would be invested elsewhere, if at all. The story of boom and bust is evident in the data used in this chapter. As mentioned previously, the

SHAREMINING variable is positively correlated with state personal income growth in the 1970s and negatively thereafter. Moreover, SHARE-MINING is positively correlated with state population growth between 1970 and 1980, $\rho = 0.31$, and negatively between 1980–2000, $\rho = -0.11$. These numbers suggest that declining prices and production, especially for oil, over the period 1977–2000 followed the standard boom/bust scenario.

A similar story pertains to agriculture, but for a different reason. Agricultural output per acre has been increasing since the beginning of the 20th century (Ruttan, 2002). While advances in technology may increase the value of land, and that is by no means certain, the proportion of the population engaged in agriculture has been declining for the past century. The simple correlation between SHAREAG and population growth between 1980 and 2000 is $\rho = -0.24$. Hence, both agriculture and mining are essentially stagnant or declining industries. States with relatively high GSP shares in either of these two sectors tend to be rural states. In general, these states do not appear to have attracted sufficient investment and population to compensate for the decline in those two sectors. Of course, the regression results presented in this chapter suggest that convergence of per capita GSP will eventually occur, but the implied time frame is long.

It could be argued that the extent to which the US experience, as described in this chapter, can be applied to the rest of the world is limited. A declining sector invites exit, and labor and capital are likely far more mobile between the states than between most countries. But if a major sector of a country's economy is undergoing decline, there is no certainty other sectors will expand rapidly enough to absorb the released factors of production and avoid a slowdown in growth. Thus, it would seem important in the search to document the resource curse that we control for whether resource sectors in the resource-abundant countries are growing or declining.

Understanding the determinants of the resource curse has important policy ramifications. If, for example, the root cause is that resource-abundant countries tend to neglect education, the remedy may lie with more extensive use of trust funds devoted to education. But if the underlying cause is associated with the boom/bust scenario and its potential for ghost towns whose costs are not fully accounted for, the remedy may call for a reduction in mining activity. Furthermore, uncertainty about the environmental impacts of natural resource use and the possibility that some of these impacts are irreversible has led many resource economists to argue for a 'precautionary principle'. A failure to understand the determinants of the resource curse lends support to those anxious to apply that principle. But advocacy of that sort appears premature. The arguments presented to date fail to sufficiently inform us as to whether, on net, resource-abundant countries are blessed or cursed, and what margins are relevant.

NOTES

1. See the volume edited by Auty (2001b) for a recent survey of these studies as well as the contributions contained therein. Those papers offer a variety of explanations for and extensions to the literature on resource abundance and economic development. But, also see Mikesell (1997) who argues there is no single or even dominant explanation for the resource curse.
2. This result may be more tenuous than Sachs and Warner indicate. See the empirical results in Leite and Weidmann (1999) and discussion in Auty (2001b).
3. Although data on GSP are available back to 1963 (see Barro and Sala-i-Martin, 1992), the Bureau of Economic Analysis does not make these data available, claiming they are not consistent with their post-1977 data.
4. In addition to natural resource rents, rents or quasi-rents can also accrue to other factors of production engaged in extraction or cultivating practices. See Johnson and Libecap (1982).
5. Real GSP was derived using the GDP deflator. The CPI index was used to obtain measures of real personal income.
6. Unfortunately, the Bureau of Economic analysis does not have comparable state-level data on investment. The more recent data series on state level investment have been largely developed by researchers and generally involve extrapolation. See, for example, Garofalo and Yamarik (2002).
7. The data on educational levels and expenditures utilized in this section are from the US Census and the *Statistical Abstract of the United States* (various issues).
8. States like Alaska and Wyoming have for years ranked near the top in terms of per pupil expenditures.
9. See, for example, Leite and Weidmann (1999), who present evidence showing a rather strong statistical relation between various indexes of corruption and natural resource abundance. Also see Deacon (1999) on the role of various institutional factors and deforestation.
10. Source, U.S. Department of Energy (2003), Energy Information Agency.
11. The Tax Rate variable in Table 6.2 is for 1977. Use of the average tax rate between 1977 and 2000 yielded similar results.

REFERENCES

Auty, Richard M. (2001a), 'The political economy of resource-driven growth', *European Economic Review*, **45** (4–6), 839–46.

Auty, Richard M. (2001b), *Resource Abundance and Economic Development*, Oxford: Oxford University Press.

Barnett, Harold J. and Chandler Morse (1963), *Scarcity and Growth: The Economics of Natural Resource Availability*, Baltimore: Johns Hopkins University Press for Resources for the Future.

Barro, Robert J. (1997), *Determinants of Economic Growth: A Cross-Country Empirical Study*, Cambridge, MA: MIT Press.

Barro, Robert J. and Xavier Sala-i-Martin (1992), 'Convergence', *Journal of Political Economy*, **100** (2), 223–51.

Benson, Bruce and Ronald N. Johnson (1986), 'The lagged impact of state and local taxes on economic activity', *Economic Inquiry*, **24** (3), 389–401.

Brown, Gardner M. (2000), 'Renewable natural resource management and use without markets', *Journal of Economic Literature*, **38** (4), 875–914.

Brown, Gardner M. and Barry C. Field (1978), 'Implications of alternative measures of natural resource scarcity', *Journal of Political Economy*, **86** (2), 229–43.
Deacon, Robert T. (1999), 'Deforestation and ownership: evidence from historical accounts and contemporary data', *Land Economics*, **75** (3), 341–59.
Easterly, William (2001), *The Elusive Quest for Growth: Economists' Adventures and Misadventures in the Tropics*, Cambridge, MA: MIT Press.
Garofalo, Gasper A. and Steven Yamarik (2002), 'Regional convergence: evidence from a new state-by-state capital stock series', *The Review of Economics and Statistics*, **84** (2), 316–23.
Goldin, Claudia and Lawrence F. Katz (2000), 'Education and income in the early twentieth century: evidence from the prairies', *Journal of Economic History*, **60** (3), 782–818.
Gylfason, Thorvaldur (2001), 'Natural resources, education, and economic development', *European Economic Review*, **45** (4–6), 847–59.
Halvorsen, Robert and Tim R. Smith (1984), 'On measuring natural resource scarcity', *Journal of Political Economy*, **92** (5), 954–64.
Irwin, Douglas A. (2000), 'How did the United States become a net exporter of manufactured goods?', National Bureau of Economic Research, working paper no. 7638.
Johnson, Ronald N. and Gary D. Libecap (1982), 'Contracting problems and regulations: the case of the fishery', *American Economic Review*, **72** (5), 1005–22.
Krautkraemer, Jeffrey A. (1998), 'Nonrenewable resource scarcity', *Journal of Economic Literature*, **36** (4), 2065–107.
Leite, Carlos and Jens Weidmann (1999), 'Does Mother Nature corrupt? Natural resources, corruption, and economic growth', *International Monetary Fund*, working paper no. 99/85.
Mikesell, Raymond F. (1997), 'Explaining the resource curse with special reference to mineral-exporting countries', *Resources Policy*, **23** (4), 191–9.
Neary, Peter J. and Sweder Van Wijnbergen (1986), *Natural Resources and the Macroeconomy*, Cambridge, MA: MIT Press.
Ruttan, Vernon W. (2002), 'Productivity growth in world agriculture: sources and constraints', *Journal of Economic Perspectives*, **16** (4), 161–84.
Sachs, Jeffrey D. and Andrew M. Warner (1997), 'Natural resource abundance and economic growth', National Bureau of Economic Research, working paper no. 5398.
Sachs, Jeffrey D. and Andrew M. Warner (2001), 'The curse of natural resources', *European Economic Review*, **45** (4–6), 827–38.
U.S. Department of Agricultural (various years), *Agricultural Statistics*, Washington, DC: Government Printing Office.
U.S. Department of Commerce (2002), *Regional Accounts Data, 1977–2000*, Washington, DC: Bureau of Economic Analysis.
U.S. Department of Commerce (various years), *Statistical Abstract of the United States*, Washington, DC: Government Printing Office.
U.S. Department of Energy (2003), *State Severances Taxes, 1985–1993*, Washington, DC: Energy Information Agency, online, http://www.eia.doe.gov/emeu/sevtax/ chap 1.html, cited 20 March, 2003.
Wasylenko, Michael (1997), 'Taxation and economic development: the state of the economic literature', *New England Economic Review*, **March/April** (2), 37–52.

7. Fishes and trees, or continuous vs. discrete harvesting[1]

Martin L. Weitzman

1 GARDNER BROWN AND THE HARVESTING OF RENEWABLE NATURAL RESOURCES

Gardner Brown has been one of the great early pioneers in developing and applying dynamic economic tools (in particular, optimal control theory) to the analysis of how best to develop and harvest natural resources.[2]

Gardner was, at a young age, attracted to the interface between human beings and the natural environment that surrounds and nurtures them. That is to say, early on Gardner was relatively most interested in the part of environmental economics having to do with the combining of economics with 'nature', as opposed to, say, the combining of economics with pollution–health issues, which might be called 'EPA-type' environmental economics. What then could be a more 'natural' (no pun intended) field for Gardner to specialize in than the harvesting of renewable natural resources?

This is not to say that Gardner has not done outstanding work in lots of other areas of economics. It is just that I think that the 'love of his life' has been in this area of how to balance human interests and the interests of 'nature'.

I first met Gardner in the autumn of 1963, at a picnic, through a mutual acquaintance. He was then a graduate student at UC Berkeley. I remember chatting with him then, and being impressed by three things. First of all, he obviously had an abiding love of the outdoors. Secondly, Gardner seemed very directed in this goal of combining economics with the natural environment. The third (and most important for me) impression was that this natural economics goal of his seemed very intriguing, and maybe I (who was at Stanford in statistics at the time) should think about something like it too as a field of study or even a career. I do not want to say 'the rest is history', because that is off the mark for several reasons, but this first conversation with Gardner definitely made a lasting impression on me.

When Gardner entered the field, the economic harvesting of natural resources was still in its murky infancy. The basic ideas were 'out there', for sure, but they were far from being in the nicely-packaged reduced form we now know and teach to students. Every model seemed special, and disconnected from every other. It was not clear what were the basic unifying underlying principles. Were they just specific particularly exotic examples of capital theory, or was there some deeper connection with the rest of dynamic economics?

It is fair to say that Pontryagin's maximum principle, which was just then beginning to be applied to economics, and which Gardner latched on to very early, forced us economists to 'see' the capital-theoretic unity of all such natural resource problems. First of all, just using the maximum principle made us put all dynamic problems into a canonical form that was almost automatically a useful way of seeing the underlying unity. More importantly, the maximum principle itself is a set of duality conditions with a natural, and very important, economic interpretation centered on the co-state variables, which are competitive-like prices to us. The maximum principle has a direct economic interpretation as describing a dynamic competitive equilibrium, while other forms of dynamic optimality conditions (for example, Euler-type equations) essentially must be transformed into a maximum principle-like form to give them economic meaning.

Thus, by using the maximum principle, we economists were led to a rich understanding of the connections between the optimal regulation of a renewable fishery resource, the optimal extraction of an exhaustible mineral resource, and the neoclassical theory of optimal growth – to name just three famous models that thereby became interconnected. However, one famous and very important model that we natural resource economists knew and loved remained somehow outside this maximum principle-contained orbit of (almost) all other dynamic resource allocation models. This was the famous Faustmann–Wicksell model of optimal forestry rotation.

Forestry models seemed somehow 'different' from the other models of natural resource harvesting or extraction. The forestry models focus sharply on the age structure of a cohort, and are essentially discrete. The 'harvesting' of a tree or forest is the discrete act of cutting it down and bringing it to market. The 'renewal' of a tree or forest is the discrete act of planting seedlings. This seems very different from the continuous harvesting and renewal that characterizes, say, the classical model of the fishery.

There is an air of intellectual disappointment in not being able to combine fishery and forestry models under some unifying umbrella. At least this was the case for me. Gardner was also puzzled about this seeming dichotomy between the continual harvesting and renewal of the fishery and the discontinuous harvesting and renewal of the forest. Why should these two core models of the economics of renewable resources seem so different in structure?

What I want to show in what follows is that there exists a way to connect the two models by turning the classical Faustmann–Wicksell forestry model into an equivalent continuous harvesting version. We will then be able to see how the maximum principle applied to this equivalent continuous harvesting version of the forestry rotation problem is just another form of the famous Faustmann–Wicksell first-order conditions telling us when to cut down the trees.

In the next section, we recapitulate the problem of the sole owner of the fishery as an optimal control problem that is linear in net investment, and hence supports a most-rapid-approach bang-bang solution. The more interesting and novel part, which follows in the third section, shows that the classical forestry problem is also an optimal control problem that is linear in net investment, and hence this problem also supports a most-rapid-approach bang-bang solution. In this way, we show that the mathematical structure of these two famous problems of the harvesting of natural resources is essentially isomorphic. Both are linear-in-investment optimal control problems whose solution is the most rapid approach to their respective stationary states.

2 OPTIMAL MANAGEMENT OF THE FISHERY

The classical dynamic economic problem of optimal fishery management is typically presented as if seen through the eyes of a fictitious 'sole owner', who may be conceptualized as being either a private firm or a government regulatory agency. The sole owner is assumed to be seeking a harvesting policy that maximizes net present discounted profits.

The problem here is to choose the harvesting flow rate $\{h(t)\}$ to

maximize
$$\int_0^\infty \pi(x)h(t)e^{-\rho t}dt \tag{7.1}$$

subject to

$$\dot{x}(t) = F(x(t)) - h(t), \tag{7.2}$$

and

$$\underline{h} \le h(t) \le \bar{h}, \tag{7.3}$$

and with the given initial condition

$$x(0) = x_0. \tag{7.4}$$

For this model, $x(t)$ represents the stock of fish at time t, and $h(t)$ is the harvest flow taken at time t. In condition (7.3), $\bar{h}$ is some more-or-less-arbitrary upper bound on harvesting; the lower bound $\underline{h}$ is perhaps somewhat less arbitrary because $\underline{h} \equiv 0$, at least, has a natural interpretation. (The upper and lower bounds are needed to make sense of the problem for technical reasons, so in a way it does not matter what they are.) The function $F(x)$ represents the net biological increase of the fish population, in the absence of any harvesting. The function $\pi(x)$ gives the net profits per fish caught when the stock of fish is x.

In the fisheries literature it is standard to take as unit profit the difference between price and catch cost, so that

$$\pi(x) = P - c(x), \tag{7.5}$$

where P represents the exogenously given price of fish and $c(x)$ represents per unit 'locating and harvesting cost' as a function of fish density x. A reader typically sees the form of the right-hand side of (7.5), rather than our more concise notation $\pi(x)$.

To reduce the problem of the sole owner of the fishery to a canonical form, it is useful to reformulate it in terms of net investment. In this situation, net investment is the natural biological increment of the fish population *minus* the amount of fish being caught or harvested. (It is perhaps not yet entirely clear why we might want to take a problem out of the form in which it naturally suggests itself and recast it in the form of a prototype economic problem where net investment is considered to be the control variable; the reason is that this canonical form always permits the solution to be understood quickly, easily, and in the most economically intuitive way.)

With the change of variables $K \equiv x$ and $I \equiv F(x) - h$, and specifying $m(K) \equiv F(K) - \bar{h}$ and $M(K) \equiv F(K) - \underline{h}$, the optimal fishery harvesting problem is a prototype-economic problem with gain function

$$G(K, I) = \pi(K)[F(K) - I]. \tag{7.6}$$

The stationary rate of return on capital is defined to be

$$R(K) \equiv \frac{G_1(K, 0)}{-G_2(K, 0)}. \tag{7.7}$$

It can readily be shown that net investment should be positive if $R(K) > \rho$, negative if $R(K) < \rho$, and zero if $R(K) = \rho$. Once the stationary rate of return on capital has been calculated, the qualitative direction of investment (positive, negative, or zero) is determined. The only remaining question is how fast to go to a stationary state. For the linear-in-investment renewable resource problems under investigation here, the answer is 'as fast as possible'.

From applying formula (7.7) to (7.6) (and remembering to evaluate at $I = 0$), the stationary rate of return on capital for this model of optimal fishery management is

$$R(K) = F'(K) + F(K)\frac{\pi'(K)}{\pi(K)}. \tag{7.8}$$

Equation (7.8) can be interpreted as saying that the stationary rate of return $R(K)$ consists of two terms representing the two economic effects that come from having a higher amount of fish capital here. The first effect, $F'(K)$, represents the increment of new fish population that comes with a higher parent fish stock. The second term on the right-hand side of (7.8) represents the additional profit from the lower unit harvesting cost that attends a larger fish population, since it is easier to locate and catch fish when there are more of them.

Let $\hat{K}$ represent the stationary solution where

$$R(\hat{K}) = \rho. \tag{7.9}$$

As is well known for a problem linear in net investment, the optimal policy is a most rapid approach to the stationary solution $\hat{K}$.

This description of the management of the fishery is familiar, because we are (by now) accustomed to seeing the classical fishery model as a linear-in-investment optimal control problem with a bang-bang solution. What is less familiar, and less obvious, is that the optimal forest rotation problem is also a linear-in-investment optimal control problem with a bang-bang solution. Hence, the mathematical structure of the two renewable resource harvesting problems is essentially the same.

3 THE OPTIMAL TREE HARVESTING PROBLEM

Another model whose gain function is linear in investment is the *optimal tree harvesting model*. This problem can be posed and solved directly, without invoking optimal control theory, so a formulation in terms of optimal control theory serves more to enrich an intuitive understanding of the maximum principle (as capital theory) than to act as a mechanism for actually solving a problem that could not otherwise be solved.

Suppose that, when it is cut down and brought to market, a tree of age T yields a net value given by the function

$$F(T). \tag{7.10}$$

Frequently in the forestry literature, $F(T)$ is specified in the form

$$F(T) = Pf(T) - c + v, \tag{7.11}$$

where P is the given market price of wood and $f(T)$ is (in forestry termi-nology) the 'merchantable volume' of wood yielded by a tree of age T. The parameter c represents the total economic cost of cutting down the tree, processing it for sale, and bringing the wood to market. (In the forestry lit-erature, the expression $Pf(T)-c$ is called the *net stumpage value* of the tree.) The parameter v stands for the *opportunity value* (in lumbering terminol-ogy the *land expectation* or *site value*) of the land being freed for its best subsequent economic use after the tree is felled, which 'best subsequent economic use' might well be the replanting of a sapling to start the tree-growing cycle anew.

The famous *Wicksell problem* of capital theory is to choose the time of cutting T to

maximize $e^{-\rho T}F(T).$ (7.12)

It might appear perverse to force such a direct statement as (7.12) into the seemingly more arcane form of an optimal control problem. However, an optimal control formulation will serve to reinforce economic intuition and to highlight quite dramatically the underlying unity of *all* time-and-capital problems. In particular, it will allow us to see sharply the relation-ship between the two most famous models of renewable resources: optimal harvesting of the fishery and optimal harvesting of the forest.

In the optimal control version of the Wicksell problem, the 'capital stock' is the *age of the tree* (more precisely, it is the tree of that age). The corre-sponding 'investment' here means allowing the tree to grow older by a year.

Suppose we fancifully imagined that 'the forest' could be continuously harvested in the spirit of 'the fishery'. For this fishery-like forest, the 'harvest flow' generalization of the Wicksell problem in capital theory is to control the 'investment rate' $\{I(t)\}$ to

maximize $\displaystyle\int_0^\infty \rho F(K(t))[1 - I(t)]e^{-\rho t}dt$ (7.13)

subject to

$$\dot{K}(t) = I(t), \tag{7.14}$$

and

$$0 \le I(t) \le 1, \tag{7.15}$$

and with the given initial condition

$$K(0) = 0. \tag{7.16}$$

The original Wicksell formulation in effect limits the investment $I(t)$ to be a step function, which takes on value one when the tree is growing (or until it is cut), and takes on value zero thereafter. As we will see, the above 'harvest flow' generalization yields the Wicksell solution anyway. For now it suffices to note that the Wicksell problem is a special case of (7.13)–(7.16); therefore, if the optimal solution of (7.13)–(7.16) is a step function, as will turn out to be the case, then it must also represent the solution of the more restricted Wicksell problem (7.12).

It is useful to pose the Wicksell model formally as an optimal control model of capital accumulation because it highlights the underlying connection between growth and aging processes where *capital is time* (aging of wine is another well-known example) and the bulk of *all other* capital-theoretic models that can be formulated as simple optimal control problems where capital is *not* time. Posing the problem this way allows us to see rigorously what we otherwise can only intuit in models of tree cutting, wine aging, animal raising, and many other problems of growth and aging: the important idea that in many situations *age is capital*, but that otherwise the same general principles of capital theory apply.

So, for this Wicksell problem, let us identify 'capital' with 'age'. Applying the definition (7.7) to the gain function

$$G(K, I) = \rho F(K)[1 - I], \tag{7.17}$$

which appears in (7.13), the stationary rate of return on capital in the optimal tree cutting problem is

$$R(K) = \frac{F'(K)}{F(K)}. \tag{7.18}$$

From the general consideration that the gain function of the Wicksell problem is linear in investment, we know that the optimal solution involves a most rapid approach to the stationary state $\hat{K}$ where $R(\hat{K}) = \rho$, which by (7.18) is equivalent to the condition

$$\frac{F'(\hat{K})}{F(\hat{K})} = \rho. \tag{7.19}$$

Let us see what is happening specifically in this particular optimal control problem by formally applying the maximum principle. The Hamiltonian here is

$$H = \rho F(K)[1 - I] + pI, \tag{7.20}$$

where p stands for the marginal value of letting a tree of age K grow for one more year.

The next step is to calculate the maximum value of the Hamiltonian over all feasible values of I. This part is easy because we are maximizing a linear function over the unit interval. With $\tilde{I}(p)$ denoting the Hamiltonian-maximizing value of investment as a function of its price, from (7.20) there are three possibilities:

$$p > \rho F(K) \; implies \; \tilde{I}(p) = 1 \; implies \; \tilde{H}(K, p) = p, \tag{7.21}$$

or

$$p < \rho F(K) \; implies \; \tilde{I}(p) = 0 \; implies \; \tilde{H}(K, p) = \rho F(K), \tag{7.22}$$

or, the case of an indeterminate solution where $\tilde{I}(p)$ can be *any* feasible value,

$$p = \rho F(K) \; implies \; 0 \le \tilde{I}(p) \le 1 \; implies \; \tilde{H}(K, p) = \rho F(K). \tag{7.23}$$

It is now not difficult to guess at the form of an optimal policy. Just from glancing at (7.21), (7.22) and (7.23), an intuitive chain of reasoning is that

$$K < \hat{K} - \frac{F'(K)}{F(K)} > \rho \; implies \; p > \rho F(K) \; implies \; \tilde{I}(p) = 1$$
$$implies \; \tilde{H}(K, p) = p, \tag{7.24}$$

in which case we have

$$-\frac{\partial \tilde{H}}{\partial K} = 0, \tag{7.25}$$

and therefore the dual differential equation condition here becomes

$$\dot{p}(t) = \rho p(t), \tag{7.26}$$

with the 'terminal condition'

$$p(\hat{K}) = \rho F(\hat{K}). \tag{7.27}$$

Combining (7.26) with (7.27) yields

$$p(t) = \rho F(\hat{K}) e^{\rho(t - \hat{K})}. \tag{7.28}$$

By the optimality of $\hat{K}$ for the problem (7.12), we must then have that for $K(t) < \hat{K}$

$$F(K(t))e^{-\rho t} < F(\hat{K})e^{-\rho \hat{K}}. \tag{7.29}$$

Combining (7.29) with (7.28), we obtain the basic result that for $K(t) < \hat{K}$

$$p(t) > \rho F(K(t)). \tag{7.30}$$

From (7.30) we can say that the signal *not* to cut down the tree is that the shadow *indirect value of allowing the tree to grow exceeds the direct value of harvesting it*. (It is *never* optimal to *allow* a tree to grow to an age T where $F'(T)/F(T) < \rho$, but *if we acquired* such an 'economically overripe tree' having $T > \hat{K}$ from a nonprofit-maximizing owner, the signal to cut it down immediately would be that the shadow *indirect value of allowing the tree to grow is less than the direct value of harvesting it*.)

We now make some important observations about the role of the hitherto obscure parameter v, which stands for the *opportunity value* of the land being freed for its best subsequent economic use after the tree is felled. Suppose that, instead of being concerned about the fate of an individual tree, which is the Wicksell problem, we are interested in the infinite horizon optimal *rotation* of a one-tree lot (or, more realistically, of a woodlot consisting of a stand of cohort trees). In this case, the opportunity value v of the land being freed for its best subsequent economic use after the tree is felled is the present discounted value of an infinite horizon rotation policy beginning with the replanting of a sapling to start the tree-growing cycle anew.

Suppose the parameter c now includes all costs of replanting (as well as logging, processing, and transportation costs). The *competitive market value v* of the land (in forestry terminology the *land expectation* or the *site value*), right after it has been cleared and a new sapling has just been replanted, satisfies in competitive equilibrium the recursive equation

$$v = e^{-\rho \hat{K}}[Pf(\hat{K}) - c - v], \tag{7.31}$$

which is equivalent, after rearrangement, to

$$v = \frac{e^{-\rho \hat{K}}[Pf(\hat{K}) - c]}{1 - e^{-\rho \hat{K}}}. \tag{7.32}$$

If $\hat{K}$ is the optimal age to cut down a tree *given* the competitive market value v of the site, then it seems plausible that $\hat{K}$ is chosen to *maximize* present site value, so that

$$v = \underset{K}{\text{maximum}} \; \frac{e^{-\rho K}[Pf(K) - c]}{1 - e^{-\rho K}}, \tag{7.33}$$

which yields the first order condition

$$\frac{P'f(\hat{K})}{Pf(\hat{K}) - c} = \frac{\rho}{1 - e^{-\rho \hat{K}}}. \tag{7.34}$$

Equation (7.34) is the famous *Faustmann formula* for the optimal rotation length $\hat{K}$. Rewriting the optimization problem (7.33) in the equivalent form of an infinite geometric series, we have

$$v = \underset{K}{\text{maximum}} \sum_{j=1}^{\infty} e^{-j\rho K}[Pf(K) - c]. \tag{7.35}$$

In effect, equation (7.35) defines the *Faustmann model* of optimal forest rotation, whose solution satisfies the Faustman formula (7.34).

In the forestry literature, the Faustmann model and the Faustmann *formula* are typically contrasted with the Wicksell model and the Wicksell formula. In a serious sense, this is a false dichotomy. The Wicksell model ostensibly takes the site value as exogenously given, often as zero, although there is evidence that Wicksell himself understood that it would be fallacious to perform comparative statics when treating v as if it were constant.[3] The Faustmann and Wicksell models are *identical* when proper account is taken of the market site value of forest land. We showed above that the Wicksell model with competitive market site value yields the Faustmann solution; the converse can readily be shown by substituting the Faustmann formula for site value into the Wicksell formulation and confirming directly that the Wicksell-optimal cutting time satisfying condition (7.19) is exactly the Faustmann-optimal cutting time satisfying condition (7.34). The two models represent two equivalent ways of looking at optimal forestry management. The Wicksell approach emphasizes how to think about harvesting an individual tree. The Faustmann approach emphasizes how to think about the harvesting cycle of an ongoing stand of trees. So long as the opportunity value of the woodlot is properly assessed and included, the two models yield identical conclusions. It is essentially a case of looking at two sides of a single problem that more properly should be called 'the Faustmann–Wicksell model' of forestry management.

What has been shown here is that the Faustmann–Wicksell model of optimal tree harvesting has essentially the same form as the standard model of the sole owner of the fishery. Both can be seen as optimal control models linear in net investment, and both have the same form of most rapid approach to their respective stationary solution. Of course the

Faustmann–Wicksell model can be developed without optimal control theory, but applying the maximum principle to the forestry rotation problem allows us to see it as a harvesting problem of the same generic form as the standard fishery model. Thus, the two most famous models in the economics of renewable resources – the fishery and the forest – are essentially two forms of the same underlying optimal control problem.

NOTES

1. This chapter was prepared for the conference in honor of Gardner Brown, 5 April 2003 and is essentially a repackaged version (with different emphases) of some material contained in my book *Income, Wealth, and the Maximum Principle*, Cambridge, MA: Harvard University Press, 2003.
2. See, for example, Brown (1974).
3. See the interesting historical discussion in Löfgren (1999).

REFERENCES

Brown, Gardner, Jr (1974), 'An optimal program for managing common property resources with congestion externalities', *Journal of Political Economy*, **82** (1), 163–73.
Löfgren, Karl-Gustaf (1999), 'Ohlin versus Heckscher and Wicksell on forestry: one win (points) and one draw', Department of Economics, Umeå University, December.

8. The grand unified theory of natural resource economics: a special case

Mark L. Plummer

Natural resource economics is inevitably broken into two distinct sets of models, one for renewable resources and the other for nonrenewable resources. This division is reflected in how economists teach this subject, with textbooks and syllabi inevitably bifurcated into separate treatments of the two types of resources.

On the one hand, this division is quite logical, for renewable and non-renewable resources differ in an obvious, fundamental way: the former are capable of growth while the latter are not. This distinction means, as Harold Hotelling noted, that 'the indefinite maintenance of a steady state rate of production is a physical impossibility' for one type of resource but is quite possible for the other.[1] In short, the division between renewable and non-renewable resources makes sense from a physical point of view, and so economists have developed distinct sets of models accordingly.

On the other hand, this division makes no sense at all. 'Growth' is a characteristic that varies along a continuum. Agricultural crops have a relatively high rate of growth; trees, a relatively moderate one; minerals, a zero rate; and harvested strawberries and peaches, a negative rate. Viewed in this way, a nonrenewable resource falls squarely within a continuum, unique only in being located at one point along the continuum rather than another – unique, in other words, just as any other resource is unique. Why, then, do we need a special model of economic behavior for this point? There is no obvious reason, which means we should be able to place nonrenewable resource use in the context of a more general model of resource use, distinguished only by the fact that a particular parameter is set to a particular value.

In this chapter, I give an example of such a model. To provide some measurable content to the notion of 'growth', I use a specific example: a resource that has the property of logistic growth.[2] This example produces a parameter, r, that effectively measures a resource's intrinsic growth rate (a term I define below). Varying r then illustrates how economic behavior varies along a continuum, encompassing both renewable ($r > 0$) and non-renewable ($r = 0$) resources.

Before introducing the example of logistic growth, consider more generally the problem of allocating the consumption of a resource across time. Let Q_0 be the initial stock of the resource and $G(Q)$ the growth function, that is, $\partial Q / \partial t = G(Q)$. The resource can be consumed at zero cost, and so the problem is one of choosing a path of consumption, $q(t)$, that maximizes the present value of the utility of consumption, $U(q)$. I place the usual restrictions on U, so that $U_q > 0$ and $U_{qq} < 0$. The problem is then to maximize

$$\int_0^\infty U(q)e^{-\rho t}dt \tag{8.1}$$

subject to

$$\dot{Q} = G(Q) - q$$
$$Q(0) = Q_0,$$

where ρ is the discount rate.

The current-value Hamiltonian for this problem is

$$H = U(q) + \lambda(G(Q) - q), \tag{8.2}$$

where λ has the standard interpretation of the current (shadow) value of a marginal relaxation of the resource constraint. The corresponding maximum and adjoint (costate) equations are then

$$H_q = U_q(q) - \lambda = 0, \tag{8.3}$$

$$H_Q = \lambda G_Q = \rho\lambda - \dot{\lambda}. \tag{8.4}$$

Equation (8.4) can be rearranged to give

$$\frac{\dot{\lambda}}{\lambda} + G_Q = \rho, \tag{8.5}$$

which holds along the optimal consumption path.

Equation (8.5) produces a fundamental result that spans both renewable and nonrenewable resources, and is (obviously) general to any form of G_Q. If $G(Q) \equiv 0$, then $G_Q \equiv 0$ and we have the classic example of a nonrenewable resource. In this case, equation (8.5) produces the Hotelling rule,

$$\frac{\dot{\lambda}}{\lambda} = \rho. \tag{8.6}$$

If the resource is capable of a high enough rate of growth (explained below), a stationary solution ($\dot{\lambda} = 0$) to the maximization problem is possible and equation (8.5) becomes

$$G_Q = \rho \tag{8.7}$$

at the equilibrium point. This is the classic solution for a renewable resource.

The case in-between is one in which the resource is capable of growth but 'not enough' to support a stationary solution. In this case, we have a mixed resource, one that is renewable but for which the optimal behavior is to treat it as if it was nonrenewable. This is, of course, the case of the optimal extinction of a renewable resource such as a population or species that grows too slowly, so to speak.

None of these results taken individually is novel, of course; indeed, equation (8.5) appears elsewhere in one form or another.[3] What makes this presentation interesting is considering the family of functions, $G(Q,r)$, where r is a parameter that measures growth, and extending the family to encompass its natural endpoint, $G(Q, 0) \equiv 0$.

To better illustrate this point, I now consider the special case of the logistic growth function:

$$G(Q) = rQ\left(1 - \frac{Q}{K}\right), \tag{8.8}$$

where K represents a limit on the growth of the resource, or carrying capacity, and r is the growth parameter, also called the 'intrinsic' growth rate. This form has two well-known properties that are worth repeating. First, $G(Q)$ reaches a maximum at $Q = K/2$. This stock level is called the maximum sustained yield level, or Q_{MSY}. Second, G_Q reaches a maximum at $Q = 0$, where $G_Q = r$. The parameter r is thus the 'intrinsic' growth rate in the sense that r is the rate of growth for the resource as it comes into existence, so to speak. Figure 8.1 illustrates how variation in r affects $G(Q)$, holding K constant ($= 500$). Setting $r = 0$ produces the case of a nonrenewable resource.

Substituting the logistic form of $G(Q)$ into equation (8.5) then gives

$$\frac{\dot{\lambda}}{\lambda} + r\left(1 - \frac{2Q}{K}\right) = \rho. \tag{8.9}$$

We can use this equation to illustrate how different values of r affect the optimal consumption of Q. First, what value of r is sufficiently high to

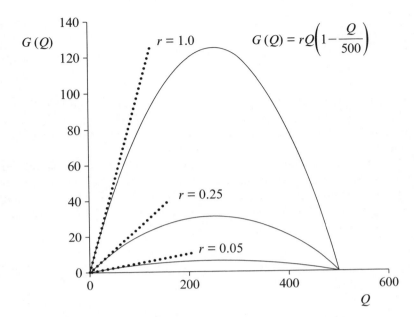

Figure 8.1   Variation in the growth function, G(Q), *with respect to the intrinsic growth rate,* r

produce a stationary solution? Such a solution comes from the following system of equations:

$$\dot{Q} = rQ\left(1 - \frac{Q}{K}\right) - q = 0, \tag{8.10}$$

$$\dot{\lambda} = \rho\lambda - \lambda\left[r\left(1 - \frac{2Q}{K}\right)\right] = 0. \tag{8.11}$$

Equation (8.3) can be solved implicitly for q as a function of λ, $q(\lambda)$. Substituting $q(\lambda)$ into equation (8.10) reduces the variables in this system to λ and Q, giving us two loci for (λ, Q). The intersection of these two loci then constitutes a stationary solution, (λ^*, Q^*).

Note, however, that the locus for equation (8.11) ($\dot{\lambda} = 0$) is determined by Q alone:

$$\rho - \left[r\left(1 - \frac{2Q}{K}\right)\right] = 0, \tag{8.12}$$

so that

$$Q^* = \frac{K}{2}\left(1 - \frac{\rho}{r}\right). \tag{8.13}$$

For $\rho > 0$, equation (8.13) implies that $Q^* < K/2$ for any r, but that $Q^* \geq 0$ only if $r \geq \rho$. This case is illustrated in Figure 8.2. If $r < \rho$, no stationary solution exists,[4] and given the special case of no consumption costs, the resource will be exhausted.

Now consider the dynamics of equation (8.9) over time as consumption moves along the optimal path. For convenience, assume that the initial stock of the resource, Q_0, equals $K/2$ ($> Q^*$). At $t = 0$, $G_Q(Q_0) = 0$, so that $\dot{\lambda}(0)/\lambda(0) = \rho$. Again for convenience, assume that if $Q^* = 0$, exhaustion occurs in finite time.

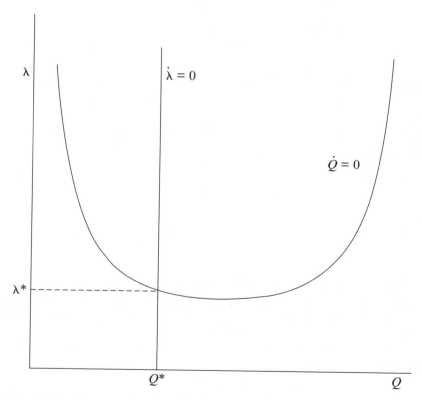

Figure 8.2   Stationary solution for the case of $r \geq \rho$

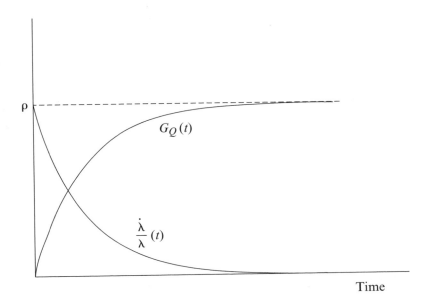

Figure 8.3   The paths over time of $\dot{\lambda}(t)/\lambda(t)$ *and* G_Q *for the case* $r \geq \rho$

Figure 8.3 illustrates the paths of $\dot{\lambda}(t)/\lambda(t)$ and G_Q for the case of $r \geq \rho$ ($Q^* \geq 0$). Along the optimal path, equation (8.9) holds. This means that $\dot{\lambda}(t)/\lambda(t)$ falls and G_Q rises until Q^* is reached. After this point, the paths continue with $\dot{\lambda}(t)/\lambda(t) = 0$ and $G_Q = \rho$.

If $r < \rho$ ($Q^* = 0$), similar paths can be traced for $\dot{\lambda}(t)/\lambda(t)$ and G_Q. These paths terminate in finite time, when the resource is exhausted, and reach terminal values that vary with the value of r. Figure 8.4 illustrates these paths for three values of r, with $r_3 < r_2 < r_1 < \rho$. Figure 8.5 illustrates the collapse of a renewable resource ($r > 0$) to a nonrenewable resource ($r = 0$). Both $\dot{\lambda}(t)/\lambda(t)$ and G_Q approach and eventually merge into the horizontal lines, $\dot{\lambda}(t)/\lambda(t) = \rho$ and $G_Q = 0$, respectively. This evolution is smooth and continuous, giving the case of $r = 0$ the characteristic of being merely one of an infinite number of possible 'resource' pathways.

Finally, consider the relation between the intrinsic growth rate, r, and the dynamics of the two components of equation (8.9) at the terminal time (either exhaustion or the stationary equilibrium). Figure 8.6 illustrates the fundamental point of this chapter: As r varies continuously in the range $[0,\rho]$, there is a continuous tradeoff between $\dot{\lambda}(t)/\lambda(t)$ and G_Q. Once r equals and then exceeds ρ, $\dot{\lambda}(t)/\lambda(t) = 0$ and $G_Q = \rho$ in the stationary equilibrium. There is no sharp division between a nonrenewable and renewable resource.

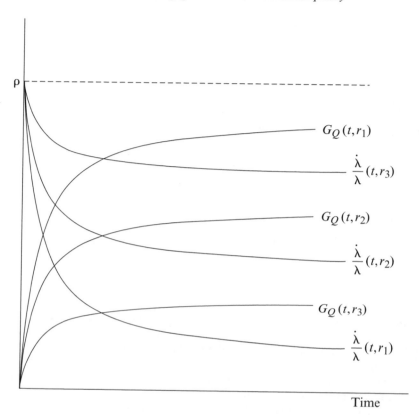

Figure 8.4   The paths over time of $\dot{\lambda}(t)/\lambda(t)$ and G_Q for three cases of $0 < r < \rho$

Still, we do in fact like to break things up in order to put them in their own boxes. And so rather than try to meld renewable and nonrenewable resources, which might wreak havoc in the textbook market, perhaps a slight modification to our resource economics boxes is in order. The optimal consumption of any type of resource exists as a member of the same family, $q^*(r)$, in which the parameter r measures the capability of the resource to grow. For $r \geq 0$, membership in this family can be divided, adapting the observation of Harold Hotelling, by the following characteristics: whether a stationary solution to the consumption problem is a physical possibility, and whether a stationary solution is an economically optimal one. These characteristics give us the mapping for the economics of natural resources shown in Table 8.1. In the special case of logistic growth and no consumption costs, these boxes correspond to particular values of r relative to the

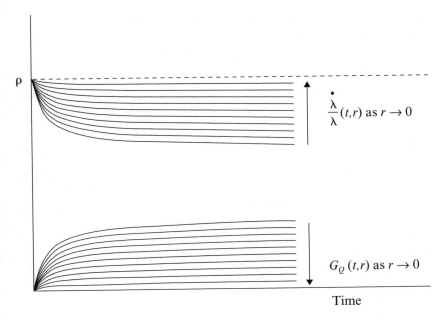

Figure 8.5   The paths over time of $\dot{\lambda}(t)/\lambda(t)$ and G_Q as r approaches zero

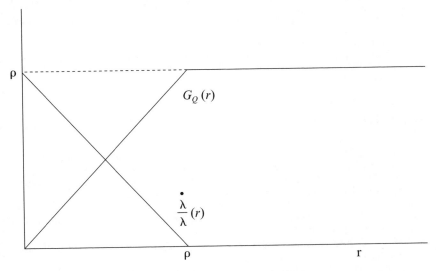

Figure 8.6   Variation in $\dot{\lambda}(t)/\lambda(t)$ and G_Q at the terminal time with respect to r

Table 8.1   A new mapping for the economics of natural resources

		Economically Optimal Solution	
		Stationary	Non-stationary
Physically Possible Solution	Stationary	Renewable resources such as timber and fish ⇒ Classic renewable resource framework	Low growth resources such as large mammals or old growth trees ⇒ Extinction
	Non-stationary	Empty	Nonrenewable resources such as minerals and oil ⇒ Classic Hotelling framework

discount rate, ρ. In the more general case, the exact relations will be more complicated but the correspondences will still be there.

NOTES

1. Hotelling (1931), p. 139.
2. Using a logistic growth model is not novel, of course. Clark (1990) uses it as a fundamental example for fisheries, although he does not take the next step of letting the growth parameter, r, go to zero.
3. See, for example, Silberberg and Suen (2001), eqn. (20–54). See also Cropper *et al.* (1979) and Swanson (1994).
4. No stationary solution exists where $Q^* \geq 0$, that is. As long as $U(0) < \infty$, the locus (λ, Q) defined by equation (8.10) extends into the negative Q-plane. A stationary solution exists for $Q^* < 0$, but we impose the constraint that $Q(t) \geq 0$, and so the solution $Q^* = 0$ is in fact a corner solution.

REFERENCES

Clark, C. (1990), *Mathematical Bioeconomics: The Optimal Management of Renewable Resources*, 2nd edn, New York: John Wiley & Sons, Inc.

Cropper, M.L., D.R. Lee and S.S. Pannu (1979), 'The optimal extinction of a renewable natural resource', *Journal of Environmental Economics and Management*, **6**, 341–9.

Hotelling, H. (1931), 'The economics of exhaustible resources', *The Journal of Political Economy*, **39**, 137–75.

Silberberg, E. and W. Suen (2001), *The Structure of Economics*, 3rd edn, Boston: Irwin McGraw-Hill.

Swanson, T.M. (1994), 'The economics of extinction revisited and revised: a generalised framework for the analysis of the problems of endangered species and biodiversity losses', *Oxford Economic Papers*, **46**, 800–821.

PART III

Theory and practice of valuation

9. Environmental valuation under dynamic consumer behavior

Jinhua Zhao and Catherine L. Kling

Ever since the publication of Hammack and Brown (1974), economists have documented significant divergences between willingness to pay (WTP) and willingness to accept (WTA) measures of welfare in valuing environmental goods. While the divergence observed in contingent valuation studies has been (and in some cases continues to be) cited as evidence against the non-market method itself, divergences documented in laboratory experiments where goods are actually traded have been employed to refute the core of modern welfare analysis, namely Hicksian welfare theory. The literature includes two lines of responses to the challenge. One calls for alternative paradigms such as prospect theory (Kahneman and Tversky, 1979; Tversky and Kahneman, 1991) and expected utilities with rank-dependent (Quiggin, 1982) or nonadditive probabilities (Schmeidler, 1989). The other approach tries to enrich Hicksian theory to accommodate decision environments that give rise to the divergences, such as lack of substitutes (Hanemann, 1991) and the existence of future information and commitment costs (Zhao and Kling, 2001, 2004).

In this chapter, we extend the commitment cost framework that we presented in Zhao and Kling (2004) to formulate a theory of welfare measurement when consumers make dynamic decisions facing uncertainty and future information. We argue that the application of static Hicksian welfare theory in a dynamic setting can yield incorrect welfare assessments and policy recommendations. Although there are many goods for which this scenario seems likely to hold, this issue may be particularly important in environmental valuation. Specifically, many decisions relating to the environment are inherently dynamic, with uncertain benefits and significant transaction costs associated with reversing the decisions that are made. If agents expect that more information can be gathered in the future, they may wish to delay their decision until such information is available. If they are forced to act now, they will change their WTP or WTA to incorporate compensation for their lost learning opportunity, as well as their implicit valuation of the good (that is, expected compensating variation (CV) or equivalent variation (EV)). Thus, static Hicksian theory, when applied to such dynamic settings, can produce predictions that (1) are inconsistent with the empirical evidence, such as the WTP/WTA divergence, and (2) may be inappropriate for policy assessment.

Even for decisions that are easy to reverse in the future, uncertainty and future learning may still affect the agent's demand curve. For example, deciding the number of trips to a park this year will not directly restrict the future visits to the park. However, future learning may affect the agent's intertemporal allocation of her lifetime income among the visits in different time periods. Then the demand curve for the current period will also be contingent on the agent's current information.

We consider two kinds of goods or services, perishable goods which can only be consumed in the current period if purchased, and non-perishable goods which can be consumed forever if purchased now. For perishable goods, the current consumption level does not have direct consequences for future consumption; consumption can be freely adjusted in each period. For non-perishable goods, the consumption level, if chosen now, will be fixed for lengthy periods of time (unless there is immediate and costless reversal). The major distinction between the two is that the consumption level based on the current information will have long-run effects for non-perishable, but not for perishable goods. For example, if an agent is deciding how much to pay for preserving the Grand Canyon, the good of interest, that is, the Canyon, is a non-perishable good, because, if preserved, the Canyon will provide environmental amenities for a long time. If, on the other hand, the agent is asked how many trips she will make to the Canyon under certain conditions (such as the gate fee or the air quality), the good of interest, visiting the Canyon, is a perishable good. Her number of visits this year does not directly lock in her future visits.

In many cases, perishable goods are divisible and non-perishable goods are lumpy in the sense of Randall and Stoll (1980). For example, the number of visits to a park or the expenditure on such visits can be changed freely, but there is only *one* Grand Canyon.[1] Similar to Randall and Stoll (1980), we assume that there is a well functioning market for perishable goods, so that we can study the associated price effects. On the other hand, the non-perishable goods are assumed to be public goods for which a market or a price may not exist. We instead focus on the quantity effects, the WTP/WTA and their relationship to CV/EV. We show that information and future learning will have different consumer behavioral implications for the two sets of goods. However, in both cases we find that, even in the presence of stable preferences, demand and WTP will shift through time as consumers trade off the advantage of delaying action (thereby collecting more information on the substitutes available and the value of the good) with the costs of delayed consumption.

This chapter proceeds as follows. In the first section we follow Kling and Zhao (2004) to develop WTP and WTA in a dynamic setting for non-perishable goods with general utility functions. Importantly, we show that WTP and WTA can be different from CV and EV, with the difference termed 'commitment costs'. We relate the commitment costs to the quasi-option values of Arrow and Fisher (1974) and Dixit and Pindyck (1994), and distinguish them from the substitution effects of Hanemann (1991). We further illustrate the magnitudes of the commitment costs using parameters estimated from a valuation study of Clear Lake in Iowa. We conclude the section with a discussion of the implications of this finding for environmental valuation. Next, we consider the perishable goods model where we derive 'information conditioned' Marshallian and Hicksian demand curves, and show how they relate to each other and how they evolve as the consumers' information about the transaction changes. Here, commitment costs do not arise as a decision made in the first period has no carryover into the second period. Nonetheless, uncertainty and future learning may still drive a wedge between the observed consumer surplus (CS) and the true EV/CV, so that CS may not be bounded by EV and CV.

1   A MODEL OF NON-PERISHABLE GOODS

In this section, we adopt the model of Kling and Zhao (2004) where we derived the dynamic WTP and WTA loci, and obtained the dynamic WTP and WTA values from the loci. Here, we derive these values directly while using the same model setup.

Suppose an agent is deciding on how much to pay to obtain more of a non-perishable good, or to accept to forgo the opportunity of increasing her consumption of this good. Let $U(x, y, \theta)$ be her utility function, where x is the quantity of the non-perishable good, y is the quantity of a composite good, the price of which is normalized to one, and θ is a parameter which affects the marginal utility of x. In our example, θ may reflect the air quality or accessibility at the Grand Canyon. Currently the agent does not know the value of θ, only knowing that it is distributed according to $F(\cdot)$ on $\Theta \equiv [\theta_l, \theta_h]$. However, she will learn the true value of θ at the beginning of the next period. For instance, there may be a current study on the air quality at the Grand Canyon which will be released at the start of the next year.

We assume that $U(\cdot)$ is continuous and differentiable and $U_{x\theta} \neq 0$. The non-perishable good x is a public good, for which a market does not exist and currently is offered at the level x_0. Given the agent's (constant) per period income m, the agent spends all her income on y and obtains the utility $U(x_0, m, \theta)$. For simplicity, we assume away consumption smoothing across periods. That is, the per period income m cannot be shifted across periods.

1.1 Willingness to Pay

Suppose the agent is asked to state her WTP for an increase in the amount of the non-perishable good from x_0 to $x_1 > x_0$. If the agent cannot learn about θ or ignores the learning opportunities, her (annualized) WTP is determined by

$$E_\theta U(x_0, m, \theta)/\tau = E_\theta U(x_1, m - WTP^n, \theta)/\tau, \tag{9.1}$$

where r is her discount rate and WTP^n denotes the WTP under no-learning. Implicitly, we are assuming that her WTP decision is *irreversible:* if she is committed to paying a certain amount, she will have to do so in every period in the future. Alternatively, she may commit herself to pay a lump sum amount in the beginning, and WTP^n is the annualized payment of the lump sum. Equation (9.1) indicates that WTP^n is the same as the *ex ante* compensating variation (Helms, 1985), or the option price (Weisbrod, 1964), denoted by CV and defined by

$$E_\theta U(x_0, m, \theta) = E_\theta U(x_1, m - CV, \theta). \tag{9.2}$$

Note that both Helms (1985) and Weisbrod (1964) defined CV in the framework of a lump sum payment. Our definition is again the 'annualized' version of the payment. Helms (1985) further showed that, under uncertainty, the 'correct' measure of welfare should be the *ex ante* rather than the expected compensating variation.

However, if the agent recognizes her learning opportunities in the second period, her WTP will differ from $CV = WTP^n$. To see this, we first determine her maximum WTP for x_1 when she knows she can delay her purchase until the next period. Let c be a per period cost of x_1. We seek to determine the maximum c she will agree today to pay in all periods. If she decides to pay in the current period, her expected payoff is

$$V_0 = E_\theta U(x_1, m - c, \theta)/\tau. \tag{9.3}$$

If she waits until the second period when she knows the true value of θ, she will pay c if and only if $U(x_1, m - c, \theta) \geq U(x_0, m, \theta)$. In this case, she can avoid 'purchasing' the good if it turns out not to be very valuable. Let $\Theta_p(c)$

$\subseteq \Theta$ such that $U(x_1, m - c, \theta) \geq U(x_0, m, \theta)$ if and only if $\theta \in \Theta_p$, and let $\Theta_{np}(c) = \Theta \backslash \Theta_p(c)$. Then her expected payoff of waiting to decide until the second period is

$$V_1 = E_\theta U(x_0, m, \theta) + \frac{1}{(1+\tau)^\tau} [E_{\theta \in \Theta_p} U(x_1, m - c, \theta) + E_{\theta \in \Theta_{np}} U(x_0, m, \theta)]$$

$$= E_\theta U(x_0, m, \theta)/\tau + \frac{1}{(1+\tau)^\tau} E_{\theta \in \Theta_p} [U(x_1, m - c, \theta) - U(x_0, m, \theta)],$$

(9.4)

where $E_{\theta \in \Theta_p}$ represents expectation over the set Θ_p (which is not the *conditional* expectation).

It is clear from (9.3) and (9.4) that both V_0 and V_1 are monotone decreasing in c, and V_0 decreases in c *faster* than V_1. Intuitively, as the cost of x_1 increases, there will be more values of θ such that the agent will decide not to purchase x_1. Her loss from the higher c is thus lower than it would be without this opportunity to delay. In addition, $V_0 > V_1$ at $c = 0$ and $V_0 < V_1$ at $c = \infty$: due to discounting, the agent prefers to enjoy x_1 earlier if it costs nothing. If it is extremely costly, she is better off not buying x_1. Then, a *unique* c exists that equates V_0 and V_1, and this unique value is the maximum value of c such that $V_0 \geq V_1$. Thus, the value is the agent's WTP today when the opportunity to delay and learn is present, denoted as WTP^l where superscript l represents learning:

$$E_\theta U(x_0, m, \theta) = E_\theta U(x_1, m - WTP^l, \theta)$$

$$- \beta E_{\theta \in \Theta P} [U(x_1, m - WTP^l, \theta) - U(x_0, m, \theta)], \quad (9.5)$$

where $\beta = 1/1 + r$ is the discount factor.

Equation (9.5) is closely related to the quasi-option value literature (Arrow and Fisher, 1974) and Dixit and Pindyck (1994). It can be rewritten as

$$E_\theta U(x_0, m, \theta)/\tau + QOV_p = E_\theta U(x_1, m - WTP^l, \theta)/\tau, \quad (9.6)$$

where $QOV_p = (\beta/\tau)E_{\theta \in \Theta p} [U(x_i, m - WTP^l, \theta) - U(x_0, m, \theta)]$ is the (quasi) option value associated with waiting. If the agent decides not to buy x_1 in the current period, she can still buy in the next period. Thus, the expected payoff of not buying today is the direct payoff $E_\theta U(x_0, m, \theta)/\tau$ plus the option value of the future decision QOV_p.

Now it is straightforward to compare WTP^l and $CV = WTP^n$. From (9.2) and (9.5), we know $WTP^l < CV$. The inequality is strict because if $WTP^l = CV$, by (9.2), $\Theta_p(WTP^l)$ is nonempty.[2] The last term in (9.5) is then strictly positive, so (9.2) and (9.5) would contradict each other. In order for the agent to 'buy' x_1 in the *current* period, the 'price' of x_1 has to be lower to compensate for the lost opportunity of obtaining more information.

Define the *commitment cost* associated with WTP as $CC_p = CV - WTP^l$. It measures the minimum reduction in the WTP in order to compensate for the commitment of buying now and consequently giving up future information gathering. From (9.2) and (9.6), we know

$$E_\theta U(x_1, m - CV, \theta) = E_\theta U(x_1, m - CV + CC_p, \theta) - \tau QOV_p. \quad (9.7)$$

When CC_p is small, we can apply Taylor expansion around $m - CV$ and obtain

$$CC_p = \frac{\tau QOV_p}{E_\theta U_m(x_1, m - CV, \theta)}. \quad (9.8)$$

The term τQOV_p measures the annualized quasi-option value in utils. When divided by the expected marginal utility of income, the term translates into annualized quasi-option value in monetary terms. This equation thus establishes a one-to-one relationship between quasi-option value and commitment cost. They measure the same object, namely the ability to wait for more information, in two ways. QOV_p measures it through a lump-sum transfer and CC_p measures it through a price reduction.

1.2 Willingness to Accept

Similar to the case of WTP, in the case of no learning, the agent's (annualized) WTA, that is, her required compensation for continuing to consume x_0 instead of consuming x_1, is determined by

$$E_\theta U(x_0, m + WTA^n, \theta)/\tau = E_\theta U(x_1, m, \theta)/\tau \quad (9.9)$$

Again, WTA^n is the same as the *ex ante* equivalent variation (EV), or option price, defined in

$$E_\theta U(x_0, m + EV, \theta) = E_\theta U(x_1, m, \theta). \quad (9.10)$$

Consider now the case when the agent can learn about θ. Again, we need to determine the compensation she will accept in lieu of x_1. Suppose she is presented with the compensation level w: her consumption will not increase from x_0 to x_1 if she accepts ω. If she accepts now, her expected payoff is

$$\pi_0 = E_\theta U(x_0, m + w, \theta)/\tau. \tag{9.11}$$

If she waits until the second period when she observes the true value of θ, she will choose to accept only when $U(x_0, m + w, \theta) \geq U(x_1, m, \theta)$. That is, she can accept the compensation only when x_1 turns out to have low value. Define $\Theta_a(w) \subseteq \Theta$ such that $U(x_0, m + w, \theta) \geq U(x_1, m, \theta)$ if and only if $\theta \in \Theta_a(w)$. Let $\Theta_{na}(w) = \Theta \backslash \Theta_a(w)$. Then her expected payoff of waiting is

$$\pi_1 = E_\theta U(x_1, m, \theta) + \frac{1}{(1 + \tau)\tau}[E_{\theta \in \Theta_a} U(x_0, m + w, \theta) + E_{\theta \in \Theta_{na}} U(x_1, m, \theta)]$$

$$= E_\theta U(x_1, m, \theta)/\tau + \frac{1}{(1 + \tau)\tau} E_{\theta \in \Theta_a}[U(x_0, m + w, \theta) - U(x_1, m, \theta)]. \tag{9.12}$$

Note that, in the first period, while she is waiting for the new information, she enjoys x_1 but does not receive the compensation w.

Both π_0 and π_1 are increasing in ω, but π_0 increases at a faster rate. Further, $\pi_0 > \pi_1$ as $w \to \infty$ and $\pi_0 < \pi_1$ as $w \to 0$. Thus there is a unique value of w that equates π_0 and π_1. It is also the minimum value of w so that $\pi_0 > \pi_1$, or the minimum value of compensation needed for the agent to accept in the *current* period. This value is the agent's WTA with learning, given by

$$E_\theta U(x_1, m, \theta) = E_\theta U(x_0, m + WTA^l, \theta) -$$
$$\beta E_{\theta \in \Theta_a}[U(x_0, m + WTA^l, \theta) - U(x_1, m, \theta)] \tag{9.13}$$

Comparing (9.10) and (9.13), we find that $WTA^l > EV$: the agent demands additional compensation in the form of higher WTA for committing to giving up x_1 in the current period and forgoing the future learning opportunities. Again, (9.13) can be rewritten as

$$E_\theta U(x_1, m, \theta)/\tau = E_\theta U(x_0, m + WTA^l, \theta)/\tau - QOV_a, \tag{9.14}$$

where $QOV_a = (\beta/\tau)E_{\theta \in \Theta_a}[U(x_0, m + WTA^l, \theta) - U(x_1, m, \theta)]$ is the (quasi) option value associated with waiting. Define the associated commitment cost as CC_a: $CC_a = WTA^l - EV$. From (9.10) and (9.14), we know

$$CC_a = \frac{\tau QOV_a}{E_\theta U_m(x_0, m + EV, \theta)}. \tag{9.15}$$

1.3   Implications for Welfare Measurement

The results presented above are quite intuitive. They indicate that the opportunity to delay a purchase or sale until better information is available about the precise value of the good in question is valuable. To forgo this option, the consumer must be compensated (in the form of a lower price for a buyer and a higher price for a seller). When the agent's current choices have long-run effects that are hard to reverse, and when there are future learning opportunities that will make the choices more 'intelligent' later, the agent's current WTA^n and WTA^l are typically different from the static CV or EV. Although the magnitude of this difference is an empirical question, several important implications for welfare measurement of environmental goods emerge.

First, as discussed in Zhao and Kling (2001, 2004), the presence of commitment costs can potentially explain the observed divergence between WTP^l and WTA^l in experimental and contingent valuation markets, first documented by Hammack and Brown (1974). Similar to the explanation provided by Hanemann (1991), our theory suggests that these divergences are consistent with stable preferences and optimizing behavior. Specifically, if a commitment cost is present in either or both of the WTP^l or WTA^l values, there will be an observed difference between them that exceeds the amount that income effects or Hanemann's substitution effects can generate. Since the explanation for how commitment costs can generate this divergence is discussed elsewhere (Zhao and Kling, 2001), we focus here instead on the implications of this result for applied welfare measurement.

The widespread use of WTP^l in contingent valuation experiments rather than WTA^l appears largely due to the 'large' values of many WTA^l estimates (NOAA report). If these high WTA^l estimates are due to large commitment costs associated with 'selling' the environment (as would be the case if survey respondents or experimental subjects feel that, once they give up the environmental quality, it will be difficult or impossible to re-obtain it), then this observation provides justification for the use of WTP^l, rather than WTA^l, as a better approximation for CV/EV in stated preference studies. But the use of WTP^l as a closer approximation to CV/EV implies that CV/EV are the correct welfare measure for policy purposes instead of the WTP^l or WTA^l values that contain commitment costs.

When is expected CV or EV the correct welfare measure to use and when is WTP^l or WTA^l appropriate? In using a WTP question to elicit the value of a public good in a contingent valuation survey, the researcher may unwittingly induce respondents to include a commitment cost in their responses. Contingent valuation surveys generally ask action questions (for example, are you willing to pay x dollars to keep this park? Or how much would you be willing to pay to keep the park open?), instead of direct value questions (for example, how much surplus would you receive if this park is kept open?). In the absence of commitment costs, these two questions (and their answers) are equivalent, but when values are uncertain and learning is possible, asking for WTP or WTA commingles commitment costs with the implicit value of the good. So, for example, in answering a WTA question about giving up a local park, a respondent may include a large commitment cost because they have not investigated the characteristics of other local parks in the area that might provide good substitutes. Were they given adequate time to investigate these alternatives, the commitment cost might disappear. But a standard contingent valuation survey asks for a value now; under that circumstance the reported WTA^l may contain a large commitment cost.

In contrast, some decisions are inherently characterized by uncertainty and irreversibility, and contain commitment costs that are independent of the experimental or survey design. For example, the decision to build a dam contains a significant amount of uncertainty regarding the benefits and costs of the change. In such a case, a contingent valuation survey that accurately replicates the decision framework will elicit WTA^l and WTP^l measures that contain the commitment costs. But these costs should enter the welfare calculations, thus WTA^l or WTP^l are in fact the appropriate welfare measures.

The main point is that, whether a researcher is using contingent valuation studies, laboratory experiments, or market transactions data, he or she needs to be cognizant of the possible inclusion of commitment costs in WTP^l and/or WTA^l. Fundamentally, if policy-relevant option values cause the divergence between WTP^l and WTA^l, then the reliance on WTP^l when WTA^l is the more appropriate measure will generate inefficient resource allocations. On the other hand, if the divergence between WTP^l and WTA^l arises from analysis-induced commitment costs that do not have a basis in the true situation, the use of either WTP^l or WTA^l may yield inefficient outcomes. Again, the key point is that analysts must understand that option values may arise in WTP^l and/or WTA^l values and they must consciously choose which measure is appropriate.

1.4 The Effects of Functional Forms and Magnitudes of Commitment Costs

The size of the commitment costs depends on the curvature of the utility function $U(\cdot)$, in addition to uncertainty. However, unlike Hanemann (1991), the substitutability between x and y may not significantly affect the size of the commitment costs. From (9.8) and (9.15), for the same option values, the commitment costs are smaller the higher the expected marginal utility of income. The option values are conditional values of information (Hanemann, 1989), and they can be strictly positive even when there is perfect substitutability between x and y.

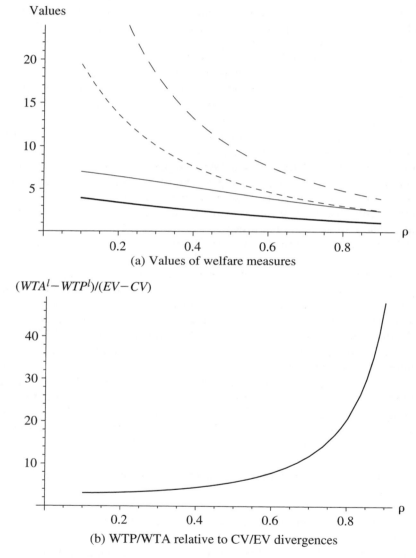

Values

(a) Values of welfare measures

$(WTA^l - WTP^l)/(EV - CV)$

(b) WTP/WTA relative to CV/EV divergences

Figure 9.1   The effects of substitutability on the divergence

To illustrate the different effects of the substitutability on CV/EV and WTP^l/WTA^l, we study numerically the modified CES utility function $U(x, y, \theta) = \theta(x^\rho/\rho) + (y^\rho/\rho)$ where $0 < \rho < 1$, and $1/(1 - \rho)$ is the elasticity of substitution. Figure 9.1 shows the effects of ρ for $m = 10$, $x_0 = 1$, $x_1 = 2$, and $\theta \in$ Uniform[0,4]. In Panel (a), the four curves are, from the top, WTA^l, EV, CV and WTP^l values. Thus, as predicted by Hanemann (1991), the divergence between EV and CV decreases as the elasticity of substitution rises. Further, the WTP^l/WTA^l divergence also goes down, possibly due to the fact that the marginal utility of income increases in ρ. However, the *ratio* between the WTP^l/WTA^l and CV/EV divergences increases in ρ. That is, as the elasticity of substitution rises, the observed WTP/WTA divergence exaggerates the true CV/EV divergence proportionally more.

To illustrate the potential magnitude of the dynamic welfare measures and their relationship to the static measures, we use estimated parameters from an actual empirical study of water quality improvements at a recreational lake in Iowa (Corrigan, 2002). Stated preference data were used to estimate the parameters of a modified CES of the form: $U(x, y, \theta) = \theta(x^\rho/\rho) + (1 - \theta)(y^\rho/\rho)$ where x is the level of public good (water quality), ρ, and θ are estimated parameters with $1/(1 - \rho)$ the elasticity of substitution $(0 < \rho < 1)$. For illustrative purposes, we take the estimated values of $\theta = 0.02$, and $\rho = 0.277$, and use the approximate sample mean income of \$50,000. We then consider the values for WTP^l, WTA^l, EV and CV under a variety of assumptions about the degree of uncertainty, risk aversion, and time preference. We assume that there are only two state-dependent outcomes and two time periods.

In Figure 9.2(a) we demonstrate the effect of uncertainty in the value of the public good, x. The figure shows the values of WTP^l; CV, CC_p, and the static option value when $x_0 = 0$, $x_1 = 1$, and θ varies about a mean of 0.02 with $(\theta^H - \theta^L)/2\theta \in [0, 2]$ plotted on the horizontal axis. The probabilities of θ^H and θ^L are both 0.5 and we use an interest rate of $\tau = 0.05$. For these parameter values, CV is about \$184 and constant over the entire range (the functional form of utility yields a CV that is linear in θ) and the static option value is quite small taking on a value less than \$0.05 over all ranges of uncertainty. The dynamic WTP (WTP^l) equals the CV when there is no uncertainty and decreases monotonically (and nearly linearly) over the range. The associated commitment cost (CC_p) is zero when there is no uncertainty and rises continuously with increasing uncertainty. Eventually, the commitment cost actually exceeds the dynamic WTP. While the range of uncertainty that may be realistic is unknown, this figure indicates that, at least over some range, the divergence between the CV and the WTP^l can be very large.

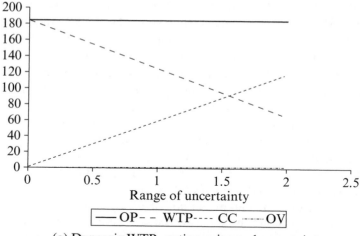

(a) Dynamic WTP, option price and uncertainty

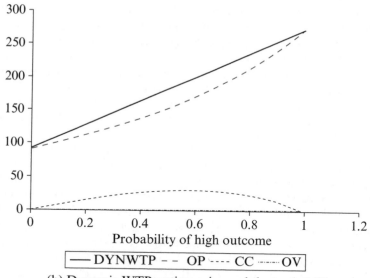

(b) Dynamic WTP option price and the probability

Figure 9.2   The numerical illustration: uncertainties and probabilities

In Figure 9.2(b), the same measures are presented. This time the uncertainty in the value is held constant at $\theta^H = 0.03$ and $\theta^L = 0.01$, but the probability of the high outcome is varied from 0 to 1 (with the associated value of the low event range from 1 to 0). At the two extremes, when $\pi = 0, 1$, there is no uncertainty and thus the dynamic WTP equals CV and $CC_p = 0$. When the probabilities are not at a corner, $WTP^l < CV$, with its peak difference occurring when the probability of low and high are about the same.

In Figure 9.3(a), we investigate the magnitude of these welfare measures with respect to risk aversion and the elasticity of substitution. Along the horizontal axis we plot the relative risk aversion coefficient ($\rho - 1$). Going from left to right on the diagram also represents an increasing degree of substitution between x and y. Note that, unlike Hanemann (1991), the substitutability between x and y may not significantly affect the size of the commitment costs. The CC_p are conditional values of information and can be strictly positive even when there is perfect substitutability between x and y. Clearly, as the risk aversion and degree of substitutability rises, the divergence between CV and WTP^l declines.

Unlike CV, WTP^l depends on the time preference of the individual. In Figure 9.3(b), we hold constant all of the parameters except the rate of time preference, $(1/(1 + \tau))$, which we vary from 0 to 1 over the horizontal axis. With an increasing preference for future consumption, the divergence between the CV and WTP^l increases. When more weight is placed on future consumption, there is more benefit from waiting and being able to employ the additional information concerning the value of θ when making the choice of whether to buy or not. Thus the consumer will need to be compensated more (pay a lower price) in the current period to forgo this learning opportunity.

Of particular interest for environmental and experimental economists is Figure 9.4, where we depict CV, WTP^l, EV and WTA^l again as a function of the range of uncertainty akin to Figure 9.2(a). The potential divergence created between WTA^l and WTP^l by the presence of commitment costs is clearly demonstrated. While the difference between CV and EV is almost imperceptible, the difference between the behavior measures, the willingness to pay and willingness to accept, are significant. At a range of uncertainty represented here, the ratio WTA^l/WTP^l ranges from 0 to 6. While this is only a simulation and it is unknown whether this is a realistic range of uncertainty, the example does illustrate that large divergences between WTP and WTA can potentially be explained by the presence of commitment costs.

2   A MODEL OF PERISHABLE GOODS

For simplicity we consider a two period model. There is a market for x, for example, the number of trips to a national park, the price of which is p. The choice of x in the current period does not directly restrict its consumption level in the second period. Further, we assume that (i) $U(\cdot)$ is

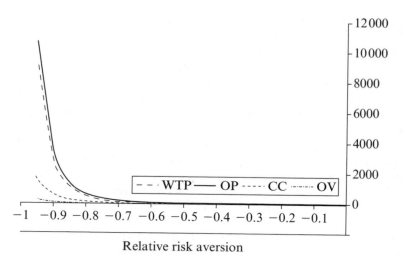

Relative risk aversion

(a) Dynamic WTP and OP with changing risk aversion

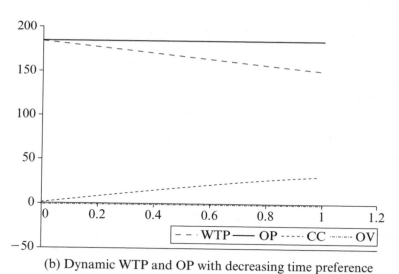

(b) Dynamic WTP and OP with decreasing time preference

Figure 9.3   The numerical illustration: risk aversion and time preference

linear in θ, (ii) $U_{x\theta} \geq 0$, and (iii) $d/d\theta(U_x/U_y) \neq 0$. Assumption (i) is for simplicity: uncertainty in θ does not change the expected utility directly if the consumption bundle is unaffected. This assumption is not as restrictive as it first appears since reparameterization of the random parameter is

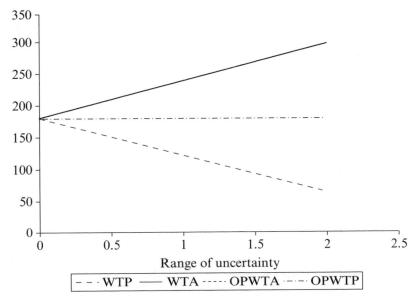

Figure 9.4 Dynamic WTP and WTA as a function of uncertainty

possible. For example, if $U(\cdot) = f(\tilde{\theta})u(x, y)$ where $f(\cdot)$ is not linear, we can redefine $\theta = f(\tilde{\theta})$ to obtain linearity in θ. Assumptions (ii) and (iii) guarantee that θ does matter in the agent's choice of the consumption bundles: θ affects the marginal utility of x, and the marginal rate of substitution between x and y. Thus given the same income level, the agent will choose a different bundle if θ changes. Without these conditions, a model of learning is uninteresting as learning would not affect the agent's optimal choices. Note that (iii) does exclude some common utility functions, such as the Cobb–Douglas utility function $U(x, y, \theta) = \theta x^{\alpha} y^{\beta}$. Learning about θ is irrelevant for such utility functions since it does not affect the agent's choices.

2.1 The Case of No Learning

Consider first the case when the agent cannot learn or ignores the learning possibilities in deciding her consumption bundle in the first period. Her decision problem is

$$\max_{x_1, y_1, x_2, y_2} U(x_1, y_1, \bar{\theta}) + \beta U(x_2, y_2, \bar{\theta})$$
$$\text{s.t.} \quad \rho x_1 + y_1 + \beta(\rho x_2 + y_2) = M, \tag{9.16}$$

where $\bar{\theta} = E\theta$ is the expected value of θ, and M is the agent's lifetime income. Note that, unlike the case of a non-perishable good, the choice of x imposes no physical restrictions on x_2 or y_2. Further, $E_\theta U(x, y, \theta) = U(x, y, \bar{\theta})$ because $U(\cdot)$ is assumed to be linear in θ.

From the first order conditions of (9.16), we know

$$\frac{U_{x_1}}{U_{y_1}} = \frac{U_{x_2}}{U_{y_2}} = p, \; U_{x_1} = U_{x_2}, \text{ and } U_{y_1} = U_{y_2}.$$

Thus $x_1 = x_2 = x$ and $y_1 = y_2 = y$: the agent chooses the same consumption bundle in both periods. Substituting the solution back to the budget constraint in (9.16), we know the agent allocates her income between the two periods *equally*, adjusted by the discounting factor. In particular, the choice of her first period's consumption bundle in (9.6) can be represented as

$$\max_{x_1, y_1} U(x_1, y_1, \bar{\theta})$$
$$\text{s.t.} \quad px_1 + y_1 = \bar{M} \equiv \frac{M}{1 + \beta}. \tag{9.17}$$

Note that the income allocated to the first period $M_1 = \bar{M}$ is *independent* of the price p or the value of θ. This is where the simplifying assumption of linearity in θ is particularly useful. In studying the agent's demand function for the goods in the first period, we can ignore the dynamic nature of the problem, and simply work in the static framework of (9.17). As a result, the standard results for Marshallian and Hicksian demand functions, such as the associated expenditure and indirect utility functions and the Slutsky equation, apply to the dynamic model without learning through (9.17).

To be comparable with the case of learning about θ, the dynamic model in (9.16) can also be written *recursively* in the following form:

$$\max_{x_1, y_1} \left\{ U(x_1, y_1, \bar{\theta}) + \beta \max_{x_2, y_2} E_\theta \{ U(x_2, y_2, \theta), \right.$$

$$\left. \text{s.t.} \; \beta(px_2 + y_2) = M - px_1 - y_1 \} \right\}. \tag{9.18}$$

Given $\{x_1, y_1\}$, the agent maximizes her expected utility in the second period subject to the income of $M - px_1 - y_1$. Thus, what affects the agent's second period choices is the *expenditure* of the first period, instead of the particular bundles chosen.

2.2 The Case of Learning

Consider now the case where the agent learns about the true value of θ at the beginning of the second period. Her decision problem becomes

$$\max_{x_1, y_1}\left\{U(x_1, y_1, \bar{\theta}) + \beta E_\theta \max_{x_2, y_2} \{U(x_2, y_2, \theta),\right.$$

$$\left.\text{s.t. } \beta(px_2 + y_2) = M - px_1 - y_1\}\right\}, \tag{9.19}$$

where the difference between (9.19) and (9.18) is the location of the expectation operator in the second term: the maximization in (9.19) is conducted *after* observing θ. Let $V(p, m, \theta)$ be the indirect utility function in the second period, and let $M_2 = (M - px_1 - y_1)/\beta$. The two objective functions in (9.19) and (9.18) can be represented as

$$\max_{x_1, y_1} U(x_1, y_1, \bar{\theta}) + \beta E_\theta V(p, M_2, \theta), \tag{9.19'}$$

$$\max_{x_1, y_1} U(x_1, y_1, \bar{\theta}) + \beta V(p, M_2, \bar{\theta}). \tag{9.18'}$$

The expected payoff is higher under learning as $V(\cdot)$ is convex in θ, that is, $E_\theta V(p, M_2, \theta) > V(p, M_2, \theta).$[3] This says simply that when the consumer has the opportunity to make a decision under better information, she can achieve higher utility.

The demand functions for x_1 and y_1 under learning and no-learning are given by the respective first order conditions:

(Learning) $\quad U_x(x_1, y_1, \bar{\theta}) = pE_\theta V_m(p, M_2, \theta); \quad U_y(x_1, y_1, \bar{\theta}) = E_\theta V_m(p, M_2, \theta)$

(No-learning) $U_x(x_1, y_1, \bar{\theta}) = pV_m(p, M_2, \bar{\theta}); \quad U_y(x_1, y_1, \bar{\theta}) = V_m(p, M_2, \bar{\theta}).$

$$\tag{9.20}$$

Similar to the case of no learning, the allocation of first period's expenditure between x_1 and y_1 is independent of the second period consumption or learning: $U_x/U_y = p$. Thus, learning affects the optimal x_1 or y_1, only through changing the portion of the total income M that is allocated to the first period.

To show how income M is allocated between the two periods and how the allocation depends on learning, note that the no-learning optimization problem (9.16) can be rewritten as

$$\max_{M_1, M_2} V(p, M_1, \bar{\theta}) + \beta V(p, M_2, \bar{\theta})$$
$$\text{s.t. } M_1 + \beta M_2 = M, \tag{9.21}$$

and the learning problem (9.19) can be rewritten as

$$\max_{M_1, M_2} V(p, M_1, \bar{\theta}) + \beta E_\theta V(p, M_2, \theta)$$
$$\text{s.t. } M_1 + \beta M_2 = M \tag{9.22}$$

It is clear from (9.21) that the optimal income allocation without learning is $M_1 = \bar{M}$. However, the allocation with learning must satisfy the following first order condition:

$$V_m(p, M_1^*, \bar{\theta}) = E_\theta V_m(p, M_2^*, \theta). \tag{9.23}$$

Since $V(\cdot)$ is increasing and concave in M, $M_2^* > M_1^*$ if $V_m(\cdot)$ is convex in θ and $M_2^* < M_1^*$ if $V_m(\cdot)$ is concave in θ.

Proposition 1 *If the indirect utility function is such that $V_m(p, m, \theta)$ is convex (or concave) in θ, learning about θ reduces (or raises) the income allocated to the first period, thereby shifting in (or out) the (Marshallian) demand curves of both x_1 and y_1. If $V_m(\cdot)$ is linear in or independent of θ, learning does not affect the income allocation.*

Intuitively, since income is 'more useful' when the agent has more information about θ, and since the extra information occurs in the second period, we might expect that income will be moved from the first period into the second to take advantage of this efficiency, that is, $M_2^* > \bar{M} > M_1^*$. Suppose the agent is given a little more income. If she simply ignores the new information about θ, she would allocate the additional income according to the ratio $U_x(x, y, \tilde{\theta})/U_y(x, y, \tilde{\theta}) = p$, and obtains more utility from additional consumption of x and y. But if she recognizes the information about θ, she will allocate the additional income differently according to the realized value of θ. In expectation, she should obtain more utility from the additional income if she puts it into the second period because it is allocated more 'efficiently'. However, this result is not assured. It is also possible that it could be efficient to move income from the second period into the first as the increase in efficiency in the second period is equivalent to an increase in total purchasing power or total income. Then she may prefer to allocate more nominal income to the first period since utility $V(\cdot)$ is concave in income m.

Thus, specific functional forms and parameter values may be needed to characterize the convexity or concavity of $V_m(\cdot)$ in θ. Below we present examples where $V_m(\cdot)$ is independent of, linear or convex in θ.[4] We utilize the relation $V_m = U_y(x^*, m - px^*, \theta)$ derived from the Envelope theorem, where x^* is the optimal level of x.

Example 1 (Independence)
Consider a quasi-linear utility function $U(x, y, \theta) = \theta \ln x + y$. In this case, it is straightforward to verify that the indirect utility function is $V(p, m, \theta) = \theta \ln(\theta/p) + M - \theta$. Although $V(\cdot)$ is convex in θ, $V_m = 1$ is independent of θ. Thus learning does not affect the demand functions of x_1 or y_1.

Example 2 (Linear)
Suppose the utility function is given by $U(x, y, \theta) = \theta x + \ln y$. Then $V_m = 1/y^*$ with the optimal solution $y^* = p/\theta$. Thus $V_m = \theta/p$ which is linear in θ.

Example 3 (Convexity)
Consider the modified CES utility function $U(x, y, \theta) = \theta(x^\rho/\rho) + (y^\rho/\rho)$ where $0 < \rho < 1$ is the elasticity of substitution. We can show that the indirect utility function is $V(p, m, \theta) = A(p, \theta)m^\rho$ where

$$A(p, \theta) = \frac{\theta}{\rho}\left(\frac{1}{p + \theta^{-1/1-\rho}p^{1/1-\rho}}\right)^\rho + \frac{1}{\rho}\left(\frac{1}{1 + \theta^{1/1-\rho}p^{-\rho/1-\rho}}\right)^\rho.$$

$V(\cdot)$ being convex in θ implies that $A(p, \theta)$ is convex in θ. Thus $V_m = A\rho m^{\rho-1}$ is also convex in θ. In this case, learning about future θ reduces the income allocated to period one and thus the demand functions of x_1 and y_1.

Let $\Delta(p, M)$ be the 'additional' net income allocated away from period one to period two, relative to $\bar{M}$, determined in (9.23). That is,

$$V_m(p, \bar{M} - \Delta, \bar{\theta}) = E_\theta V_m(p, \bar{M} + \Delta/\beta, \theta). \tag{9.24}$$

Suppose $V_m(\cdot)$ is indeed convex in θ. Then, as the agent expects more information in the second period, for example as the variance of $F(\cdot)$ increases, Δ increases and the demand functions of x_1 and y_1 are shifted inwards more. In a multiple period model, as the agent's information increases over time, her demand function also shifts out. Further, providing more information to the agent will increase the demand in the early periods.

These results establish the fact that, when a consumer is forward looking, her demand function and associated welfare measures will shift through time as she acquires more information. This occurs despite stable preferences, prices, and income.

2.3 The Effects of a Price Change

In neoclassical economic theory, the demand and welfare responses to price changes based on $x^n_1(p, m)$ have been analyzed through the Slutsky equation, willingness to pay and accept, and compensating and equivalent variation. In this section, we study how these standard results based on $x^n_1(p, m)$ need to be modified for $x^l_1(p, m)$ given learning.

When p changes, in addition to the standard income and substitution effects, the income allocation across periods may also change. Applying the implicit function theorem to (9.24), we get

$$\frac{\partial \Delta(p, m)}{\partial p} = \frac{V_{mp}(\cdot, \cdot, \bar{\theta}) - E_\theta V_{mp}(\cdot, \cdot, \theta)}{V_{mm}(\cdot, \cdot, \bar{\theta}) + E_\theta V_{mm}(\cdot, \cdot, \theta)/\beta}.$$

Thus, similar to Proposition 1, the allocation depends on whether $V_{mp}(p, m, \theta)$ is convex or concave in θ. Higher p reduces (or increases) $\bar{M}$ if $V_{mp}(\cdot)$ is convex (or concave) in θ. That is, the allocation depends on whether learning makes the additional income 'more useful' as p increases.

The convexity of V_{mp} depends on the specific utility function and parameter values. Intuitively, as $p \to \infty$, little will be spent on x and a further increase in p will not matter much, regardless of the value of θ. More information about θ will not affect the allocation of the income between x and y, or the response of the allocation to the price changes. Thus, learning is of little value and $V_{mp}(\cdot)$ should be close to being linear in θ. Similarly, as $p \to 0$, most of the income will be spent on x, regardless of small increases in p or the value of θ. Again, learning does not matter much in the allocation of income between x and y and in the response of the allocation to p. $V_{mp}(\cdot)$ should again be close to being linear in θ.

In our two examples, $V_{mp}(\cdot)$ is independent of θ if $U(\cdot)$ is quasi-linear, and it may be convex or concave depending on the value of p. Figure 9.5 illustrates the latter example with parameter values $\rho = 0.9$ and $p = 4$. It is clear that, while $A(\cdot)$, that is, $V_m(\cdot)$, is always convex in θ, $A_p(\cdot)$, or $V_{mp}(\cdot)$, can be convex and concave in θ.

If $V_{mp}(\cdot)$ is not linear or independent of θ, the Slutsky equation needs to be extended to incorporate the additional effect of a price change on the income allocation between the two periods. Let $x_1(p, m)$ be the Marshallian demand for x_1 given income m, and $h_1(p, u)$ be the corresponding Hicksian demand. Let $x^l_1(p, m(p, M))$ be the Marshallian demand under learning,

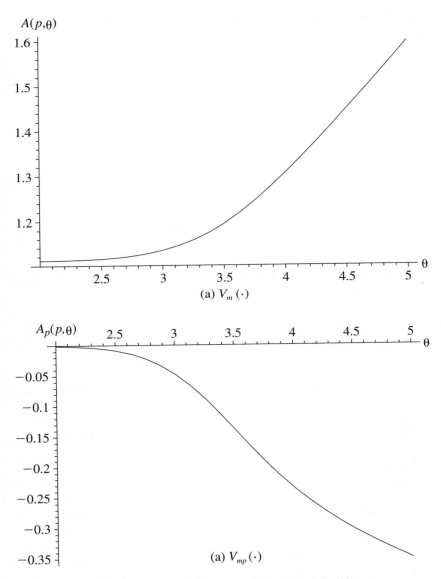

Figure 9.5   The convexity and concavity of $V_m(\cdot)$ and $V_{mp}(\cdot)$ in θ

where income allocated to period one is $m(p, M) = \bar{M} - \Delta(p, M)$. The standard Slutsky equation relating x_1 and h_1 is

$$\frac{\partial x_1(p, M_1)}{\partial p} = \frac{\partial h_1(p, u)}{\partial p} - \frac{\partial x_1(p, M_1)}{\partial m} x_1.$$

Since

$$x_1^l(p, m(p, M)) = x_1(p, \bar{M} - \Delta(p, M)), \tag{9.25}$$

we know

$$\frac{\partial x_1^l(p, m(p, M_1))}{\partial p} = \frac{\partial x_1(p, \bar{M} - \Delta)}{\partial p} - \frac{\partial x_1(p, \bar{M} - \Delta)}{\partial m} \frac{\partial \Delta(p, M)}{\partial p}$$

$$= \frac{\partial x_1(p, \bar{M} - \Delta)}{\partial p} - \frac{\partial x_1^l(p, m(p, M_1)) \partial \Delta(p, M)}{\partial m}{\frac{}{\partial p}},$$

where the second equality follows from (9.25). Substituting the previous equation into this one, we obtain the modified Slutsky equation for x_1^l:

$$\frac{\partial x_1^l(p, m(p, M))}{\partial p} = \frac{\partial h_1(p, u)}{\partial p} - \frac{\partial x_1^l(p, m(p, M))}{\partial m} \left(x_1^l + \frac{\partial \Delta(p, M)}{\partial p} \right), \tag{9.26}$$

where u, the utility level, is fixed at $V(p, \bar{M} - \Delta, \bar{\theta})$. Thus, in addition to the standard substitution and income effects associated with a price increase, there is an income reallocation effect. If $V_{mp}(\cdot)$ is concave in θ, lower p would reduce M_1, offsetting the increase in x_1 due to the standard substitution and income effects.

Figure 9.6 illustrates these effects graphically for the case when $V_{mp}(\cdot)$ is concave in θ. As p decreases to p', the income allocated to the first period decreases. The increase in the consumption of x_1 is lower than without the income reallocation effect. The distance between x_1^l and h_1 measures the substitution effect, while that between h_1 and $x_1^{2'}$ measures the traditional static income effect. However, as p changes to p', income allocated to the first period decreases, shifting the budget constraint in and moving the consumption of x to x_1^2. This distance is due to the learning effect.

2.4   Welfare Measurement

Consider two decision environments an agent faces. In the first case, she is allowed to gather complete information about θ in the beginning of the first

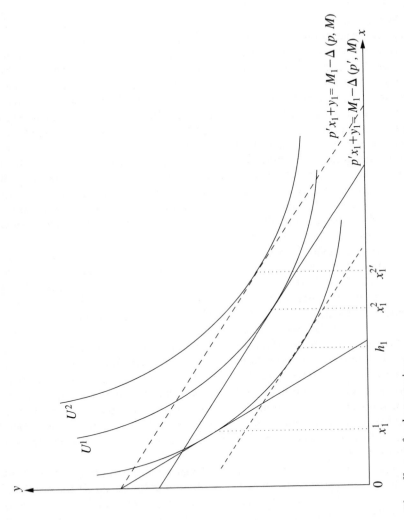

Figure 9.6   The effects of a decrease in p

period. Thus, her decision problem is without uncertainty, and is the same as the problem in (9.16) with $\bar{\theta}$ replaced by the true θ. In the second case, she is forced to make her first period decision without complete information, but gathers the information only in the second period. Her decision problem is the same as in (9.19).

When answering a contingent valuation or contingent behavior question, the latter case could be viewed as applicable. In this situation, she is asked to respond to a set of questions in a limited time frame, forgoing the opportunities of gathering more information about the environment amenity being valued or its substitutes and complements. Suppose the agent is asked to consider the introduction of a new park near her home and she is asked how many trips she would take to that park next year if the park were to open. Equivalently, she might be asked how much she would be willing to pay next year to visit the park. As is typical of contingent behavior or valuation questions, she would be expected to provide this answer in a short time, either immediately if the survey is done via phone or in a few days if it is a mail survey. In any event, she is likely to provide a response to the question before she has gathered as much information about the prospective park as she would if she were to actually make the decision about how many trips to take to the park.

Suppose that she responds to the survey, recognizing that there is potential for learning in the second period. She provides an answer based on $x^l_1(p, m)$ as illustrated in Figure 9.3 (the figure is drawn assuming that $V_m(\cdot)$ is convex in θ). Suppose that everyone in the sample responds to this hypothetical question in the same way. Then the demand function estimated from the survey data will reflect the dynamic nature of the agent's decisions, and the analyst will have data to estimate $x^l_1(p, m(p, M))$. However, the 'true' demand function, in expectation, should be $x_1(p, \bar{M})$. From (9.25), we know $x^l_1(p, m(p, M)) < x_1(p, \bar{M})$, as illustrated in Figure 9.7. Survey restrictions in this case result in an underestimation of the demand and the value of CV/EV for the environmental good. In this scenario, the fact that a response is elicited from the respondents before they have time to complete their information set generates an underestimate of the value and the observed use.

However, in some cases, the lack of learning opportunity is *not* imposed by the survey instrument but rather is inherent in the nature of the problem. For example, the agent may be actively thinking about visiting the park, and she will not have time to gather the relevant information before making her decision. In this case, the estimated demand $x^l_1(p, m(p, M))$ is in fact the relevant function for welfare measurement. The Hicksian demand functions associated with the two price levels p_0 and p_1 are $h_1(p, u^0)$ and $h_1(p, u^1)$, where $u^0 = V(p_0, \bar{M} - \Delta(p_0, M), \bar{\theta})$ and $u^1 = V(p_1, \bar{M} - \Delta(p_1, M), \bar{\theta})$.

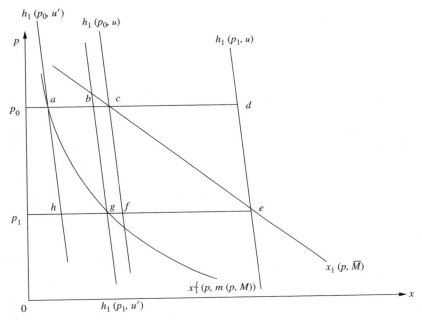

Figure 9.7   The effects of ignoring the delay opportunity on demand

Not surprisingly, in the case where survey restrictions result in the inappropriate use of $x_1^i(p, m(p, M))$, the true compensating and equivalent variation measures may not bound the estimated consumer surplus. It is possible that the estimated CS is lower than both CV and EV for the associated price change. That is, the standard Willig bounds may not work once learning is introduced. In our example, the observed CS is p_0agp_1, while CV is p_0cfp_1 and EV is p_0dep_1.

The implications for welfare measurement described here are similar to those of the non-perishable goods model in that the requirement imposed in surveys (and experiments) to form a willingness to pay or accept value without adequate time to learn can, in both cases, lead to biased estimates of welfare. However, the cause of the bias differs. In the case of non-perishable goods, the fact that a purchase or sale of a good in the current period commits the agent to future consumption levels generates a commitment cost which causes a divergence between the willingness to pay for a good, the willingness to sell, and the respective CV/EV. However, in the case of perishable goods, commitment costs do not arise since the current decisions do not have long-run consequences. Then learning about θ will not significantly alter the divergence between WTP and WTA. Rather, differences between the reported willingness to pay and the true willingness to pay arise from income reallocation between the two periods.

3 DISCUSSION AND CONCLUSIONS

In this chapter, we have presented two simple models of dynamic consumer behavior and considered the implications for welfare measurement when agents can delay transactions while obtaining additional information. In the first model, the consumer is assumed to face the decision of purchasing or selling a good which is non-perishable, implying that the level of consumption of the good chosen in the current period will be consumed in the future periods. In this setting, the well understood equivalence between the static Hicksian welfare measures of CV and EV and their behavioral counterparts, WTP and WTA, no longer holds. These results have important implications for understanding the presence of a divergence between WTP and WTA as well as when the divergence should disappear or be small.

In the second model, we study a situation where the good is perishable, implying that the quantity of consumption can vary freely in each period. Even in this case we find that the availability of information at the time that the consumption decision must be made has important implications for welfare measurement. Fundamentally, when the agent must make a decision today when she knows that additional information will be available later, she may change her income allocation to take advantage of the future information. This will alter her reported welfare values and projected demand.

In both cases, the information available to respondents at the time they answer a stated preference question relative to the information they will ultimately obtain about the good is key. To the extent that there is a difference in the information sets at these different times, there is the potential for erroneous welfare assessment. This finding has implications for researchers designing and analyzing data from stated preference surveys. Specifically, researchers need to be aware of whether the requirements of the survey instrument might generate commitment costs or generate information-restricted demands.

Finally, it is important to note that the theoretical possibility of these information effects does not imply that they will be of significant magnitude in any particular case to warrant concern. Further empirical investigation is needed to understand the circumstances under which these magnitudes are likely to be large and therefore of practical concern.

NOTES

1. There are exceptions: books and sportcards are non-perishable but divisible goods.
2. Otherwise, if $\Theta p(CV) = \phi$, $U(x_1, m - CV, \theta) > U(x_0, m, \theta)$ for all $\theta \in \Theta$, which implies that $E_\theta U(x_1, m - CV, \theta) > E_\theta U(x_0, m, \theta)$, violating (9.2).
3. To show the convexity of $V(\cdot)$, let $\{x^1, y^1\}$ be the optimal second period's bundle given θ^1. Consider another value of θ, $\theta^2 > \theta^1$. If the consumption bundle is fixed at (x^1, y^1), the payoff would change (say, increase, without loss of generality) linearly in θ. Thus, V will increase more than linearly in θ as the optimal consumption bundle (x^2, y^2) will generate higher payoff than (x^1, y^1) at θ^2. That is, $V(\cdot)$ is convex in θ.
4. We have not yet been able to identify functional forms where $V_m(\cdot)$ is concave in θ.

REFERENCES

Arrow, Kenneth J. and Anthony C. Fisher (1974), 'Environmental preservation, uncertainty, and irreversibility', *Quarterly Journal of Economics*, **88**, 312–19.

Corrigan, Jay R. (2002), 'Disparities in empirical welfare measures: the effects of time and information', PhD dissertation, Iowa State University.

Dixit, Avinash K. and Robert S. Pindyck (1994), *Investment Under Uncertainty*, Princeton, NJ: Princeton University Press.

Hammack, Judd and Gardner Brown (1974), *Waterfowl and Wetlands: Towards Bioeconomic Analysis*, Baltimore, MD: Johns Hopkins University Press.

Hanemann, W. Michael (1989), 'Information and the concept of option value', *Journal of Environmental Economics and Management*, **16**, 23–37.

Hanemann, W. Michael (1991), 'Willingness to pay and willingness to accept: how much can they differ?', *American Economic Review*, **81**, 635–47.

Helms, L. Jay (1985), 'Expected consumer's surplus and the welfare effects of price stabilization', *International Economic Review*, **26**, 603–17.

Kahneman, Daniel and Amos Tversky (1979), 'Prospect theory: an analysis of decision under risk', *Econometrica*, **47** (2), 263–91.

Kling, Catherine L. and Jinhua Zhao (2004), 'Welfare measures when consumers can learn: a unifying theory', working paper, Iowa State University.

Quiggin, John (1982), 'A theory of anticipated utility', *Journal of Economic Behavior and Organization*, **3**, 323–43.

Randall, Alan and John R. Stoll (1980), 'Consumer's surplus in commodity space', *American Economic Review*, **70**, 449–55.

Schmeidler, D. (1989), 'Subjective probability and expected utility without additivity', *Econometrica*, **57**, 571–87.

Tversky, A. and D. Kahneman (1991), 'Loss aversion in riskless choice: a reference-dependent model', *Quarterly Journal of Economics*, **106**, 1039–61.

Weisbrod, Burton A. (1964), 'Collective-consumption services of individual consumption goods', *Quarterly Journal of Economics*, **78**, 471–7.

Zhao, Jinhua and Catherine L. Kling (2001), 'A new explanation for the WTP/WTA disparity', *Economics Letters*, **73**, 293–300.

Zhao, Jinhua and Catherine L. Kling (2004), 'Willingness-to-pay, compensating variation, and the cost of commitment', *Economic Inquiry*, **42**, 503–17.

10. Caught in a corner: using the Kuhn–Tucker conditions to value Montana sportfishing

Craig Mohn and Michael Hanemann

Economists are often called upon to supply estimates of changes in measures of consumer well-being under counterfactual scenarios that affect the quality of a public good. Sometimes this is in response to an unplanned change in conditions that has already occurred (such as a toxic spill), and sometimes it is to evaluate a potential policy change (such as a dam or habitat preservation). While these two types of analysis pose different problems regarding data collection and in the development of an accurate description of the alternative scenarios for the model, they share two fundamental requirements. The demand analysis must incorporate quality attributes and it must also explicitly consider the possibility that consumption of one or more good may change to or from zero as a result of the change in quality.

In the field of recreational demand, the customary approach to this problem has been to use random utility-based choice models to answer the question, 'how is total consumption of the item allocated among the alternative brands?' and then apply a separate model (often a count model) to analyze the total consumption of the item. The two separate aspects of consumer choice can be modeled in different ways, but all such approaches have the notable drawback that they do not explicitly specify how the underlying utility function aggregates across time. Moreover, any apparent preference for variety comes from the stochastic 'noise' in the utility function rather than from a systematic desire for variety itself.

The consumer choice can also be modeled in an integrated, single-step approach. The usual method of directly estimating demand systems has been to solve a hypothesized utility function for the demand equations (or equivalently, to find a set of demand functions which satisfy the requisite integrability conditions). Because consumers differ in their choices, this deterministic model must be augmented with stochastic terms. The most straightforward way to do this is to attach an 'error-in-quantity' stochastic term to each demand equation. The inequalities can then be handled with the usual truncated variable methods, using Amemiya's (1974) extension of Tobin's approach. There are, however, several problems with this formulation that may lead to inconsistent estimates of the parameters of the model. Most obviously, changes in consumption levels cannot be treated as independent, or the consumers' budget constraints will not be met. And it is virtually certain that changed levels of consumption for one good will not affect all other demands equally: properly specifying the covariance structure for the stochastic part of the model requires knowledge of the deterministic part being estimated.

An alternative method of estimation was proposed independently by Hanemann in 1978 and Wales and Woodland in 1983. In this approach, the stochastic terms are put inside the utility function, either as random coefficients in the utility model (Wales and Woodland, 1983) or as random variations in a quality index which is part of a utility function (Hanemann, 1984b; Phaneuf, Kling and Herriges, 2000). The Kuhn–Tucker inequalities are employed to derive probability inequalities in prices and quantities. In this model, the stuff that is unknown to the analyst drives the consumer's plan rather than merely his implementation of that plan, as is the case in the Amemiya–Tobin framework.

This chapter will give an example of a Kuhn–Tucker-type model by examining sportfishing in the state of Montana, specifically looking at consumer welfare losses from a long-term disruption to the Clark Fork River fishery which is a legacy of past mining activity. The model uses a functional form which has been used in previous studies of this sort; however, we allow a heteroscedastic error structure, addressing a potential source of bias.

1   THE UPPER CLARK FORK RIVER

Over the past century, mining activities in and around the city of Butte created significant heavy-metal contamination in both Silver Bow Creek and the Clark Fork River from its source at Warm Springs Pond downstream to Missoula. These toxics damage aquatic vegetation and impact fish populations in several ways. Arsenic salts leaching from the mining waste are directly toxic to wildlife. Copper salts poison streambed plant life and may have a direct impact on piscine reproduction. Ore tailings from a large smelter site in Anaconda have washed into the creek and river, leaving unsightly piles, known as 'slickens', in the middle of the stream. These tailings seal the interstitial spaces between the rocks on the bottom of the streambed, depriving aquatic insects of the environment they need to prosper, thus depleting the stream of the food that would support a large trout population for sportfishing. In the worst affected area, which is immediately around Silver Bow Creek, in addition to the damage to aquatic life the terrestrial vegetation has been destroyed and the site appears to contain no plant or insect life – it has aptly been described as a 'moonscape'. In 1991, the State of Montana brought suit against Atlantic Richfield Oil Corporation (ARCO), which had acquired the mining company responsible, to recover losses to the public welfare, including the value of the reduced sportfishing opportunities on the affected streams. In 1999, Montana and ARCO settled the suit for $129 million, an amount which was to cover both restoration and compensation for lost use.

2   BEYOND THE REPEATED CHOICE FRAMEWORK

Each time a consumer goes shopping and buys food, she makes an economic choice of where to go and what to buy. From one perspective, it is possible to view each of these choices as separate decisions. However, there could be some important interactions among these decisions, in which case it would be more sensible to view them as collectively determined. If so, the sequence of choices as a whole involves a quantitative choice of how many units of foods as well as a qualitative choice of which types of foods, and this must be reflected by incorporating quantity into the utility function explicitly. For example, when faced with a choice of goods at a favorite bakery, many people will choose different items on different visits. The fact that they had a chocolate croissant yesterday may make a blueberry muffin look more favorable today. Having had scones twice in the past week or two may make shortbread seem less attractive. Knowing that a seasonal pastry will be available next week may lead one to avoid similar products this week. Aggregated past choices and future options can enter into consumption decisions. While it is possible to use a multi-period choice model with a sufficiently rich covariance structure to describe these decisions, it may not be the most natural way of proceeding. In many cases, the drive for variety is only dependent on what was consumed in the recent past, not the particular order of consumption. Multi-period modeling introduces a substantial structure that is not necessarily directly relevant to the problem, and this in turn may create unreasonable data requirements.

Another way of looking at the problem is to view the consumer as having preferences over consumption bundles, the aggregated product of many choices. These preferences are represented by a utility function that is defined in terms of the number and quality of goods consumed in some time frame. This model of consumers as forward- and backward-looking agents requires that the analyst define any utility function in terms of a 'natural' time interval – long enough that it includes enough purchases so that the interaction between them is captured, and short enough so that consumption at the end is still impacted by consumption at the beginning. In reality, this is not so burdensome: on many occasions there is a natural 'season' delineating events. This has not generally been considered a significant problem in the practice of modeling systems of demand equations.

It is not always appropriate to model consumer choices as a system of demand equations. If choices are made repeatedly, but sufficiently far apart to have very little influence on each other, then classic discrete choice modeling is the appropriate tool. It is important to consider the number of actual decisions in a complex choice situation. While a person may have many choices of transportation mode for her daily commute, she generally makes this decision once and then sticks to it most days thereafter with only occasional deviations due to special circumstances that are likely to be unknowable to the modeler. On the surface, it appears that there is a choice made every day, and each day there is some nonzero probability of using each possible transportation option. However, a close analysis of the decision process will reveal that for most consumers there is only a single decision made, with some contingency options if that choice becomes unavailable or inconvenient, because it is relatively costly in terms of effort to keep track of public transit schedule changes or make arrangements for car pooling. Modeling this as the consumption of a bundle of different trip-mode choices, in contrast to modeling it as a single choice, would be pointless. Treating it as a system of repeated choices would be needlessly complex, as there is essentially a degenerate relationship between the selections on each occasion.

Situations where a demand model for a bundle of goods is more appropriate than a repeated choice model include most outdoor recreational activities which are repeated several times a year, meals eaten at restaurants, and other goods where consumption decisions are made at separate points in time but are suspected to impact each other, yet there is insufficient data for a multi-period model with general inter-period covariance and state dependence. Sometimes the analyst does not believe that the interactions between the choice occasions can be embedded naturally in the covariance structure of the multi-period model. In these cases it is appropriate to estimate a demand system. Demand system models are straightforward to estimate if there is an interior solution to the utility maximization problem and the nonnegativity constraints on consumption are not binding.

This last qualification is an important one, because individual decision makers often fail to purchase some of one or more of the commodities that are available. Analyzing aggregate demand data is relatively simple, because a large population generally consumes at least some of every good. This assures that every first-order condition for demand in the system is an equality for each observation, and the likelihood of an observation conditional on the parameters depends on the density function of the underlying stochastic part of the model, which generally has a closed-form expression. However, when some of the first-order conditions are inequalities, as happens when the observed demand is zero, evaluation of the likelihood for an observation involves the integral of the underlying density function. This does not have a closed form in the most interesting and general cases, for example, when the underlying stochastic structure is described by a multivariate normal distribution. As a consequence, demand systems have rarely been estimated on disaggregated individual data. In 1986, Angus Deaton said, 'In my view, the problem of dealing with zero expenditures is currently one of the most pressing in applied demand analysis' (Deaton, 1986, p. 1809); very little work has been done on the problem since then.

Under a naïve approach which estimates quantity demands directly, the budget constraint is not met for consumers' predicted expenditures: the predicted value can exceed the budget constraint, because negative demands are pushed to zero. This can be fixed by working with expenditure shares (bounded between zero and one), but a homoscedastic specification of this model leaves the quantity demand equations heteroscedastic, with variance proportional to the budget size. In non-technical language, the usual share equation implementation of the Amemiya–Tobin model says that the rich are more careless about getting what they want than are the poor. This is a strong and counterintuitive assumption, which can be changed only if one is willing to explicitly formulate a better variance model. The key problem is that the stochastic terms in this 'errors-in-quantity' formulation of consumer behavior are not in a place that scales between individuals in an easily interpretable way. This difficulty is especially serious given that censored models are biased, often strongly biased, in the presence of unmodeled heteroscedasticity. To make matters worse, there is no way of telling the direction of the bias.

An alternative way of looking at this problem was put forth independently by Hanemann (1978) and Wales and Woodland (1983). They proposed rejecting the ad hoc tacking-on of the stochastic disturbance to the quantity (or share) function and instead placing it inside the utility function. This model specification takes the viewpoint that consumers are heterogeneous at the level of their preferences, not merely in their implementation of those preferences. It can be a straightforward exercise to use the Kuhn–Tucker necessary first order conditions to get a set of inequalities enabling estimation of the parameters of the system, as the next section of this chapter will show. The meaning of assuming homoscedastic error terms in the stochastic part of the model is clear, and lacking in any extreme implications. For a random coefficients implementation, this assumption means that consumers' utility functions are distributed in a way which is not correlated with income (or any other variable we are modeling); for random quality, the non-systematic (to the analyst) perceived-quality variations between the choices are drawn from the same distribution for all consumers.

This approach has all consumer decisions driven by utility maximization, in contrast to the conventional Amemiya–Tobin truncation models, where the consumer is implicitly assumed to maximize utility and then make mistakes in implementing the decisions. This contrast highlights the benefit of using the Hanemann/Wales and Woodland (Kuhn–Tucker) approach over the truncated-variable approach in policy formulation and compensation calculation: we can choose either to consider or to ignore the heterogeneity implicit in the K–T approach, but what is the role of consumption 'mistakes' in welfare comparisons? Do analysts work only with the representative consumer without mistakes, or do they include the expected loss of utility due to consumer errors in their calculations?

3   A KUHN–TUCKER MODEL

From the consumers' perspective, the problem of putting together an optimal consumption bundle during the relevant planning period is a simple deterministic one. The preferences as represented by the utility function are completely known, as are the prices and budget. The following lays out the notation used throughout this chapter:

individuals are indexed by $i \leq I$,
goods are indexed by $j \leq J$,
good quality attributes are indexed by $k \leq K$,
$x_{ij} \geq 0$ is the amount of good j consumed by person i,
s_{ijk} is the level of the kth attribute for good j for person i,
(note that s_{ijk} may be constant across i for good-specific characteristics, and constant across j for individual-specific characteristics which equally affect the quality index of all goods),
p_{ij} is the price consumer i pays for good j,
$z_i \geq 0$ is the total consumption of all other goods (treated as a composite) by person i,
$m_i \, (= z_i + \Sigma_j p_{ij}{}^* x_{ij})$ is person i's total income.

For compactness, the quantities and prices for consumer i will also be written as vectors $\mathbf{x}_i$, $\mathbf{p}_i$, and the product attributes will be written as a matrix $\mathbf{S}_i$.

The consumer solves the problem (suppressing the i subscript):

$$\max_{\mathbf{x}, z} \quad U(\mathbf{x}, \mathbf{S}, z) \tag{10.1}$$

$$\text{subject to } \mathbf{p}' \, \mathbf{x} \leq \mathbf{m} \tag{10.2}$$

The Kuhn–Tucker first order (necessary) conditions for a maximum are

$$\frac{\partial U(\mathbf{x}, \mathbf{S}, z)}{\partial x_j} - p_j^* \lambda \leq 0 \text{ and} \tag{10.3a}$$

$$\frac{\partial U(\mathbf{x}, \mathbf{S}, z)}{\partial z} - \lambda \leq 0, \tag{10.3b}$$

with equality holding in (10.3a) [(10.3b)] if and only if x_j [resp. z] is greater than zero. Sufficient conditions for U to have a unique global maximum are concavity in x and z.

The economist, however, does not know the consumers' preferences exactly, and assumes that they can be represented by a function $U(\mathbf{x}, \mathbf{S}, z, \boldsymbol{\theta}, \varepsilon)$, where $\boldsymbol{\theta} \in \mathbf{R}^M$ is a vector of parameters and $\varepsilon \in \mathbf{R}^N$ is a random variable. In this case the Kuhn–Tucker inequalities become

$$\frac{\partial U(\mathbf{x}, \mathbf{S}, z, \boldsymbol{\theta}, \varepsilon)}{\partial x_j} - p_j^* \lambda \leq 0 \quad \text{and} \tag{10.3a$'$}$$

$$\frac{\partial U(\mathbf{x}, \mathbf{S}, z, \boldsymbol{\theta}, \varepsilon)}{\partial z} - \lambda \leq 0. \tag{10.3b$'$}$$

With any reasonable definition of 'income' and 'other consumption', we can assume that $z > 0$, so (10.3b$'$) gives an expression for the marginal utility of money:

$$\lambda = \frac{\partial U(\mathbf{x}, \mathbf{S}, z, \boldsymbol{\theta}, \varepsilon)}{\partial z}. \tag{10.4}$$

This can be combined with the budget constraint to eliminate z from (10.3a$'$) and (10.3b$'$), yielding a system of J equalities and inequalities in the quantities, prices, attributes, parameters, and the random variable. These simplified equations merely state that the consumer allocates money across each good to equate the marginal utility of the last dollar spent in each category. These relations define a region in R^n that contains the values of ε which are compatible with the observed consumption bundle. This allows the calculation of the probability density function for the observed pattern of demand, given tractable distributions for ε and a sufficiently simple region defined by the Kuhn–Tucker conditions.

Substituting (10.4) into the expression in (10.3a') and using the budget constraint (10.2) to write the function in terms of income yields

$$\frac{\partial U(\mathbf{x}, \mathbf{S}, m, \mathbf{\theta}, \varepsilon)}{\partial x_j} \leq p_j \frac{\partial U(\mathbf{x}, \mathbf{S}, m, \mathbf{\theta}, \varepsilon)}{\partial z}. \tag{10.5}$$

Under some reasonable assumptions about the function U, specifically that the Jacobian $\partial^2 U/\partial x_j \partial \varepsilon_n$ is nonsingular and $\partial^2 U/\partial z \partial \varepsilon_n = 0$, the Implicit Function Theorem guarantees that the ε_j can be written as functions of the known quantities:

$$\varepsilon_j = g_j(\mathbf{x}, \mathbf{p}, \mathbf{S}, m, \mathbf{\theta}). \tag{10.6}$$

This allows the Kuhn–Tucker first order conditions to be written as

$$\varepsilon_j \leq g_j(\mathbf{x}, \mathbf{p}, \mathbf{S}, m, \mathbf{\theta}), \text{ with equality holding iff } x_j > 0. \tag{10.7}$$

Given a distribution for ε, we can use (10.7) to construct the likelihood function for estimation of the parameter $\mathbf{\theta}$. Let $f(\varepsilon)$ be the density function for the random variable. Suppose that individual i consumes positive quantities of the x_j for $j \leq L$, and $x_j = 0$ for $j > L$. By the change of variable theorem, the contribution to the likelihood function is

$$\int_{-\infty}^{g_{L+1}} \cdots \int_{-\infty}^{g_J} f(g_1, g_2, \ldots, g_L, \varepsilon_{L+1}, \ldots, \varepsilon_J) \, | J | \, d\varepsilon_{L+1} \cdots d\varepsilon_J, \tag{10.8}$$

where J is the Jacobian $[\partial \varepsilon_j/\partial y_k]$, where $y_k = x_k$ if $k \leq L$, $y_k = \varepsilon_k$ if $k > L$. This matrix has a partitioned structure, with the lower right component being the identity matrix, the upper right component being zero. Thus, the determinant is just the determinant of the $L \times L$ matrix $[\partial \varepsilon_j/\partial x_k]$.

4 MEASURES OF WELFARE

While the researcher may be interested in analyzing changes in consumer demand, there is often an interest in determining the change in consumer welfare when price or quality attributes are altered. The two basic measures of consumer welfare are the compensating variation (CV), which is the change in wealth required so that the consumer can attain the same level of utility after the change as she had before, and the equivalent variation (EV), which is the similar quantity with the post-change utility taken as the reference point. In terms of the indirect utility function $v()$, income y, initial prices p_0 and attributes S_0, and final prices p_1 and attributes S_1,

$$v(p_1, S_1, y + CV) = v(p_0, S_0, y) \quad \text{and} \tag{10.9}$$

$$v(p_1, S_1, y) = v(p_0, S_0, y - EV). \tag{10.10}$$

Calculating these numbers is relatively straightforward for the simplest Multinomial Logit and Nested Multinomial Logit models commonly used in choice-based demand analysis, where the stochastic terms are assumed to have a Gumbel distribution. Exact calculation where the underlying distribution is multivariate normal requires Monte Carlo techniques, where draws are done from the error or random parameter distribution and the quantity of interest is calculated for each draw. As Krinsky and Robb (1986) observed, these parameter values are only estimates, and the impact on the quantity of interest from small changes in these parameters can be highly nonlinear, so an accurate approach requires integration over the distribution of parameters. This integration is usually accomplished by sampling from the distribution. The asymptotic normal distribution of the parameters obtained from MLE is one possibility for this sampling. Because of the limited sample size, the asymptotic approximation may be questionable in the case analyzed in this chapter, so we use parameter draws derived from the empirical distribution obtained from bootstrapping. A further difficulty arises because CV and EV are defined implicitly in (10.9) and (10.10). There is in general no closed form expression for these quantities, so numerical techniques such as bisection must be used to find the solution. This has no real consequence other than forcing a tradeoff between computational time requirements and accuracy.

The biggest difficulty in calculating CV and EV with the Kuhn–Tucker demand model is in evaluating the indirect utility function $v()$ in the presence of corner solutions. The demand functions resulting from the presence of the nonnegativity constraints are not smooth, and do not have a simple closed form. Hanemann (1984b) demonstrated that it is sufficient to consider all subsets of goods and solve for the (restricted) utility conditional on consuming only positive quantities of those goods in each subset. If the consumer would opt to consume a negative quantity of any good in the subset in the absence of the constraints, that subset is not the utility-maximizing consumption bundle in the presence of the constraint. The overall utility associated with the given prices and characteristics will be the largest utility associated with a subset which has positive consumption for all goods. This gives an obvious recursive formulation for calculating the indirect utility, albeit one which grows exponentially in the number of goods. The most serious impact of this search over subsets lies in the fact that it must be repeated for each evaluation of the indirect utility function during the bisection (or other) search for CV or EV.

Recently, von Haefen *et al.* (2004) pointed out that, when 'other consumption' z is constrained to be nonnegative and the utility function is additively separable, then each unique value for this variable determines the marginal utility of money, and conditional on the ε (and the estimated utility function parameters θ) this determines unique levels of consumption for the goods. Since these combine to yield the total expenditure (which must equal the budget constraint by the definition of z), the problem reduces from the intractable search over all subsets to a relatively simple search in one dimension.

The welfare calculation is still computationally intensive, since it must simulate draws from the distribution of the θ (Krinsky and Robb, 1986) and must also simulate the ε.

5 FUNCTIONAL FORMS WHICH CONSIDER QUALITY

A cursory examination of detailed consumer choice data usually reveals what everyone already knew: consumers often skip the cheapest alternative in favor of some other alternative which is more expensive but of better quality. Thus it is generally important that the utility function include quality attributes of the goods in addition to their quantities. Hanemann (1984a) lays out a framework for including quality in the utility function in various ways, and discusses the implications of these. Bockstael, Hanemann and Strand (1986) give another way of including quality, a variant of the Linear Expenditure System (LES). This last formulation was used by Phaneuf, Kling and Herriges (2000), and will be discussed next. Its main subjective qualities are that marginal utility is decreasing in quantity of each good and composite other consumption, and exponentially increasing in quality. When the stochastic terms are assumed to have independent Gumbel distributions, as is the case with Logit-based choice models, there is a closed-form solution. When the structure is enriched by assuming a multivariate normal distribution, there is no closed form solution so simulation techniques are required.

In this LES formulation, preferences are represented by the strongly separable function:

$$U(\mathbf{x}, \mathbf{S}, z, \boldsymbol{\theta}, \gamma, \varepsilon) = \ln(z) + \sum_j e^{\mathbf{s}_j \boldsymbol{\theta}} e^{\varepsilon_j} \ln(x_j + \gamma), \qquad (10.11)$$

where γ is a parameter equal to 1 if weak complementarity holds. Weak complementarity says that small changes in the attributes of goods not consumed have no impact on utility. The strong separability of the utility function means that any deviation from $\gamma = 1$ has an obvious interpretation as 'non-use value', as in Phaneuf, Kling, and Herriges (2000), but this may also be an artifact of the fact that the log function used to capture the diminishing marginal utility of quantity is ultimately just an approximation of the true preference ordering.

The functions mapping from the x_j to the ε_j are given by

$$\varepsilon_j = g_j(\mathbf{x}, \mathbf{p}, \mathbf{S}, m, \boldsymbol{\theta}, \gamma) = \ln(p_j) + \ln(x_j + \gamma) - \ln(m - \sum_j x_j p_j) - \mathbf{S}_j \boldsymbol{\theta}$$

$$(10.12)$$

and the elements of the Jacobian in the integral (10.8) are given by:

$$\frac{\partial \varepsilon_j}{\partial x_j} = \frac{1}{x_j + \gamma} + \frac{p_j}{m - \sum_i x_i p_i}, \qquad (10.13a)$$

$$\frac{\partial \varepsilon_j}{\partial x_k} = \frac{p_k}{m - \sum_i x_i p_i} \text{ for } j \neq k. \qquad (10.13b)$$

6   DATA

Our data were originally generated in the course of litigation between the State of Montana and ARCO Petroleum, the owner of the Anaconda copper mining company which historically had operated in Butte Montana and which the state considered responsible for the environmental damage in the Upper Clark Fork Basin. The Research Triangle Institute, a consultant to ARCO, conducted an extensive and detailed survey of outdoor recreation activity by residents of Montana in 1992–93, referred to as the Montana Outdoor Recreation Survey (MORS).[1] In July and August of 1992, Montana residents were contacted by telephone from a list of 5000 random phone numbers. The 2071 who were contacted were asked a series of demographic and opinion questions, and then asked to participate in a 14-month survey about recreational behavior. A total of 1149 panelists were active outdoor recreators who agreed to participate. They were asked to record their recreation behavior in bimonthly surveys. These activities included boating, camping, hiking, game-hunting, waterfall-hunting, and trapping. Respondents indicated the primary purpose of each trip, as well as other activities taking place on the trip. During each of the seven reporting periods, between 895 and 698 forms were returned, with some evidence of attrition. Respondents were paid five dollars for each returned survey, whether or not they recreated during the two-month period. A total of 861 people reported some activity in some bimonthly period. By design, the panel included a larger proportion of participants from the area around Butte than the rest of Montana, since this was the most severely affected region.

The data include demographic information about the panel members, including age, gender, race, home zip code, level of educational attainment, and occupation. It also includes such things as whether the individual has things such as cabins and boats, the opportunity to fish on the way home from work, or can take time away from work to recreate. Data about each trip includes the destination, the target species, whether it was a fly-fishing trip, the vehicle taken, and the actual time and costs incurred in getting to the fishing site.

Recreators indicated the location of their trip destinations by attaching stickers to a map of the state of Montana, and also by making further descriptive comments in the questionnaire. Working with local fishing experts, we were able in many cases to use this descriptive information to better characterize the specific location identified by the stickers. These corrections had a surprisingly large impact (approximately 10 percent) on the consumer surplus measures calculated using a traditional travel-cost choice model. This indicates the importance of using either more precise locating mechanisms or bringing in local expertise.

Quality measures for the sites are difficult to obtain. Objective measures of biomass and scenic attributes for the state are both highly disaggregated and very incomplete, and there is no obvious way of combining these different measures from different locations within a broadly-defined site. We consulted several fishing guidebooks, notably *Fishing Montana* (Sample, 1997), which offers ratings as to which streams offer outstanding fishing experiences. While these ratings may seem less rigorous than objective measures such as number of fish, they may best be viewed as a distillation of numerous factors which strongly affect the fishing experience, any of which may not be obvious to the non-angler analyst. Our analysis uses the quality indices derived from this guidebook.

Another source of data on fishing pressure is a survey done every two years by the Montana DFWP (Department of Fish, Wildlife and Parks). This survey recruits panel members by placing postcards on the windshields of vehicles parked near fishing sites. Participants do not remain in the panel for an entire season, and the amount of information about them is extremely limited, so these data were used primarily to check year-to-year patterns of fishing variability and to check the average participation level of the MORS survey panelists. The data suggest that the MORS data under-report actual per-angler fishing effort by 50 percent, while overstating the number of Montanans who are active anglers by 75 percent (Hanemann, 1995). These data can also be used to construct exogenous measures of congestion, popularity and catch rate, which may be useful in extending the methods used here.

As is usual in revealed-preference travel-cost modeling, the survey responses on travel cost appear to be unreliable and are not used in this analysis. Instead we use travel costs and travel times generated by PC-Miler, a computer program that determines the optimal highway route to get between two points. This is done to make prices comparable between observed alternatives and options not selected. PC-Miler works with locations defined by zip code or major highway intersections.

The MORS data contain 513 subjects who engaged in fishing during the 14-month sample period. The data contain information about two different sorts of fishing trips: those where the primary purpose was identified as fishing, and those where fishing occurred, but the primary purpose was identified as some other outdoor recreation activity. Participants were asked to keep track of all fishing, boating, camping, hiking, game-hunting, waterfowl-hunting, trapping and other recreational trips.[2] It is clear that many trips will involve multiple activities, and whether a particular trip is categorized as fishing or boating may be arbitrary. We examined all reported trips and used any where fishing was reported as one of the activities. There were 2656 trips involving fishing reported by the 513 individuals. The mean number of trips per active angler was five, with half reporting one or two trips. A total of 492 anglers fished during the first 12 months of the survey, and were used in the analysis.

Income was available in terms of broad categories, so we defined annual income as the midpoint of the category. The budget constraint reflects income plus the value of all free time, since the value of travel time is included as a cost. The value of time is assumed to be the hourly wage, with some adjustments made for retirees, students, and part-time workers. People are assumed to allocate 14 hours per day toward productive or consumptive activities.

The application of the model in this chapter will be the demand for outdoor recreation trips in Montana. The goods considered are trips to different potential fishing sites having different characteristics, along with aggregated other consumption. The consumers have diverse vehicles and live varying distances from each of the sites, so fishing at these destinations requires different expenditures of time and money – the consumers see different prices for the goods.

Trips from 492 consumers who supplied adequate demographic information were classified as to their destination, based primarily on stickers which the anglers attached to a map which accompanied the survey forms. The stickers were mapped to USGS 7.5 minute quadrangles which were the basis for site definition. In many cases, supplemental information (highway names, landforms, and other landmarks) entered on the survey forms allowed for a more precise location of the consumer's destination.

The trips are sorted into sites sharing similar characteristics. The river fishing sites are the same as the 59 such locations used in Desvouges and Waters (1995). The 38 lake fishing sites used in Desvouges were combined into five geographically-defined aggregates, because lake fishing is thought to be a more distant substitute for river fishing than fishing on a different river, and thus it was not worth increasing the computational complexity by using all of the lake sites. The travel cost to get to one of these aggregated sites is defined as the minimum of the costs to get to one of the component sites; each composite site is seen as having several main fishing spots, and the consumer is assumed to care only about the cost of getting to the closest such location. This is consistent with the usual practices of travel-cost modeling.

Table 10.1 lists the sites by the main river or stream contained within. Minor tributaries are included with the bigger river in the site description. Two of the 59 river sites used in Desvouges' analysis are omitted because there were no usable trips to them, which precludes meaningful estimation of the variance of the site-specific stochastic term under the assumption that these terms are not identically distributed.

7   RESULTS

The LES demand model described above was estimated using GAUSS 5.0. The parameter γ is constrained to be 1, since any other value implies that existence value is a factor in valuation. We wanted to eliminate this from the present analysis because we do not believe that revealed preference data about the sites people visited provide an appropriate basis for assessing any non-use value they may place on these and other fishing sites in Montana.

The quality index for a composite site is a function of the number of the constituent sites which are premier trout streams (as determined by *Fishing Montana* (Sample, 1997)), the density of campgrounds and state

Table 10.1   River and lake sites used in model

River and Lake Sites

Kootenai River	Upper Big Hole River
Yaak River	Lower Big Hole River
Upper Flathead River	Beaverhead River
Stillwater and Whitefish Rivers	Ruby River
Flathead River	Jefferson River
M Fk Flathead River	Madison River
St. Mary, Milk, Two Medicine Rivers	Missouri River
Lower Clark Fork River	Upper Madison River
St. Regis River	Gallatin and Lower Gallatin Rivers
Flathead River	Upper Gallatin River
Middle Clark Fork River	Upper Yellowstone River
Swan River	Middle Yellowstone River
South Fork Flathead River	Boulder River (Yellowstone)
Teton River	Stillwater River
Sun River	Red Rock River
Lower Missouri River	Little Bitterroot River
Smith River	Lower Yellowstone River
Belt Creek	Silver Bow Creek
Lower Bitterroot River	Missouri River (Ft Benton)
Rock Creek (Clark Fork)	Bighorn River
Blackfoot River	Clarks Fork Yellowstone River
Clark Fork River (W Springs to Garrison)	Yellowstone River (Billings)
Clark Fork River (Garrison to Miss)	Bearpaw Mountains
Flint Creek	Missouri River (5 lakes)
Warm Springs Creek	Red Lodge and Willow Creeks
Little Blackfoot River	Ashley Creek
Tenmile and Prickly Pear Creeks	Northwest Lakes
Boulder River	Southwest Lakes
Judith River	Central Lakes
Musselshell River	Northeast Lakes
Upper Bitterroot River	Southeast Lakes

recreational areas, and demographic variables. The *Fishing Montana* rating for the Clark Fork between Garrison and Missoula is reduced to non-premier for current conditions, based on conversations with several fishing experts in the region.

The site-specific stochastic terms are assumed independently normally distributed with non-identical variances (INID), which is a generalization of previous modeling efforts. We also estimate the model with independent identically distributed error terms (IID). Allowing the variances to differ is important because of the functional form of the utility equation: the stochastic term is exponentiated, and thus has an expected value which increases with variance. Cursory inspection of the functional form reveals that the scale of the variance parameter affects the constant and other coefficient estimates. In particular, imposing a too-large variance on a subset of the observations forces them to pull the constant term estimate downward. Even though the utility function is strongly separable, the variance parameters from the goods interact through their impact on the constant term. Incorrect assumptions about variance bias the estimated coefficients, and thus the welfare results. And identical variance is an unreasonable assumption in this case: it says that the idiosyncratic component of people's preferences has the same distribution over all alternatives. This is implausible: people have different levels of familiarity with different sites, and this will almost certainly force a divergence of the variance in these terms. The estimated model indicates significant differences in the variance of the idiosyncratic component of utility among the different goods. The model variables and coefficients are presented in Table 10.2 below.

A likelihood ratio test that the variances are equal strongly rejects that hypothesis with an LR-statistic of 240.2, which is distributed chi-squared with 61 degrees of freedom.

To explore the welfare implications of this model we consider a counterfactual scenario where the trout population is doubled for both Clark Fork River sites, and the portion of the river which is upstream from Garrison is upgraded to a 'major' trout stream (the river below Garrison is already 'major'). These conditions reflect one possible scenario as to what conditions would be like in the absence of the environmental degradation. The value of the welfare change induced by the mining activities was estimated using a standard binary search for the compensating variation (CV) that would make a panel of demographically identical consumers whole for the damage to the Clark Fork River. The welfare changes were calculated based on 2000 draws from the distributions for the stochastic part of each consumer's preferences. We use the point estimate of the coefficients rather than using the Krinsky–Robb (1986) procedure to account for uncertainty in estimation. This is done both to ensure comparability with other results, and to simplify the comparison between the IID and INID versions of our model.

Using the IID model, the mean loss in welfare was $8.97 per angler for the first 12 month period of the survey. Assuming 140 000 active anglers in Montana (Hanemann, 1995), this brings the total loss per year to $1.3 million. Desvouges and Waters (1995) also estimated a discrete choice and obtained an estimated annual loss of $0.13 million; they used a different

Table 10.2   Coefficients for the Kuhn–Tucker demand model

Covariate	INID stochastic terms	IID stochastic terms
	Coefficient (T-stat)	Coefficient (T-stat)
Trout biomass	0.15 (2.5)	0.11 (4.9)
'Major' trout stream	1.33 (5.5)	0.42 (4.8)
Restricted species in stream	−0.20 (−1.7)	0.15 (3.9)
Campground density	0.50 (0.9)	0.09 (0.6)
State rec. area density	−0.58 (−1.5)	0.09 (0.7)
Natural logarithm of area	−0.03 (−0.2)	0.36 (5.7)
ASC for NW lake region	3.22 (6.5)	3.60 (13.3)
ASC for SW lake region	2.13 (4.5)	2.55 (9.5)
ASC for central lake region	2.31 (4.7)	3.15 (11.5)
ASC for NE lake region	2.61 (5.1)	2.90 (10.0)
ASC for SE lake region	2.77 (5.6)	2.56 (10.0)
Constant	−11.78 (−27.2)	−12.48 (−52.5)
Fly fisher	0.34 (3.8)	0.37 (4.0)
Truck owner	0.38 (4.2)	0.43 (4.4)
Trout fisher	0.37 (3.7)	0.34 (3.2)
Female	0.13 (1.7)	0.12 (1.5)
Retired	0.14 (1.1)	0.13 (1.0)
Can fish on way home from work	0.09 (1.3)	0.09 (1.1)
Urban dweller	−0.18 (−2.5)	−0.19 (−2.3)
Eastern Montanan	0.56 (3.7)	0.70 (4.5)
Disabled	0.57 (1.7)	0.57 (1.4)
Fly fisher – lake site interaction	−0.49 (−3.2)	−0.55 (−3.4)
Trout fisher l lake site interaction	0.02 (0.1)	0.09 (0.5)
Variance	0.67–7.79	4.02
(Range for all 62 sites for INID model)	(1.7–8.5)	(26.3)

counterfactual scenario which included a larger change in fish biomass but ignored changes in other aesthetic attributes or expert rankings. When probable changes to the site aesthetics are included, their estimate of annual loss would be $0.63 million. Correcting their data for misclassification of destinations and re-estimating their model, using their damage scenario, raises their loss estimate by roughly 10 percent. It is likely that a similar increase would apply when probable changes to site aesthetics are added to the damage scenario, yielding an annual loss estimate with their model of $0.69 million. Using their own survey data on anglers, the state of Montana's consultants estimated a discrete choice model for sportfishing with a different structure from that used by Desvousges and Waters (1995). Their final estimate was a welfare loss of $0.44 million. Because our model in this chapter takes diminishing marginal utility of consumption into account, and because we include more fishing trips from more participants in the data, it is not surprising that our estimate is higher than the estimates from these other studies.

The welfare impact is dramatically affected by allowing the stochastic part of recreators' preferences for different sites to have different variances. As the larger coefficient on biomass and the much larger coefficient on the 'major' classification would suggest, the CV measure is much larger. When the assumption of identical variances is relaxed, the welfare change per angler increases to $95.53 per year; this raises the estimate of total annual loss to $13.4 million. Figure 10.1 is a histogram showing the percentage of the draws in the simulation of the stochastic part of the preference function which have a nonzero welfare impact. Most of the time, the changes to the systematic part of the utility function do not have an impact, because they are not sufficient to push demand for the good into the interior. If a good is not consumed in either the baseline or counterfactual scenario, changes to its attributes have no affect on a consumer's welfare. When the stochastic term in the utility function for an affected good happens to be large, that good is more likely to be moved into or out of the set of goods consumed, and thus affect welfare. So the variance of the stochastic terms in the utility function can greatly affect welfare measures.

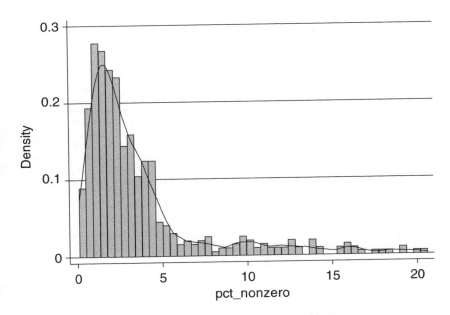

Figure 10.1   Histogram showing percentage nonzero CV

8 CONCLUSION

We have found that Kuhn–Tucker models yield welfare measures which are comparable to those obtained by traditional choice-modeling methods. The value of the hypothetical changes were quite a bit larger, as is to be expected since simple choice models cannot take into account any systematic preference for variety, nor can they allow for diminishing marginal utility from recreational consumption, which makes the first trip or two more valuable. This last fact matters in a world where averages are skewed by a few people who took many trips.

Allowing consumers to have different levels of unobserved taste variation for the separate goods is a step towards modeling more general correlations in the stochastic structure. In some cases the impact on welfare measures can be very large. This is one direction for further exploration, although efforts are perhaps better applied toward exploring the rich variety of functional forms that arises from the shift from the instantaneous notion of utility inherent in choice models to one based on tradeoffs over a time interval. There are many ways to represent diminishing marginal utility and preference for variety, and thus much room for innovation in modeling of demand systems with disaggregated data. This is an approach with considerable promise, and warrants further exploration.

NOTES

1. The data subsequently became available through the discovery process. We were brought in as consultants by the State of Montana to analyze these data after the discovery had occurred. The State of Montana hired Hagler Bailly Consulting, Inc. to conduct its own damage assessment, which was based on a less ambitious and less expensive effort restricted to a survey of anglers identified on-site. These data were analyzed by Morey and Rowe (1995) and Morey and Waldman (1998); we were not asked to analyze these data.
2. The MORS survey explicitly covered all these other outdoor recreation activities, but the non-fishing recreation data do not appear to have been systematically analyzed by ARCO's consultants and they were not turned over to the State of Montana in a sufficiently transparent manner and with sufficient documentation to permit us to analyze the other activities.

REFERENCES

Amemiya, T. (1974), 'Multivariate regression and simultaneous equation models when the dependent variables are truncated normal', *Econometrica*, **42**, 999–1012.
Bockstael, N.E., W.M. Hanemann and I.E. Strand (1986), 'Measuring the benefits of water quality improvement in a recreational demand framework', *Water Resources Research*, **23**, 951–60.

Deaton, Angus (1986), 'Demand analysis', in Z. Griliches and M.D. Intrilligator (eds), *Handbook of Econometrics*, vol. III, New York: North-Holland, pp. 1767–839.

Desvouges, William H. and Stephen M. Waters (1995), 'Report on the potential economic losses associated with recreation services on the Upper Clark Fork river basin', Triangle Economic Research, Research Triangle, North Carolina.

Hanemann, W. Michael (1978), 'A methodological and empirical study of the recreation benefits from water quality improvement', PhD dissertation, Department of Economics, Harvard University.

Hanemann, W. Michael (1984a), 'Discrete/continuous models of consumer demand', *Econometrica*, **52**, 541–61.

Hanemann, W. Michael (1984b), 'Multiple site demand models. Part I: some preliminary considerations', Giannini Foundation working paper no. 336, Department of Agricultural and Resource Economics, University of California, Berkeley.

Hanemann, W. Michael (1984c), 'Multiple site demand models. Part II: review of existing models and development of new models', Giannini Foundation working paper no. 337, Department of Agricultural and Resource Economics, University of California, Berkeley.

Hanemann, W. Michael (1995), 'Review of Triangle Economic Research Report on Economic Loss to Recreational Fishing in the Upper Clark Fork Basin', State of Montana Natural Resource Damage Program, Helena, Montana.

Krinsky, Itzhak and A. Leslie Robb (1986), 'On approximating the statistical properties of elasticities', *Review of Economics and Statistics*, **68**, 715–19.

Morey, Edward R. and Robert D. Rowe (1995), 'Assessment of Damages to Anglers and Other Recreators from Injuries to the Upper Clark Fork River Basin', Prepared for the State of Montana Natural Resource Damage Litigation Program, January.

Morey, Edward R. and Donald M. Waldman (1998), 'Measurement error in recreation demand models: the joint estimation of participation, site choice, and site characteristics', *Journal of Environmental Economics and Management*, **35**, 262–76.

Phaneuf, Daniel J., Catherine L. Kling and Joseph A. Herriges (2000), 'Estimation and welfare calculations in a generalized corner solution model with an application to recreation demand', *Review of Economics and Statistics*, **82** (1), 83–92.

Sample, Michael S. (1997), *Fishing Montana*, Missoula, MT: Falcon Press.

von Haefen, Roger H., Daniel J. Phaneuf and George R. Parsons (2004), 'Estimation and welfare analysis with large demand systems', *Journal of Business and Economic Statistics*, **22** (2), 194–205.

Wales, T.J. and A.D. Woodland (1983), 'Estimation of consumer demand systems with binding non-negativity constraints', *Journal of Econometrics*, **21**, 263–85.

11. The economic valuation of shoreline: 30 years later

Raymond B. Palmquist and Charles M. Fulcher

Over his career so far, Gardner Brown has contributed to the frontiers of environmental economics in many areas, as the many topics in this volume demonstrate. He has revisited some of the areas over and over, while in other areas he made an innovative contribution and then moved on. An excellent example of the latter category is the work that he did with Henry Pollakowski on the 'Economic Valuation of Shoreline' in the mid-1970s.

The use of property values as a means to infer the value of non-market goods was in its infancy. Hedonic studies had been used previously to study differentiated products in a variety of other areas,[1] but Ridker and Henning (1967) were the first to apply hedonic techniques to an issue in environmental economics, namely air pollution. Their study inspired numerous other similar studies of air pollution, such as Anderson and Crocker (1969, 1971) and a number of unpublished studies referred to in Freeman (1979, 1982). The technique was also applied to other environmental problems. For example, Gamble et al. (1973) studied highway noise and Nelson (1975) considered both airplane and highway noise. Havlicek et al. (1971) studied solid waste. Finally, Dornbusch and Barrager (1973) attempted to use property values to study water pollution, with mixed success.[2]

However, the study by Ridker and Henning also generated a good deal of controversy about the theoretical interpretation of their results. Freeman (1971, 1974a), Small (1975) and Polinsky and Shavell (1975) all contributed to that debate and improved our understanding of the hedonic model. During this period the first theoretical models of hedonic pricing were developed. Simultaneously and independently, Rosen (1974) and Freeman (1974b) vastly improved our understanding of what was being estimated by hedonic regressions and what results could be derived from them.

In this period, our theoretical understanding of hedonic modeling had rapidly evolved, but the empirical implementation was still at a somewhat rudimentary stage. Most (but not all) of the existing studies used census tract data, which meant using averages of owner estimates of house values. The measures of characteristics were limited and were census tract averages.

It is in this setting that the contribution of Brown and Pollakowski can be appreciated. Their article was one of the first to use micro data on individual sales. In addition to avoiding the problems with the aggregation and proxies in census data, it also allowed them to consider an issue that was at a much finer spatial scale than most previous studies.

Another innovation by Brown and Pollakowski was that they were studying an amenity. Today, the study of amenities, such as open space, is extremely common, but at that time almost all environmental hedonic studies were of major pollutants, especially air pollution. Valuing amenities was new. In addition, Brown and Pollakowski incorporated the recent theoretical insights in interpreting their results, something which few previous studies had done. Even when they were forced to make strong assumptions, these were clearly acknowledged and the possible effect on the interpretation was discussed. Finally, they considered the policy implications of their study and the conclusions that could and could not be drawn from their work. The standards were raised for hedonic studies that followed.

It is important to remember the technological conditions under which this work was done. Recall that the article was written in 1975, although it was published in 1977. Those were the days of mainframe computers, keypunch machines, and decks of computer cards. Rather than the multifaceted statistical packages we have today, there were Fortran programs written in the department. The simplest OLS regressions with less than 100 observations had to be run overnight to keep costs down. It is important to keep these conditions in mind in thinking about the Brown and Pollakowski work on valuing shoreline.

Their data allowed them to consider two types of lakes. One of the lakes they studied, Green Lake, was surrounded by public park land of varying depths, which they called setback. There were 90 observations here. The two other lakes were surrounded by private land, so there was no setback. Data on houses surrounding these two lakes had to be combined to yield 89 observations. Linear regressions were run, and the variables of interest, distance to waterfront and individual setback size, were entered in log form. The results were extremely plausible, and the relationships between the magnitudes of the coefficients made intuitive sense. In both cases, the coefficient on waterfront distance was significantly negative. The coefficient was larger in absolute value where there was no public land. For Green Lake where there was public land, the depth of the public land had a positive effect on property values, although it did not fully offset the negative effect of distance from the waterfront.

These results are what one would expect. If there is no public land, the benefit to a home owner would decline rapidly with distance to the lake because the only one who would benefit from the lake would have to have direct access to the lake or, at least, a view of the lake. On the other hand, when the lake is surrounded by public land, the benefits can extend further back from the lake because of the possibility of access from houses located further back. This means that the effect would not decline as rapidly with distance when there were public lands. In addition, views of public parkland have value, just as do the views of the lake. Combining the information in the two coefficients for Green Lake shows that, if the land between the house and the lake is public, distance from the water has a much smaller negative effect at the boundary of the park than if it was private land.

1 HEDONICS 30 YEARS LATER

Since the mid-1970s the basic rationale for hedonic price studies has changed very little.[3] However, there has been extensive progress in data availability, computer power, and econometric techniques.

With respect to data, in the 1970s the main sources involved extensive effort on the part of the researchers unless they were willing to use census tract averages and estimated property values. One of the best sources was county records. However, this often required physically copying the records of the property characteristics from the tax assessor's cards. The sales information was often in another office where the deeds were registered. That has all changed in most urban counties today. Large structured databases contain all the details on the properties and the sales.

In the 1970s, obtaining spatial information usually involved using rulers and blueprint maps. Today, the data on the properties are already integrated into a Geographical Information System, so that the property boundaries can be located exactly. Then sophisticated GIS programs allow distances to be calculated as straight-line distance or highway distance measured in miles or travel time. Almost all features, from parks and lakes to shopping centers, are digitized and can be readily linked. Data collection can be much easier and much more complete than previously. This has made it possible to compile much larger data sets with many more observations.

At the same time computing power has increased exponentially. Instead of an ordinary least squares regression with a hundred observations having to be run overnight on a mainframe, we can now run complex spatial econometrics problems with a hundred thousand observations on a desktop computer in a few hours using sparse matrix techniques.

This has allowed some significant developments in the econometric techniques used in property value studies. Economists have long been aware that the characteristics of the neighborhood surrounding a house could influence the value of the house. Neighborhood characteristics were included in hedonic regressions in some of the earliest studies and are an important part of almost all hedonic studies today. Nevertheless, even with these impressive data sets, there remain unobserved characteristics of houses and locations that influence sale prices. Often these unobserved characteristics are spatially correlated. This is obvious for neighborhood characteristics, but it is also true for structural characteristics. Within a subdivision there will be correlated unobservable characteristics because of codes and covenants, identical or similar builders, and similar customers. All of these factors lead to the error terms in hedonic regressions being spatially correlated, and ordinary least squares will be inefficient. We will refer to these models that control for this spatial error correlation as 'spatial error' models.

One can deal with spatial errors in various ways. The two most common approaches are to model the error covariance matrix directly (direct representation) and to model the spatial process. The first approach is common in the statistics literature and has been used in economics applications, particularly by Robin Dubin in a series of articles (for example, Dubin, 1988, 1992). Here the correlation between the error terms is specified to be a decreasing function of distance between the houses. This function is typically negative binomial, Gaussian, or spherical (for example, Dubin *et al.*, 1999). While direct representation can estimate the parameters of the distance decay function, a limitation of this approach is that the dense variance–covariance matrix must be inverted in the likelihood function. This places a limitation on the number of observations for which such estimation is feasible.

The second approach is more common in economics and is more tractable with large data sets. A set of neighbors for each observation is defined and the interaction between neighbors is specified. Luc Anselin (for example, Anselin, 1988) has been the most influential proponent of this approach.[4] Implementing this approach requires specifying a weights matrix, W, that, for each observation, gives the neighbors and their relative weights. W is specified, not estimated, and the diagonal elements are zero. If it is row-standardized, the weights assigned to the neighbors sum to one. There can be a fixed number of neighbors for each observation or all observations within a given distance can be considered neighbors. All neighbors can be assigned equal weight, or the weight can decline with distance.

Obviously, there is a great deal of flexibility in the specification, but since it is a maintained hypothesis it is not possible to test the choice.

Let the vector of prices (or transformations of the prices) for the houses be **P** and the matrix of characteristics for the houses be z. Let β be the vector of coefficients of the characteristics and let ε be the vector of error terms. The hedonic equation is

$$\mathbf{P} = z\beta + \varepsilon.$$

If there are spatially correlated errors, then

$$\varepsilon = \lambda\mathbf{W}\varepsilon + \mathbf{u},$$

where λ is a scalar parameter to be estimated and

$$\mathbf{u} \sim N(0, \sigma^2 \mathbf{I}).$$

Thus,

$$\mathbf{P} = z\beta + (\mathbf{I} - \lambda\mathbf{W})^{-1}\mathbf{u},$$

which gives the estimating equation.[5]

Several factors make this estimation tractable. The estimating equation can be written as

$$\mathbf{u} = (\mathbf{I} - \lambda\mathbf{W})(\mathbf{P} - z\beta),$$

and thus

$$\partial\mathbf{u}/\partial\mathbf{P} = \mathbf{I} - \lambda\mathbf{W}.$$

Thus, the Jacobian term in the log likelihood function is

$$ln\ |\mathbf{I} - \lambda\mathbf{W}| = \Sigma_i\ ln\ (1 - \lambda\omega_i),$$

where w_i are the eigenvalues of **W** and the simplification on the right is due to Ord (1975). Further, because the elements of the **W** matrix are predominantly but not exclusively zero, it is possible to use sparse matrix programming techniques as implemented by programs such as Matlab. This makes it possible to use maximum likelihood techniques even with very large data sets. James LeSage has written a number of Matlab programs for spatial econometrics that provide a useful starting point.[6]

2 STUDY AREA AND DATA

Brown and Pollakowski used Seattle, where the University of Washington is located, for their study areas. In keeping with that tradition, we have used Raleigh, the home of North Carolina State University, for ours. Wake County is located in the Piedmont in central North Carolina. Raleigh is the State Capitol of North Carolina. The Neuse River flows through the county, and there are numerous lakes, almost all man-made. Parts of the county are fully developed, while other parts are more rural. However, the urban influence is felt throughout the county, and agriculture is no longer a significant part of the economy.

The data used were from 1992 to 1999 throughout Wake County.[7] The Wake County Assessor's Office provided data on all sales prices of single-family residential properties during that period. In addition to data on the characteristics of the structures and lots, the parcel centroids were recorded. Using additional GIS data on the parcel boundaries, local hydrography and public lands, each parcel in the data set was linked with its distance to all lakes and streams, parks, shopping centers, and other features of the surrounding areas. The U.S. Census of Population and Housing provided data on the neighborhood (block group). The 1990 and 2000 censuses bound the interval, and linear interpolation was used to estimate the levels of the census variables in the intervening years. Local property tax rates by jurisdiction and year were obtained from the local governments within the county.

The variables used are defined in Table 11.1. Semi-logarithmic equations were used for the functional form. Work with this and other hedonic data sets has shown this to be the best of the simple functional forms. Using Box–Cox forms in combination with the spatial econometrics used here would introduce complex estimation issues with little expected payoff.

The specification of the characteristics of the structures was more complete than almost all existing hedonic studies, in that the square feet of living space was separated into primary living space, basements, and attics, and these were separated into heated and unheated components. The areas of garages, carports, storage areas, patios, decks, and various types of porches were also used. Thanks to this completeness, the specification could replicate the information buyers and sellers use in pricing houses. Linear and squared terms were used for primary living area, age, and lot area because theory and empirical experience suggest nonlinearities in valuing these characteristics.

The lot area also was treated differently than in most other studies. In simple theoretical models with a monocentric city, land value is functionally related to the distance to the central business district (CBD). Many

Table 11.1   Variable definitions

lprice	log (sale price of property)
baths	Number of bathrooms
regheatarea	Main heated living area in thousands of square feet
sqregheat	regheatarea squared
age	Age of structure, calculated as sale year–year built
sqage	age squared
acreage	Lot size in acres
sqacre	acreage squared
bsmtheat	Basement heated area in square feet
bsmtunheat	Unheated basement heated area in square feet
atticheat	Attic heated area in square feet
atticunheat	Attic unheated area in square feet
otherunheatarea	Other unheated areas (for example, unfinished rooms) in square feet
walldum1	Dummy variable indicating presence of brick walls
bsmtdum1	Dummy variable indicating presence of full basement
bsmtdum2	Dummy variable indicating presence of partial basement
heatdum6	Dummy variable indicating house has limited/partial heating
heatdum7	Dummy variable indicating house has no heating
acdum1	Dummy variable indicating house has air conditioning
story	Number of stories
detgarage	Dummy variable indicating presence of detached garage
condadum	Dummy variable indicating house is of condition A
condcdum	Dummy variable indicating house is of condition C
condddum	Dummy variable indicating house is of condition D
carport	Carport area in square feet
encporch	Enclosed porch area in square feet
scrporch	Screened porch area in square feet
opnporch	Open porch area in square feet
garage	Garage area in square feet
storage	Storage area in square feet
patio	Patio area in square feet
deck	Deck area in square feet
stoop	Stoop area in square feet
fireplaces	Number of fireplaces
poolres	Dummy variable indicating presence of swimming pool
grade	Numeric grade assessed by Revenue Department
perc_nonwhite	Percent non-white for 1990 census block group
medianvalue	Median house values for census block group
medttw	Median time to work for census block group in minutes

Table 11.1   (continued)

perc_under 18	Percent of population under age of 18 for census block group
perc_owner_ occ	Percent owner-occupied housing for census block group
nearestpark	Distance to nearest park in thousands of feet
nearestsc	Distance to nearest shopping center in thousands of feet
bigparkdistance	Distance to nearest large park (larger than 70 acres) in thousands of feet
taxrate	Property tax rate per $100 in value
lakedistindex	Transformed distance to nearest lake

hedonic studies include distance to the CBD as a characteristic. However, modern polycentric cities are more complex. One could include the distance to the many employment centers and other attractions, but identifying the centers and interactions between the centers is a daunting task. Instead, we separated the county into 15 zones using maps from the real estate Multiple Listing Service. These zones are defined to divide the county into subareas within the real estate market. For each of the 15 zones we estimated coefficients for acreage and acreage squared. This allowed land values to vary throughout the county and with the size of the lot.

The distance of the houses to the lakes is obviously central to this study. If the house is located on or near a lake this may be an amenity for the residents, which may influence property values. To allow for this, we used an ArcView shapefile of all lakes in the county provided by Wake County Geographic Information Services. As was previously alluded to, the distance of each house from all lakes was calculated and the distance to the nearest lake was determined. Since the amenity effect of lake proximity would decline rapidly with distance from the lake and would fall to zero at some distance, an index for lake proximity was developed. The index is $\text{Max}\{1 - (d/d_{\text{max}})^{1/2}; 0\}$ where d is the distance of the house from the nearest lake and d_{max} is the maximum distance where the lake has any effect on the house value. This index is between zero and one and is convex. A value of 2640 feet (one-half mile) was used for d_{max}. The reason for having it decline to zero at that distance was that, once a house is more than half a mile from a lake, the value of the house probably depends on more general considerations of access to recreation and amenities rather than access to a particular lake.[8] Distance to the nearest park and distance to the nearest large park (greater than 70 acres in size) were included in the specification to allow for this type of access.

Table 11.2 provides some summary statistics on a subset of the variables. The data cover eight years with just under 100 000 sales. A range of houses

Table 11.2   Selected summary statistics

Variable	Mean	Std. dev.	Min	Max
SQ. FT.	1936	725	400	9075
BATHS	2.5	0.76	1	10.5
AGE	9.8	14.7	0	98
ACREAGE	0.5	0.89	0.04	97.5

Year	Mean price ($)	No. of obs
1992	136 085	9 460
1993	143 276	11 107
1994	155 278	12 169
1995	165 761	11 147
1996	169 914	12 125
1997	177 739	13 417
1998	184 481	14 866
1999	194 087	12 294
Total		96 585
Range	(14 000–2 727 000)	

Percent of houses within distances to the nearest lake and index values

Distance in feet	Percent of houses	Index value
100	0.33	0.8054
500	1.84	0.5648
1 000	5.00	0.3845
2 000	14.84	0.1296
5 000	54.88	0

is represented. For the current study, a statistic on the percentage of the houses that were within varying distances of the nearest lake is provided and the value of the lake distance index at that distance is given.

3   RESULTS

Table 11.3 gives the results when the hedonic regressions use the data aggregated over the eight years. Columns 2 and 3 report the results using ordinary least squares, while columns 4 and 5 are the results with the spatial error model. These results are provided as an illustration, but for the current study we will also be interested in the separate hedonic regressions for each year. With the aggregated data the maintained assumption is that the relative values of the characteristics remained constant during the period. Changes in the general price level are captured by including dummy variables that represent the year in which the sale took place (yrdum92–yrdum98). Since the dummy variable for 1999 was omitted, that was the base year for the local real estate price index that would be generated from the coefficients of these dummy variables.

The results accord well with expectations. The value per square foot of living space on the main floors is greater than comparable space in basements or attics. Heated space in the basement or attic is more valuable than

Table 11.3   Hedonic estimates combining data from 1992–99

Variable	OLS		Spatial error model	
	Coefficient	t stat.	Coefficient	Asymptotic t-stat
intercept	10.5085	1475.2818	10.6566	1002.0814
baths	0.0274	38.2647	0.0227	32.1559
regheatarea	0.4572	175.0661	0.4042	156.2027
sqregheat	−0.0460	−97.3841	−0.0369	−79.6307
age	−0.0064	−76.0528	−0.0069	−161.5024
sqage	0.0001	47.4626	0.0001	0.0000
bsmtheat	0.0001	30.4758	0.0001	36.5655
bsmtunheat	0.0000	−1.8938	0.0000	−0.0639
atticheat	0.0002	64.6699	0.0001	66.3752
atticunheat	0.0001	15.1059	0.0001	17.2399
otherunheatarea	0.0002	16.6588	0.0001	17.4542
walldum1	0.0159	12.4964	0.0176	14.9789
bsmtdum1	0.0908	42.0379	0.0833	43.1949
bsmtdum2	0.0818	45.1874	0.0739	45.2628
heatdum6	−0.0774	−11.9349	−0.0584	−9.9445
heatdum7	−0.1691	−20.0739	−0.1513	−19.9474
acdum1	0.0652	25.0546	0.0548	22.9510
story	−0.0300	−26.4799	−0.0277	−26.0057
detgarage	0.0465	22.6281	0.0462	24.9933
condadum	0.0428	21.6227	0.0488	21.1172
condcdum	−0.0873	−37.9544	−0.0797	−35.1442
condddum	−0.2986	−50.9776	−0.2698	−49.3453
carport	0.0001	13.0104	0.0001	15.4559
encporch	0.0002	17.6036	0.0002	19.3459
scrporch	0.0002	31.7968	0.0002	28.6656
opnporch	0.0001	22.8846	0.0001	24.5041
garage	0.0002	87.3667	0.0002	83.6290
storage	0.0001	6.5271	0.0001	4.4792
patio	0.0000	8.5994	0.0000	10.4659

Table 11.3 (continued)

Variable	OLS		Spatial error model	
	Coefficient	t stat.	Coefficient	Asymptotic t-stat
deck	0.0001	42.1331	0.0001	35.3390
stoop	0.0002	11.9490	0.0002	10.4788
fireplaces	0.0379	33.4276	0.0303	28.1275
poolres	0.0258	8.1146	0.0304	10.8203
grade	0.0054	193.9447	0.0050	165.9457
perc_nonwhite	−0.0008	−24.7984	−0.0013	−22.5379
medianvalue	0.0000	45.4933	0.0000	1605.1241
medttw	−0.0010	−6.5125	−0.0017	−6.1148
perc_under18	−0.0018	−14.8114	−0.0009	−5.1173
perc_owner_occ	0.0003	10.1820	0.0001	2.2222
nearestpark	−0.0025	−11.7561	−0.0012	−2.6613
nearestsc	−0.0005	−2.2116	−0.0007	−1.4054
bigparkdistance	−0.0006	−12.0994	−0.0008	−9.6421
taxrate	0.0142	7.6347	0.0163	5.4925
yrdum92	−0.3205	−191.1986	−0.2969	−87.0752
yrdum93	−0.2743	−173.7960	−0.2573	−82.2084
yrdum94	−0.2022	−133.1802	−0.1936	−63.2106
yrdum95	−0.1380	−91.9098	−0.1336	−43.6859
yrdum96	−0.1023	−70.3518	−0.0970	−32.2728
yrdum97	−0.0685	−49.0599	−0.0594	−20.6990
yrdum98	−0.0360	−26.6403	−0.0269	−10.6757
lakedistindex	0.0389	14.8386	0.0468	11.2537

acreage and acreage squared were entered separately for each of 15 Multiple Listing Service zones (results are available from the authors)

Lambda			0.6412	
R-squared	0.9395		0.9510	
Log-likelihood	109 591.50		117 579.37	
Dependent variable	ln(price)		ln(price)	
Number of observations	96 585		96 585	

unheated space there.[9] The value of living space on the main floors increases at a decreasing rate as the size of the house increases. Increases in the age of the house lead to reductions in the price, although the rate of depreciation falls as the house ages. Greater distances to parks and shopping reduce the value of the house. Increasing mean travel times to work reduces house

Table 11.4   Percentage increase in housing prices because of lake proximity

Distance in feet	Index value	Percentage increase
100	0.8054	3.84
500	0.5648	2.68
1 000	0.3845	1.82
2 000	0.1296	0.6
5 000	0	0

prices. All of these relationships are as expected. Almost all of the characteristics are highly significant statistically. The results that allow for spatially correlated errors yield a value for λ, the coefficient for the spatial correlation, of 0.64, and a likelihood-ratio test indicates that the spatial error model is a significant improvement on the non-spatial model.

The coefficients of the lake distance index in the aggregated models can be used to illustrate the interpretation of the results. The index ranges between one at the water's edge and zero at 2640 feet from the lake. The index can be calculated for any distance between those bounds. Given the semi-log specification, $\mathbf{P} = \exp(\mathbf{X}\beta)\exp(\mathbf{I}\gamma)$ where $\mathbf{X}$ represents the matrix of all the characteristics of the houses other than the lake index, $\mathbf{I}$ is the vector for the lake index, and γ is the estimated coefficient of the index. Thus, for any observation, relative impact of the lake proximity is $\exp(\mathbf{I}\gamma) - 1$.[10] The percentage impacts at various distances are reported in Table 11.4, using the estimate from the spatial error model. It seems appropriate that the impact of lake proximity is a percentage of the value of the house rather than an absolute amount because there is evidence that the income elasticity of demand for amenities is greater than one and higher incomes are correlated with more expensive houses. The magnitude of the premium for lake proximity also seems plausible. Finally, the spatial econometrics has a substantial effect on the estimated lake proximity effect. For example, for houses in close proximity to a lake the estimated value is 20 percent greater when one controls for the spatial correlation (3.84 percent vs. 3.18 percent).

The data were also analyzed separately for each year. Rather than report the complete hedonic results, Table 11.5 has the coefficients for the lake distance index for each year and for the aggregated years. Again, the likelihood-ratio tests of the hypothesis that the constraint implicit in the OLS model is valid soundly reject the hypothesis for all years. One would expect that the value of lake proximity would be relatively stable over time, changing slowly as the population and the opportunities with respect to lakes changed. With the OLS estimates the pattern is different than with the

Table 11.5   Nonlinear lake distance index coefficients

Year(s)	OLS	Spatial error	Lambda	LR test
92–99	0.03889	0.04682	0.64117	15 976
	(14.84)	(11.25)		
92	0.05278	0.05534	0.62870	1 310
	(6.78)	(4.57)		
93	0.05278	0.05859	0.61750	1 745
	(7.04)	(5.13)		
94	0.05530	0.05484	0.60700	1 602
	(7.38)	(4.74)		
95	0.03349	0.05404	0.60189	1 381
	(4.71)	(5.00)		
96	0.02338	0.02998	0.56999	1 285
	(3.25)	(2.73)		
97	0.02752	0.05080	0.51638	1 072
	(3.92)	(5.02)		
98	0.02750	0.02555	0.57957	1 574
	(4.21)	(2.59)		
99	0.04113	0.04187	0.61608	1 490
	(4.88)	(3.88)		

R^2s = 0.93 to 0.96

spatial error model. For four of the years the value is high and for four it is low. With the spatial error model, the value is more consistently high, although there are two years that are low. Without focusing on the index, the spatial model is preferable, and for most years the more stable index coefficients seem more plausible. However, the two anomalous years suggest that more research is needed.

4   CONCLUSIONS

The innovations in Brown and Pollakowski (1977) began the long line of research on using property values to value amenities. A great deal has changed since that time, but looking back one can still see how important that work was and how it has influenced subsequent work. In honoring that work, we again have analyzed the value of lake proximity, while taking advantage of the improved data, computer power, and econometrics that are available today. The plausible estimates again confirm the insights from that original article.

The work we have reported can still be extended in a variety of directions. Lakes of different sizes may have different effects. The important issue of public vs. private land surrounding the lakes and the effect of setbacks should be addressed, as they were in Brown and Pollakowski. Other types of surface water, such as rivers and streams, could be incorporated. Finally, the water quality differences in these features need to be addressed. There is still a lot of fertile ground in this research area introduced by Brown and Pollakowski.

NOTES

1. Most attribute the earliest hedonic study to Waugh (1928), where he studied the value of the characteristics of vegetables, although we continue to find early examples (Colwell and Dilmore, 1999, cite land value studies dating back to 1922). A.T. Court (1939) was the first to use the somewhat unfortunate term 'hedonics' for his study of automobile prices. Griliches was the leader in popularizing the technique for estimating price indexes for differentiated products, particularly automobiles (see Griliches, 1961).
2. For an overview of many early policy applications of property value techniques, see Palmquist and Smith (2002).
3. There have been alternatives to the hedonic methodology that have been developed and used with property value data. The innovations in discrete choice modeling have been adapted in random utility models and random bidding models. See Palmquist (2005) for an overview of these types of studies. There have also been models of locational equilibrium, such as Sieg *et al.* (2004), that embed property value considerations in a more general equilibrium model. Nonetheless, hedonic studies of property values continue to dominate the literature by a vast margin.
4. See Anselin and Bera (1998) for a useful summary of the issues.
5. It is also possible to incorporate spatial lags, where the price of the house is influenced by the prices of the neighbors. In this case, the hedonic equation would be $\mathbf{P} = \rho\mathbf{WP} + \mathbf{z}\beta + \mathbf{u}$, where ρ is the spatial parameter to be estimated. The estimating equation becomes $\mathbf{P} = (\mathbf{I} - \rho\mathbf{W})^{-1}\mathbf{z}\beta + (\mathbf{I} - \rho\mathbf{W})^{-1}\mathbf{u}$. In this case, the spatial correlation leads to bias and inefficiency. It is also possible to estimate a general spatial model with both spatial lags and spatial errors when the weights matrices differ between the two processes.
6. http://www.spatial-econometrics.com/.
7. These data were assembled for a research project funded by the Wake County Assessors Office and were used in Fulcher (2003).
8. For example, see Smith *et al.* (2004).
9. Note that, because of the squared term, regheatarea was measured in thousands of square feet, while other areas were measured in squared feet.
10. While the context here is different, the issues are similar to those discussed in Halvorsen and Palmquist (1980).

REFERENCES

Anderson, Jr., R.J. and T.D. Crocker (1969), 'Air pollution and housing: some findings', Institute for Research in the Behavioral, Economic, and Management Sciences, Krannert Graduate School of Industrial Administration, Purdue University.

Anderson, Jr., R.J. and T.D. Crocker (1971), 'Air pollution and residential property values', *Urban Studies*, **8**, 171–80.

Anselin, L. (1988), *Spatial Econometrics: Methods and Models*, Dordrecht: Kluwer.

Anselin, L. and A.K. Bera (1998), 'Spatial dependence in linear regression models with an introduction to spatial econometrics', in A. Ullah and D.E.A. Giles (eds), *Handbook of Applied Economic Statistics*, New York: Marcel Dekker, pp. 237–89.

Brown, Jr., Gardner M. and Henry O. Pollakowski (1977), 'Economic valuation of shoreline', *Review of Economics and Statistics*, **59**, 272–8.

Colwell, Peter F. and Gene Dilmore (1999), 'Who was first? An examination of an early hedonic study', *Land Economics*, **75**, 620–26.

Court, A.T. (1939), 'Hedonic price indexes with automotive examples', *The Dynamics of Automobile Demand*, New York: General Motors, pp. 98–119.

Dornbusch, D.M. and S.M. Barrager (1973), 'Benefit of water pollution control on property values', report to Office of Research and Monitoring, U.S. Environmental Protection Agency, EPA-600/5-73-005.

Dubin, R.A. (1988), 'Estimation of regression coefficients in the presence of spatially autocorrelated error terms', *Review of Economics and Statistics*, **70**, 466–74.

Dubin, R.A. (1992), 'Spatial autocorrelation and neighborhood quality', *Regional Science and Urban Economics*, **22**, 433–52.

Dubin, R., R.K. Pace and T.G. Thibodeau (1999), 'Spatial autoregression techniques for real estate data', *Journal of Real Estate Literature*, **7**, 79–95.

Freeman, A.M. (1971), 'Air pollution and property values: a methodological comment', *Review of Economics and Statistics*, **53**, 415–16.

Freeman, A.M. (1974a), 'Air pollution and property values: a further comment', *Review of Economics and Statistics*, **56**, 554–6.

Freeman, A.M. (1974b), 'On estimating air pollution control benefits from land value studies', *The Journal of Environmental Economics and Management*, **1**, 277–88.

Freeman, A. Myrick (1979), *The Benefits of Environmental Improvement: Theory and Practice*, Baltimore: Resources for the Future.

Freeman, A. Myrick (1982), *Air and Water Pollution Control: a Benefit–Cost Assessment*, New York: Wiley.

Fulcher, C.M. (2003), 'Spatial aggregation and prediction in the hedonic model', PhD dissertation, North Carolina State University.

Gamble, H.B., C.J. Langley, Jr., R.D. Pashek, O.H. Sauerlender, R.D. Twark and R.H. Downing (1973), 'Community effects of highways reflected by property values', report to the Federal Highway Administration, U.S. Department of Transportation.

Griliches, Zvi (1961), 'Hedonic prices for automobiles: an econometric analysis of quality change', *The Price Statistics of the Federal Government*, Government Series Nl. 73, New York: Columbia University Press for the National Bureau of Economic Research.

Halvorsen, R. and R.B. Palmquist (1980), 'The interpretation of dummy variables in semi-logarithmic equations', *American Economic Review*, **70**, 474–5.

Havlicek, Jr., J., R. Richardson and L. Davies (1971), 'Measuring the impacts of solid waste disposal site location on property values', *American Journal of Agricultural Economics*, **53**, 869.

Nelson, J.P. (1975), 'The effects of mobile-source air and noise pollution on residential property values', report to the U.S. Department of Transportation.

Ord, J.K. (1975), 'Estimation methods for models of spatial interaction', *Journal of the American Statistical Association*, **70**, 120–26.

Palmquist, Raymond B. (2005), 'Property value models', in Karl-Göran Mäler and Jeffrey Vincent (eds), *Handbook of Environmental Economics, volume II*, Amsterdam: Elsevier.

Palmquist, Raymond B. and V. Kerry Smith (2002), 'The use of hedonic property value techniques for policy and litigation', in Tom Tietenberg and Henk Folmer (eds), *International Yearbook of Environmental and Resource Economics*, Cheltenham, UK and Northampton, MA, USA: Edward Elgar, pp. 115–64.

Polinsky, A.M. and S. Shavell (1975), 'Air pollution and property value debate', *Review of Economics and Statistics*, **57**, 100–105.

Ridker, R.G. and J.A. Henning (1967), 'The determinants of property values with special reference to air pollution', *Review of Economics and Statistics*, **49**, 246–57.

Rosen, S. (1974), 'Hedonic prices and implicit markets: product differentiation in pure competition', *Journal of Political Economy*, **82**, 34–55.

Sieg, H., V.K. Smith, H.S. Banzhaf and R. Walsh (2004), 'Estimating the general equilibrium benefits of large changes in spatially delineated public goods', *International Economic Review*, **45** (4), 1047–77.

Small, K.A. (1975), 'Air pollution and property values: further comment', *Review of Economics and Statistics*, **57**, 105–7.

Smith, V.K., D.J. Phaneuf and R.B. Palmquist (2004), 'Choice margins and the measurement of ecological benefits: the case of urban watersheds', paper presented at the EPA Workshop, Valuation of Ecological Benefits: Improving Science behind Policy Decisions, Washington, DC, October.

Waugh, F. (1928), 'Quality factors influencing vegetable prices', *Journal of Farm Economics*, **10**, 185–96.

12. From ratings to rankings: the econometric analysis of stated preference ratings data

David F. Layton and S. Todd Lee[1]

1 INTRODUCTION

The Stated Preference (SP) method, widely used in environmental valuation, market research, and transportation research, asks respondents to express their preferences over a set of alternative goods or services. Each alternative is defined by a bundle of underlying attributes. For example, the alternatives may be different recreational trips with typical attributes being the cost of the trip, travel distance, and measures of trip quality. Marketing applications commonly look at preferences for some consumer good (such as shampoo or soda), where the alternatives are different brands or models, and the attributes might be price, packaging characteristics, coupons, or flavors. Transportation research might consider alternatives such as mode of transportation, and the attributes are trip cost, waiting time, and length of trip. The SP approach can be used to forecast the demand for new products, to estimate the welfare impacts of changes in the availability or quality of existing alternatives, or used to examine the public's preferences regarding different governmental policies. Louviere (1988) offers a comprehensive review of the SP approach in transportation research, and Batsell and Louviere (1991) review the use of SP methods in market research.

The general SP method encompasses a variety of different preference elicitation methods. The earliest applications in economics were based on an open-ended elicitation of willingness to pay (WTP) and came to be known as the Contingent Valuation Method (CVM) in the economics literature. Gardner Brown was one of the earliest CVM pioneers with applications to the valuation of migratory waterfowl (Brown and Hammack, 1973) and to sport fishing in Washington State (Brown and Mathews, 1970). We are pleased to follow in his footsteps in discussing our application to sport fishing in Washington State. More recently, SP approaches have favored a number of different discrete choice formulations. These include asking respondents to compare two alternatives (paired comparisons), choose the most preferred from a set of alternatives (choice), rank a set of alternatives (ranking), or to rate on an integer scale (for example, from 1 to 10) each alternative (ratings). The ratings and ranking approaches are often associated with conjoint analysis (Green and Rao, 1971); for a review of the use of conjoint analysis see Green and Srinivasan (1990). To avoid possible confusion, we will use the term 'Stated Preference' (SP) to refer to any survey-based approach that is used to elicit preferences over a set of alternatives and describe the various elicitation methods as rating, ranking, or choice.

A natural question to ask is under what circumstances is a particular elicitation method 'best'? The best approach depends upon the amount of information collected from each respondent, the ability to administer the method reliably, and the availability of econometric methods that are appropriate for each type of data. This chapter is concerned with the latter issue. In particular, it examines appropriate models for ratings-based SP surveys, where the objective is to estimate an aggregate model (not individual models) using the responses from many individuals.

While many economists are more comfortable with preference revelations based on some kind of ordinal comparison, there may be good reasons for using ratings. Many people are familiar with rating exercises from prior experience (for example, customer satisfaction surveys, class evaluations and so on). It also may be a less daunting elicitation technique for respondents than rankings if the number of alternatives is large. Furthermore, in some circumstances such as in a phone survey, choice or ranking exercises may be difficult to administer, necessitating the use of ratings if the researcher wishes the respondent to evaluate a number of alternatives. However, using a rating scale to elicit preferences has come at the cost of imposing, at least some, cardinality on utility functions, and in many applications engaging in interpersonal utility comparisons. These pitfalls have been unavoidable since the frequent presence of tied ratings makes it impossible to convert ratings to the unique rankings required for rank-ordered econometric models. Furthermore, all standard econometric models that are applicable to ordered responses (ratings) impose some degree of cardinality upon preferences.

In this chapter we develop a new approach for recovering preferences from ratings data that are based solely on their ordinal content. This approach is ordinal utility theoretic as it does not require cardinal interpersonal utility comparisons of the kind implied by the use of the standard models (that is, OLS or ordered probit/logit models). This new model also allows for meaningful comparisons of ratings with choices or rankings. In developing our model, we highlight the subtle differences between the ordered probit or logit models that are commonly used to analyze ratings data, and *rank*-ordered logit models commonly used to analyze ordinal rankings.

In the next section we discuss the basic econometric approaches used to recover preferences from ratings and rankings. In section 3 we discuss the difficulties in extracting the ordinal content of ratings data. Section 4 characterizes the ordinal content of ratings data as censored rankings and develops an econometric model suitable for estimation. In section 5 we present an empirical application of our method and compare the results to several ratings models that have been used in the literature. Section 6 concludes with suggestions for extensions and further research.

2   SP ELICITATION METHODS AND STANDARD ECONOMETRIC MODELS

There are two important and related questions about ratings data. First, what is the best approach to recover the preferences over the underlying attributes as revealed by the rating of each alternative? Second, if we asked another set of respondents to choose or rank the same set of alternatives, how can we compare the results of the ratings experiment with a choice or ranking experiment? The typical econometric models used in the analysis of ratings data use fundamentally different information than choice or ranking models. Answering this second question requires developing an approach to extracting the ordinal content of ratings data. This new approach proves to be a useful method for recovering preferences, thus answering the first question.

Our approach begins by assuming task-independence of preferences: preferences over the alternatives are unaffected by the elicitation task (ratings, choice, or rankings). Different tasks result in different observed indicators of preferences, but do not affect preferences themselves. This is a necessary condition if these valuation techniques are to be reliable. If preferences are affected by the elicitation task (task-dependence), then we do not know which are the 'right' preferences. In applications, preferences could be task-dependent; then the task-independence assumption provides a useful null-hypothesis from which to test for departures. Formalizing this, assume that there is a common Random Utility Model (RUM) underlying any elicitation method. From this common unobserved RUM, the different elicitation methods yield different observable responses.

The RUM assumes that individual *i*'s utility associated with each alternative *j*, U_{ij}, are jointly distributed random variables, and that the probability that any U_{ij} equals any *Uik* is zero (see, for example, Block and

Marschak, 1960; Yellot, 1980; Mcfadden, 1981). These assumptions rule out the possibility of ties in unobserved utility. Assume that each individual faces M alternatives, and the total utility is composed of a deterministic component, V_{ij}, which is a function of observable attributes, and a stochastic component, ε_{ij}. Total utility can then be written as:

$$U_{ij} = V_{ij} + \varepsilon_{ij}. \tag{12.1}$$

We assume that we can represent the unobserved utility of any alternative by (12.1). Different elicitation methods yield different *observed* indicators of preferences, Y_{ij}, which are non-invertible transformations of the unobserved U_{ij}. The Y_{ij} for a rating question is a number from the rating scale; the Y_{ij} for a choice experiment can be either viewed as the label of the most preferred alternative or as a vector of dummy variables that equal 1 if the alternative is the most preferred and 0 otherwise; the Y_{ij} for a ranking experiment can be represented as a vector indicating the position of each alternative j in person i's ranking. In order to recover estimates of the V_{ij}, from a given elicitation task, the researcher typically specifies a distribution of the ε_{ij} and then estimates the appropriate model by maximum likelihood.

For SP rank-ordered data, the probability of person i ranking M alternatives, a through m, from most to least preferred, can be represented as

$$P_{i,ab\ldots lm} = Prob\,(U_{i,a} > U_{i,b} > \ldots > U_{i,l} > U_{i,m}). \tag{12.2}$$

Under the assumption of Type I extreme value errors in (12.1), the rank-ordered logit model of Beggs *et al.* (1981) and Chapman and Staelin (1982), which is the rank-ordered extension of McFadden's (1974) conditional logit model, results. Then the probability of a given ranking equals

$$P_{ir} = \prod_{j=1}^{p} \frac{e^{V_{ij}}}{\sum_{k=j}^{m} e^{V_{ik}}}, \tag{12.3}$$

where there are p ranks (p is at most $m-1$) and the alternatives have been ordered from most to least preferred. Rank-ordered multinomial probit models based on the multivariate normal distribution can be estimated as well (Hajivassiliou and Ruud, 1994) as well as rank-ordered random coefficient logit models (Layton, 2000). For SP ratings data, OLS or double hurdle Tobit with the ratings as the dependent variable is sometimes used, but it is better to treat the ratings as ordered categories and to estimate an ordered discrete choice model (Hanemann and Kanninen, 1996). The ordered discrete choice model, first developed by Aitchison and Silvey

(1957) and Ashford (1959), begins by noting that, if a rating r is given for alternative j, then the unobserved utility U_{ij} must lie in some utility interval. That is,

$$\text{if} \quad Y_{ij} = r, \text{then} \quad \alpha_r < U_{ij} < \alpha_{r+1}, \tag{12.4}$$

where the αs are constants to be estimated. Because the U_{ij} are continuous random variables, the inequalities in (12.4) are strict. If we assume a distribution, F, for the ε_{ij}, then the probability of a given alternative receiving a rating of r by person i is

$$P_{ij} = F(\alpha_{r+1} - V_{ij}) - F(\alpha_r - V_{ij}). \tag{12.5}$$

If we number the categories from 1 to R, there are $R-1$ αs to estimate since $\alpha_1 = -\infty$ and $\alpha_{R+1} = +\infty$. Typically, the errors are assumed to be logistically or normally distributed resulting in the familiar ordered logit or probit models. In our application we will assume that F is the Type I extreme value distribution in order to make the estimates from (12.5) comparable to those from the new model to be developed in section 4.

3   THE ORDINAL CONTENT OF RATINGS DATA

A   The Structure of Ratings Data

The primary difficulty with using ratings data to infer preferences is that respondents can give a wide variety of different ratings that are completely consistent with the same underlying ordering of the alternatives. This can manifest itself (1) in tied ratings, (2) in a different mean rating by different respondents, and (3) in different variances (how much of the scale they use).

Table 12.1 illustrates the typical structure of SP ratings data. In this example, 10 different respondents have rated the same seven alternatives, labeled A through G. The rating scale goes from one to ten, with one being the lowest rating and ten being the highest. Each alternative is a bundle of underlying attributes. The ten respondents are broken into pairs that have provided exactly the same ordering using different ratings (Respondent 1 and Respondent 2, Respondent 3 and Respondent 4, . . ., Respondent 9 and Respondent 10). Assuming that each respondent provides ratings that are consistent with their underlying ordering of the alternatives, we will examine each pair's implicit ordering as revealed by their preference ratings.

As is made clear by looking at each pair, there is a wide variety of ways to rate the alternatives and still provide the same underlying ordering.

Table 12.1 An example of ratings data (the ratings scale is 1 to 10)

Respondent	1	2	3	4	5	6	7	8	9	10
Alternative										
A	1	1	1	8	1	5	1	4	2	7
B	2	2	1	8	5	6	1	4	2	7
C	3	6	2	9	5	6	1	4	2	7
D	5	7	2	9	5	6	1	4	2	7
E	6	8	3	10	5	6	1	4	2	7
F	7	9	3	10	5	6	1	4	2	7
G	8	10	3	10	10	7	10	6	2	7
Ordering	Same ordering	Same ordering	Same ordering	Same ordering	Same ordering	Same ordering	Same ordering	Same ordering	Same ordering	Same ordering

Note: The number of ties varies from person to person.

Respondents 1 and 2 have implicitly provided the same, complete ranking of the alternatives (*G* is preferred to *F*, *F* is preferred to *E*, . . ., *B* is preferred to *A*). Respondents 3 and 4 have also provided the same ordering as each other, but have provided less information on the ordering than Respondents 1 and 2. For Respondents 3 and 4, we do not know how alternatives *A* and *B* compare to each other, *C* and *D* compare, and how *E*, *F* and *G* compare. Respondents 5 and 6 have provided a different type of discrimination than the first two pairs. They have implicitly provided their most and least preferred alternatives, with no discrimination among the 'middle' alternatives. Respondents 7 and 8 have provided their most preferred alternative, but we have no information about how the other six alternatives compare to each other. Respondents 9 and 10 have provided no information about the relative merit of any of the seven alternatives since they have each given all the alternatives the same rating.

It may not be obvious, but the example is constructed so that each respondent's preferences are consistent with all of the others in that all of them rate *A* as no better than *B*, *B* as no better than *C*, . . ., and *F* as no better than *G*. That is, the only difference across the five pairs is in the amount and type of discrimination in each respondent's ranking. Clearly the difficulties would be compounded in real world data with heterogeneous preferences.

B   Applying Ordered Models to Ratings Data

Consider using the standard ordered logit or probit model in (12.5) to estimate the indirect utility function for the data in Table 12.1. The model assumes that each respondent interprets the intervals in the rating scale in exactly the same way. Yet it is clear that ordinal utility theory combined with the assumption that people use the scale in a manner consistent with their own ordinal preferences imposes no such restriction on respondents. The use of the ordered model in (12.5) requires an assumption of some degree of cardinality. This assumption makes sense when evaluating the ratings of experts that agree upon the meaning of the scale beforehand. For instance, medical doctors using a rating scale could agree on how each interval is linked to the severity of some disease such as in the level of pneumoconiosis in coal miners analyzed in Crouchley (1995) from Wise and Oldham (1963).

Introspective judgments of personal utility are not subject to the same type of standardization as medical judgments. It is tempting to state that Respondent 3 likes all of the alternatives much less than Respondent 4, but this is an interpersonal utility comparison of the kind that economists typically eschew. Similarly, Respondents 9 and 10 have provided no information about their relative preferences over the alternatives, yet it is tempting to state that Respondent 10 likes all of the alternatives more than Respondent 9. But without some additional information we cannot say anything about their preferences.

The ranking model in (12.2) is fundamentally different from the ratings model of (12.4). The ratings model utilizes inequality restrictions on the U_{ij} with boundaries determined by the additional constants to be estimated. The α_r are not indexed for each person, indicating the boundaries of the interval are determined by information from all respondents, as opposed to the restrictions in (12.2) which use only the respondent's choices to form the boundaries of the intervals. The additional information that can identify ratings preferences for Respondents 9 and 10 is that they use the scale in the same way as others. This is a cardinality assumption that does not appear defensible when using a RUM. Of course it is possible that norms have developed, or surveys provide cues such that people use the scale in the same way. The method we develop in section 4 provides an opportunity for testing this hypothesis.

When based on the RUM assumptions, none of the above models allow for true indifference. In all cases, the unobserved U_{ij} never equals U_{ik} for any i, j. For Respondents 9 and 10 the observed ratings are equal, and some researchers interpret this as indifference, but this is questionable. As is clear from (12.4), if two alternatives are given the same rating, then they lie in the same interval, but this does not constitute indifference per se, but merely closeness. How close two or more tied ratings are, all of which given a rating of r, depends on the values of α_r and α_{r+1}. The unobserved utilities of two alternatives with the same rating may lie very close to each other or very far apart, especially if they lie in the first or last interval. A simple thought experiment makes this clearer. Consider an experiment in which a respondent is asked to rate a set of alternatives on a scale from 1 to 7. Assume they give two of the alternatives a rating of 7. If one were to interpret this as indifference, then if you enlarge the scale (say from 1 to 10) the respondent should still give both alternatives equal ratings no matter how much the scale is enlarged. They might do this, but on the other hand they might give one alternative a 9 and the other 10, invalidating the presumptive indifference from the 7-point scale. The actual ratings given to each alternative will not be independent of the task, but meaningful indifference should be task-independent. In the ranking and choice models, boundaries are also placed on the intervals, again indicating some degree of closeness. The primary difference is that closeness in the ranking and choice models is determined by the other alternatives available to the respondent, whereas in the rating model they are determined by the α_rs which are typically assumed to be common to all respondents. (One can parameterize the αs as functions of covariates as in Deacon and Shapiro, 1975, but then one is still asserting common αs for groups of respondents.)

Most importantly, the ordered rating models use different information than the rank-ordered ranking models. To make this clear, consider Respondents 9 and 10 once again. It is not possible for the model in (12.2) to use this information, because there is no ordinal content in these responses. However, such responses pose no problem for the rating model in (12.4) because of the identifying, but questionable, assumption of a common scale. This makes clear that the ordered logit model for ratings data is a fundamentally different model than the rank-*ordered* logit model for rankings data.

4   AN ORDINAL MODEL FOR RATINGS DATA

As discussed in section 3, ratings data often contain ties. As illustrated by Respondents 1 and 2 in Table 12.1, if there were no ties it would be a simple matter to convert the rating into an implied ranking, and then estimate the model in (12.2). In the presence of ties, no single ranking can describe the ratings data, and so the problem, simply put, is to develop a ranking model which can 'handle' the ties in ratings data or, put another way, to find a representation of ratings data with ties that can be analyzed with a ranking model. Our approach begins by observing that all of the different ways of using the rating scale result in censored or incompletely observed rankings. Censored rankings are rankings in which some portion of the ranking is unobserved by the researcher.

Consider Respondents 1 and 2 as compared to Respondents 3 and 4. The ordinal content or implicit ranking for Respondents 3 and 4 has less information, or more 'holes', when compared to the complete ranking for Respondents 1 and 2. With ties, all we know is that the alternatives that receive the same rating are required to lie in the same interval. We cannot say that the respondent is indifferent between the two alternatives; all we can say is that we do not observe their relative ranking of these two alternatives. This does not mean we have no information on tied alternatives. As long as *all* of the alternatives do not receive the same rating, there are some bounds on the intervals in which the unobserved utilities can lie. Table 12.2 illustrates the information implicit in Respondent 3's and 4's ratings and how it compares to the complete ranking for Respondents 1 and 2.

For Respondents 3 and 4, we do not know whether D is preferred to C, or C is preferred to D, but we do know that both C and D are preferred to A and B, and similarly for E, F and G. The ranking for Respondents 3 and 4

Table 12.2   Implicit rankings for respondents 1–4

Complete ranking by respondents 1 and 2	Censored ranking by respondents 3 and 4
G>F	
F>E	
E>D	G>D, F>D, E>D
D>C	G>C, F>C, E>C
C>B	D>B, C>B
B>A	D>A, C>A

Note: '>' means revealed preferred by the rating.

is censored in the sense that we lose or do not observe some portions of the complete ranking.

What makes extracting the ordinal content from ratings data difficult is not only the censoring, but the fact that each respondent can have a different form of censoring. Ratings data results in endogenously censored rankings. For example, returning to Table 12.1, Respondents 7 and 8 have a form of censoring that is easy to handle. For these persons the censored ranking can be seen to be equivalent to eliciting a most preferred choice. A most preferred choice tells the researcher what is most preferred, but provides no information on the relative ranking of the less preferred alternatives. Less familiar censored rankings such as provided by Respondents 3 and 4 can be treated with a common model for all respondents if everyone in the sample was asked to provide that type of ordering. A strange question would yield data with the ordinal content of Respondents 3 and 4: 'Please tell us what your three most preferred alternatives are, your next two, and your last two.' An econometric model for this type of data would be complicated, but at least it would have the advantage that it could be applied to all respondents since everyone provided the same type of ordering (same censored ranking). What makes ratings data so difficult is that the censoring is endogenous to each individual. An approach that can handle endogenously censored rankings is needed.

Mcfadden (1986) points out that there is a logical link between ranking probabilities and choice probabilities. (For discussions of related results, see also Barbera and Pattanaik, 1986; Block and Marschak, 1960; Falmagne, 1978; and Yellot, 1980.) First consider a standard most preferred choice problem for four alternatives where alternative a is preferred to alternatives b, c, d (we are not referring to Table 12.1). The standard choice probability, P_a, that alternative a is preferred to alternatives b, c, d, can be calculated as the sum of the probabilities of all rankings that yield *a* as most preferred. After dropping the *i* subscripts the probability that *a* is most preferred, P_a is

$$P_a = P_{abcd} + P_{abdc} + P_{acbd} + P_{acdb} + P_{adbc} + P_{adcb}, \qquad (12.6)$$

where for instance, P_{abcd} means the probability of the complete ranking $a > b > c > d$.

The sample space for *M* alternatives can be viewed as the set of all *M!* (factorial) mutually exclusive complete rankings. We can calculate the choice probability in (12.6) by summing the probabilities for each of the mutual exclusive rankings in which *a* is first. This provides the link to representing the probability of a censored ranking. The probability of any censored ranking can be represented as the sum of the probabilities of some set of complete rankings. The same form of probability in (12.6) would apply to Respondents 7 and 8 in Table 12.1 after adjusting for the number of alternatives. As another example, suppose that all we knew was that *a* was first and *d* was last out of *a, b, c, d*; then the probability of this occurrence could be represented by

$$P_a \ is \ first, \ d \ is \ last = P_{abcd} + P_{acbd}. \qquad (12.7)$$

After adjusting for the number of alternatives, (12.7) provides the form of the censored ranking probability for Respondents 5 and 6 in Table 12.1.

The general approach for defining the probability of any censored ranking amounts to summing the probabilities of all possible rankings in which all alternatives that are preferred to other alternatives are placed higher in the ranking. For each individual, the censored ranking can be defined as follows. Let $x(j)$ be a number from 1 to *M* that assigns the position of each alternative *j* in a given ranking, with $x(j) = 1$ being the highest or first rank. For *M* alternatives there are *M!* different complete rankings. Let $r(j)$ be the rating of alternative *j*, with higher ratings meaning 'more preferred'. Then the set of *Z* complete rankings needed to compute the probability of a censored ranking is defined by all permutations of $x(j)$ such that

$$x(j) < x(k) \quad \text{if} \quad r(j) \geq r(k) \ \forall \ k, j. \qquad (12.8)$$

If a respondent gives no alternatives the same rating, then the $\geq$ in the second part of the 'if' statement could be replaced by a strict inequality and the ratings data for this respondent could be represented with only one ranking.

Let n_r be the number of alternatives that a respondent gives a rating equal to r. Then, Z, the total number of rankings needed to compute the probability of the censored ranking, M, the total number of alternatives rated, and n_r, are related by

$$Z = \prod_{r=lowest}^{r=highest} n_r! \quad \text{and} \quad M = \sum_{r=lowestcategory}^{r=highestcategory} n_r \quad , \qquad (12.9)$$

where r is a particular rating category and the product is over all of the possible rating categories. Note that $0! = 1$, so that (12.9) is defined over all possible ratings, not just the ratings actually given. If we number the different rankings from 1 to Z, (in any order), then the probability P_i of observing the censored ranking for individual i is

$$P_i = \sum_{z=1}^{z=Z} P(z), \qquad (12.10)$$

where z denotes a particular ranking, and $P(z)$ is the probability of a given ranking z.

Using the data in Table 12.1, Table 12.3 shows the number of complete rankings needed to represent each respondent's censored ranking calculated using (12.9). Respondents 1 and 2 only need one complete ranking since their ranking was not censored, while Respondents 9 and 10 need the entire feasible set of rankings. Since the probability is calculated using (12.10), it is clear the probability will always sum to 1 for Respondents 9 and 10 for any indirect utility function since their set of needed rankings exhausts the sample space. This formalizes the fact that providing no ordinal information does not allow us to identify any aspect of their preferences.

Finally, if one imagines that a respondent really was indifferent between some alternatives so that the probability of picking any of them is equal, then the censored ranking model as formulated here is consistent with indifference. So while the censored ranking model does not assume that the respondent is indifferent between alternatives given the same rating, it in no way precludes it.

Table 12.3   *Number of rankings needed to represent the censored ranking for the ratings in Table 12.1**

Respondent	1	2	3	4	5	6	7	8	9	10
Number of rankings	1	1	24	24	120	120	720	720	5040	5040

Note: *Calculated using (12.9).

In (12.10), any econometric model for rankings will work. A natural candidate is the rank-ordered logit model in (12.3). It has a positive feature in that it is tractable and the probabilities of the entire set of rankings are guaranteed to sum to one. While it of course embodies the undesirable Independence of Irrelevant Alternatives assumption, we illustrate the approach based on this more tractable model. For an example of how the basic approach can be extended to alternative types of data and more complex error distributions using Markov chain Monte Carlo methods, see Layton and Levine (2003).

5 AN EMPIRICAL APPLICATION

In this section we present an empirical application of the censored ranking model, and compare the relative estimated parameter values to several ratings models that have been used in the literature. The censored ranking model which is based only upon ordinal information from each respondent is preferable to the various other models for theoretical reasons. We believe much is gained by using a fully ordinal econometric model to estimate preference parameters. Our purpose here is to demonstrate that the standard ratings model and various ratings transformations found in the literature may give quite different results, whether compared to the censored ranking model or to each other.

Our data are from an SP survey of Washington State trout anglers, by Lee (1996). All data were collected through a telephone survey that was completed in 1994. The sample we use here consists of 555 respondents. Respondents were asked to rate, on a scale from one to 10, their most recent fishing trip based on their catch, the average size of the fish caught, the number of fish they were allowed to keep, tackle restrictions and trip cost. They were then asked to rate four proposed trips composed of the same attributes, but with varying levels of the attributes. The attribute levels are presented below.

Catch per day:	{2, 5, 10, 20}
Average size (inches):	{6, 10, 14, 20}
Number allowed to keep:	{0, 2, 5}
Tackle regulations:	{any tackle, artificial flies and lures only}
Price per day ($):	{5, 15, 30, 50}

The proposed trips were constructed using a main-effect, asymmetric, fractional–factorial design (Addelman, 1962). A set of 32 trip combinations were derived out of the $4 \times 4 \times 3 \times 2 \times 4 = 384$ possible combinations. The 32 trip combinations were chosen such that the attribute vectors are orthogonal. Four of the trip attribute combinations were deemed unrealistic or possibly confusing to respondents. One attribute level of each of these trips was adjusted; 8 blocks of 4 trips each were created and randomly assigned to each respondent. For more details on the survey design, pretesting, and sampling, see Lee (1996).

Table 12.4 shows the number of respondents that require each possible combination of complete rankings to evaluate the probability of providing their censored rankings. The vast majority of the respondents (84 percent) had at least two tied ratings. The complete sample of 555 respondents require 2901 rankings to represent their censored rankings. Three people provided tied ratings to all five trips and therefore provide no ordinal information. These three respondents (and their 360 required rankings) can be dropped from the estimation resulting in 552 respondents with a total of 2541 required rankings. In the standard rating model (we call this model *Ordered Rating*), each trip rating is treated as a single observation, resulting in a total of 2775 observations (555 respondents rated an actual trip plus four proposed trips). Note that the three respondents who provided all ties can be included in this model, and we do so because in applications of ordered models they typically are included. We also estimate three models based on ad hoc ratings transformations that have been discussed in the economic valuation literature.

Table 12.4   Number of rankings needed to represent the fishing survey ratings data

Number of rankings needed	Description of ties in the ratings	Number of respondents
1	zero tied ratings	89
2	two tied ratings	232
4	two tied ratings + two different tied ratings	89
6	three tied ratings	84
12	three tied ratings + two different tied ratings	22
24	four tied ratings	36
120	five tied ratings	3
Total = 2901 (2541)*		Total = 555 (552)*

Note: *The number in parentheses is the number actually needed after dropping the three people with completely tied ratings.

A   Ad Hoc Approaches to Using Ratings Data

In an attempt to deal with the wide variation possible in ratings for the same underlying ordering, Roe *et al.* (1996) suggested that the ratings be differenced with respect to the rating for some baseline or status quo alternative. (Another motivation that Roe *et al.*, 1996, provide for differencing the ratings is based on the derivation of the compensating variation welfare measure from ratings data.) For instance, in Table 12.1 we might use alternative *A* as the baseline, and subtract its rating for each respondent from the ratings for *B* through *G*. This method will remove rating differences attributed to the use of different mean ratings by different respondents. For example, a major difference between Respondents 3 and 4 is the fact that Respondent 3 used the lower part of the scale and Respondent 4 used the upper part. For both Respondents 3 and 4, the rating for *G* minus the rating for *A* is 2. Thus for these two respondents the differencing approach resolves a major problem. However, for Respondent 5 this difference is 9 while for Respondent 6 it is only 2. So this method does not account for variation in the amount of the scale used. The rating difference model of Roe *et al.* (1996) we estimate (called *Rating_D*) is based on differencing the rating from each of the four proposed trips with respect to the rating of the angler's actual trip. For these data this expands the number of rating categories from 10 to 19, and the associated category break points (constant + αs) from 9 to 18. This model results in 2220 total observations.

Mackenzie (1993) suggested an approach to facilitate a comparison of ratings and rankings. The idea is to make the ratings look more ranking-like by contracting the rating scale so that it has the same number of categories as there are alternatives. One then interprets this new rating as indicating 'ranks', and estimates the model by a standard ordered rating model. In Table 12.1 this would mean contracting the scale to seven categories. While this ratings transformation might remove some of the noise inherent in ratings data, it does not avoid the main concerns. Clearly problems arise when respondents give two or more alternatives the same rating. The extreme case is exemplified by looking at Respondents 9 and 10. Should all of the alternatives be recoded as being ranked first or ranked last, or perhaps ranked fourth? This same problem, in a less severe but still important form, occurs with as few as two tied alternatives. Should they share the upper or lower 'rank'? As shown for Respondents 9 and 10, the ad hoc recoding process essentially involves the researcher stating how 'good' or 'bad' all the alternatives are. The model estimated by Mackenzie (1993) and subsequently by Roe *et al.* (1996) gave all tied ratings the highest ranking they can share, and then the next, if any, lower rated trips are ranked by skipping the appropriate number of ranks (the number of ties minus one). We call this model *Ordered Rank_Up*. This model reduces the number of ratings categories from 10 to five. Since there is no a priori reason to make all tied ratings share their highest rank as opposed to the lowest rank, we estimate a model where tied ratings share their lowest common rank. We call this model *Ordered Rank_Down*. Both of these models have a total of 2775 observations.

B Results

All five models are estimated by maximum likelihood in GAUSS using a linear indirect utility function. The ratings and the three ratings transformation models are estimated using the ordered categorical model in (12.5). All of the models are based on the RUM formulation in (12.1) with the errors assumed to be from the Type I extreme value distribution. For the ratings and ratings transformation models, this choice of distribution is not common, but it has been discussed by others (see Crouchley, 1995). This allows us to use the same error distribution as in our censored ranking model which is based on the rank-ordered logit probability in (12.3). Each of the model's parameter estimates and t-statistics are presented in Table 12.5. The censored ranking model ran in about 30 seconds on a PC.

All of the models perform quite well in terms of the significance of the parameter estimates. In order to compare the ordered models to the censored ranking model, we calculate a ratio of the attribute parameter estimates for each model. We divide the estimated fishing trip attributes parameters by the estimated price parameter. This ratio is particularly relevant since it provides an estimate of the marginal willingness to pay (MWTP) for each attribute. The MWTP estimates and their simulated confidence intervals are presented in Table 12.6.

Most of the ordered models provide at least one MWTP estimate that is relatively close (within 4 percent) of the censored ranking model's estimate. However, most of the models provide some MWTP estimates that are not very close to the censored ranking model's estimates. Not surprisingly, there are also some relatively large differences in the MWTP estimates among the four ordered models. The confidence intervals were simulated using the method proposed by Krinsky and Robb (1986). One might expect that, if there were comparable and useful cardinal information across respondent's ratings, the confidence intervals of the ordered models (especially the ordered rating model) would be tighter than those of the censored ranking model. With our data, we find that the censored ranking model's confidence intervals are at least as small as those of the four ordered models.

Table 12.7 shows how the MWTP estimates differ in the various ordered models in comparison to the censored ranking model. Of the four ordered

Table 12.5   Econometric model estimates*

Attribute	Econometric models				
	Censored ranking	Ordered rating	Ordered rating_d	Ordered rank_up	Ordered rank_down
Catch	0.0271	0.0135	0.0092	0.0192	0.0172
	(6.37)	(5.73)	(3.63)	(7.34)	(5.61)
Size	0.1097	0.0630	0.0400	0.0716	0.0850
	(16.12)	(14.25)	(13.39)	(16.95)	(17.33)
Keep	0.1913	0.1393	0.0614	0.1093	0.1551
	(14.11)	(17.59)	(7.97)	(13.66)	(17.61)
Reg.	−0.2034	−0.0857	−0.0805	−0.1669	−0.1861
	(−3.55)	(−2.04)	(−2.76)	(−4.22)	(−4.01)
Price	−0.0251	−0.0140	−0.0084	−0.017	−0.0193
	(−13.51)	(−10.70)	(−9.28)	(−13.49)	(−12.91)
Constant		−0.1733	1.3854	0.1945	−0.7618
α_1		0.2337	0.1416	0.6951	0.5063
α_2		0.4385	0.3583	1.3225	1.1779
α_3		0.6380	0.5687	2.1138	2.2046
α_4		1.1020	0.7926		
α_5		1.3247	1.0564		
α_6		1.6942	1.2691		
α_7		2.3958	1.5084		
α_8		2.7497	1.7656		
α_9			2.2708		
α_{10}			2.5929		
α_{11}			2.9987		
α_{12}			3.5049		
α_{13}			3.9221		
α_{14}			4.5398		
α_{15}			5.1615		
α_{16}			5.8030		
α_{17}			6.2308		
N	552	2775	2220	2775	2775
Log-L	−1700.31	−5870.96	−5894.41	−4073.53	−3987.26

Note: *t-statistics are in parentheses; the standard errors for the constant and α estimates are available from the authors by request.

Table 12.6   Attribute marginal willingness to pay (MWTP) in $ and confidence intervals*

Attribute	Model	MWTP	95% Confidence intervals	
Catch	Censored Ranking	1.08	0.74,	1.45
	Ordered Rating	0.96	0.61,	1.40
	Ordered Rating_D	1.09	0.50,	1.79
	Ordered Rank_Up	1.13	0.81,	1.50
	Ordered Rank_Down	0.89	0.56,	1.27
Size	Censored Ranking	4.37	3.69,	5.24
	Ordered Rating	4.49	3.60,	5.68
	Ordered Rating_D	4.76	3.74,	6.20
	Ordered Rank_Up	4.23	3.53,	5.16
	Ordered Rank_Down	4.40	3.66,	5.34
Keep	Censored Ranking	7.62	6.20,	9.44
	Ordered Rating	9.92	7.88,	12.81
	Ordered Rating_D	7.30	5.24,	10.16
	Ordered Rank_Up	6.45	5.09,	8.23
	Ordered Rank_Down	8.03	6.52,	9.95
Reg.	Censored Ranking	−8.10	−12.89,	−3.46
	Ordered Rating	−6.10	−12.53,	−0.14
	Ordered Rating_D	−9.57	−17.02,	−2.74
	Ordered Rank_Up	−9.84	−15.00,	−5.15
	Ordered Rank_Down	−9.63	−14.94,	−4.82

Note: *Confidence intervals were simulated using the Krinsky and Robb (1986) method with 10 000 simulations.

Table 12.7   Percentage difference in MWTP relative to the censored ranking model

Attribute	Econometric model			
	Ordered rating X	Ordered rating_d	Ordered rank_up	Ordered rank_down
Catch	−11.1	1.3	5.1	−17.4
Size	2.7	8.9	−3.3	0.7
Keep	30.3	−4.2	−15.4	5.4
Reg.	−24.7	18.1	21.5	18.9
Mean absolute percentage difference	17.1	8.1	11.3	10.6

models, the ordered rating model's results diverge the most from the censored ranking model. The mean absolute percentage difference from the censored ranking model is over 17 percent. The rating difference model appears to give the closest estimates to those of the censored ranking model. However, several of the MWTP estimates are not very close, and the mean absolute percentage difference is 8.1 percent. The two pseudo-ranking models perform about equally well overall, however their point estimates of MWTP often diverge greatly from each other. Most importantly, there is no pattern to the differences between the various rating models and the censored ranking model, and there is no method for predicting the magnitude or even the direction of the differences.

The divergence between the various ad hoc pseudo-ranking transformations will depend upon the number of ties, and the number of ties, in turn, depends upon the number of alternatives rated and the rating scale, all other things equal. In some applications, the use of pseudo-ranking transformations may not bias the results greatly, but to know this one would first have to estimate the theoretically correct model. In practice, many conjoint applications ask respondents to rate 16 or more alternatives. Combined with a seven or ten-point scale this insures a great number of ties, and therefore the ad hoc approaches are more likely to prove unsatisfactory. Finally, to reiterate, the differences between the ratings model and the correct censored ranking model depend upon the ties which are themselves endogenous, and the degree and direction of divergence will be different for different parameters, and across different data sets.

6   CONCLUSION

The SP ratings elicitation approach may have practical advantages in applications where ranking every single alternative is too hard, the survey is administered over the phone, or for other reasons. The censored ranking model we developed allows the use of ratings data, without having to resort to cardinality assumptions or interpersonal utility comparisons. The censored ranking model is tractable, and can be extended for use with any econometric model that is appropriate for handling rank-ordered data. Open questions remain about the relative efficiency and reliability of ratings-based versus rankings or choice-based survey elicitation methods. Since the censored ranking model utilizes only the ordinal content of ratings data, and is a direct extension and completely compatible with standard discrete choice or rankings models, these questions can now be rigorously examined.

NOTE

1. We thank Prasad A. Naik for very helpful comments on an earlier draft of this chapter.

REFERENCES

Addelman, S. (1962), 'Orthogonal main-effect plans for asymmetrical factorial experiments', *Technometrics*, **4**, 21–46.

Aitchison, J. and S.D. Silvey (1957), 'The generalization of probit analysis to the case of multiple responses', *Biometrika*, **44**, 131–40.

Ashford, J.R. (1959), 'An approach to the analysis of data for semiquantal responses in biological response', *Biometrics*, **15**, 573–81.

Barbera, S. and P.K. Pattanaik (1986), 'Falmagne and the rationalizability of stochastic choices in terms of random orderings', *Econometrica*, **54**, 707–15.

Batsell, R.R. and J.J. Louviere (1991), 'Experimental analysis of choice', *Marketing Letters*, **2**, 199–214.

Beggs, S., S. Cardell and J. Hausman (1981), 'Assessing the potential demand for electric cars', *Journal of Econometrics*, **16**, 1–19.

Block, H.D. and J. Marschak (1960), 'Random ordering and stochastic theories of responses', in I. Olkin, S.G. Ghurye, W. Hoeffding, W.G. Madow and H.B. Mann (eds), *Contributions to Probability and Statistics: Essays in Honor of Harold Hotelling*, Stanford, CA: Stanford University Press.

Brown, Jr., G.M. and J. Hammack (1973), 'Dynamic economic management of migratory waterfowl', *The Review of Economics and Statistics*, **55**, 73–82.

Brown, Jr., G.M. and S. Mathews (1970), 'Economic valuation of the 1967 sport salmon fishery of Washington', Washington Department of Fisheries Bulletin, Technical Report 2.

Chapman, R.G. and R. Staelin (1982), 'Exploiting rank ordered choice set data within the stochastic utility model', *Journal of Marketing Research*, **19**, 288–301.

Crouchley, R. (1995), 'A random-effects model for ordered categorical data', *Journal of the American Statistical Association*, **90**, 489–98.

Deacon, R. and P. Shapiro (1975), 'Private preference for collective goods revealed through voting on referenda', *American Economic Review*, **65**, 943–55.

Falmagne, J.C. (1978), 'A representation theorem for finite scale systems', *Journal of Mathematical Psychology*, **18**, 52–72.

Green, P.E. and V.R. Rao (1971), 'Conjoint measurement for quantifying judgmental data', *Journal of Marketing Research*, **8**, 355–63.

Green, P.E. and V. Srinivasan (1990), 'Conjoint analysis in marketing: new developments with implications for research and practice', *Journal of Marketing*, **54**, 3–19.

Hajivassiliou, V.A. and P.A. Ruud (1994), 'Classical estimation methods for LDV models using simulation', in R.F. Engle and D.L. McFadden (eds), *Handbook of Econometrics*, vol. 4, Amsterdam: Elsevier Science Publishers.

Hanemann, W.M. and B. Kanninen (1996), 'The statistical analysis of discrete-response CV data', in I.J. Bateman and K.G. Willis (eds), *Valuing Environmental Preferences: Theory and Practice of the Contingent Valuation Method in the US, EC, and Developing Countries*, Oxford: Oxford University Press.

Krinsky, I. and A.L. Robb (1986), 'On approximating the statistical properties of elasticities', *The Review of Economics and Statistics*, **68**, 715–19.

Layton, D.F. (2000), 'Random coefficient models for stated preference surveys', *Journal of Environmental Economics and Management*, **40**, 21–36.

Layton, D.F. and R. Levine (2003), 'How much does the far future matter? A hierarchical Bayesian analysis of the public's willingness to mitigate ecological impacts of climate change', *Journal of the American Statistical Association*, **98**, 533–44.

Lee, S.T. (1996), 'The Economics of Recreational Fishing', PhD dissertation, University of Washington.

Louviere, J.J. (1988), 'Conjoint analysis modelling of stated preferences', *Journal of Transport Economics and Policy*, **22**, 93–119.

McFadden, D. (1974), 'Conditional logit analysis of qualitative choice behavior', in P. Zarembka (ed.), *Frontiers in Econometrics*, New York: Academic Press.

McFadden, D. (1981), 'Econometric models of probabilistic choice', in C.F. Manski and D. McFadden (eds), *Structural Analysis of Discrete Choice Data with Econometric Applications*, Cambridge, MA: MIT Press.

McFadden, D. (1986), 'The choice theory approach to market research', *Marketing Science*, **5**, 275–97.

Mackenzie, J. (1993), 'A comparison of contingent preference models', *American Journal of Agricultural Economics*, **75**, 593–603.

Roe, B., K.J. Boyle and M.F. Teisl (1996), 'Using conjoint analysis to derive estimates of compensating variation', *Journal of Environmental Economics and Management*, **31**, 145–59.

Wise, M.E. and P.P. Oldham (1963), 'Estimating progression of coal-workers' simple pneumoconiosis from reading of radiological categories', *British Journal of Industrial Medicine*, **20**, 124–44.

Yellott, Jr., J.I. (1980), 'Generalized Thurstone models for ranking: equivalence and reversibility', *Journal of Mathematical Psychology*, **22**, 48–69.

Appendix Publications of Gardner M. Brown, Jr

'Different property rights regimes in the Lake Victoria multiple species fishery', with B. Berger and M. Ikiara, *Environment and Development Economics*, **10** (1), 53–65, 2005.

'Using antibiotics when resistance is renewable', with R. Rowthorn, in R. Laxminarayan (ed.), *Battling Resistance to Antibiotics and Pesticides: An Economic Approach*, Resources for the Future, 2003.

'A market solution for preserving biodiversity: the black rhino', with D. Layton, in Shogren and J. Tschirardt (eds), *Protecting Endangered Species in the United States: Biological Needs, Political Realities, and Economic Choices*, Cambridge University Press, 2001.

'Economics of antibiotic resistance: a theory of optimal use', with R. Laxminarayan, *Journal of Environmental Economics and Management*, **42**, 183–206, 2001.

'Heterogeneous preferences regarding global climate change', with D. Layton, *Review of Economics and Statistics*, **82**, 616–24, 2000.

'Renewable natural resource management and use without markets', *Journal of Economic Literature*, **38** (4), 875–914, 2000.

'Why economics matters for endangered species protection and the ESA', with J. Shogren, J. Tschirhart *et al.*, *Conservation Biology*, **13** (6), 1257–61, 1999.

'When a high discount rate encourages biodiversity', with R. Rowthorn, *International Economic Review*, **40** (2), 315–32, 1999.

'Economics of the Endangered Species Act', with J. Shogren, *Journal of Economic Perspectives*, **12** (3), 3–20, 1998.

'A metapopulation model with private property and a common pool', with J. Roughgarden, *Ecological Economics*, **22** (1), 65–71, 1997.

'Benefits of biodiversity evaluation: why biodiversity valuation is imperative', *Investing in Biological Diversity: The Cairns Conference*, OECD, 1997.

'Management of wildlife and habitat in developing economies', in P. Dasgupta and K.-G. Mäler (eds), *Environment and Emerging Development Issues*, Oxford University Press, 1997.

'Resistance economics: social cost and the evolution of antibiotic resistance', with D. Layton, *Environment and Development Economics*, **1** (3), 349–55, 1996.

'Biodiversity, economic growth and the discount rate', with R. Rowthorn, in T. Swanson (ed.), *The Economics and Ecology of Biodiversity Decline*, Cambridge University Press, 1995.

'Economic values of biodiversity', with E. Barbier *et al.*, in V.H. Heywood (ed.), *Global Biodiversity Assessment*, United Nations Environment Programme, Cambridge University Press, 1995.

'An ecological economy: notes on harvest and growth', with Jonathan Roughgarden, in C. Perrings, K.-G. Mäler, C. Folke, C.S. Holling and Bengt-Jansson (eds), *Biodiversity Loss, Economic and Ecological Issues*, Cambridge University Press, 1995.

'Estimating non-use values requires interdisciplinary research', in B. Burgenmeier (ed.), *Economy, Environment and Technology: A Socioeconomic Approach*, M.E. Sharpe, 1994.

'The marginal cost of species preservation: the northern spotted owl', with C. Montgomery and D. Adams, *Journal of Environmental Economics and Management*, **26**, 1994; reprinted in K. Willis, K. Button and P. Nijkemp (eds), *Environmental Valuation*, vol. 1, Edward Elgar, 1999; The International Library of Environmental Economics and Policy, *Economics of Forestry*, Ashgate Publishing Ltd, 2003.

'The inefficiency of decentralized non-renewable resource extraction: the case of soviet timber', with K.-Y. Wong, *Journal of Environmental Economics and Management*, **25** (3), 212–34, 1993.

'Economics of natural resource damage assessment: a critique', in R. Kopp and V.K. Smith (eds), *Valuing Natural Assets: The Economics of Natural Resource Damage Assessment*, Resources for the Future, 1993.

'The viewing value of elephants', in E.B. Barbier (ed.), *Economics and Ecology: New Frontiers and Sustainable Development*, ch.9, Chapman and Hall, 1993.

'Rural amenities and the beneficiaries-pay-principle', Rural Development Program, OECD, 1993.

'Economics of species preservation', with C. Montgomery, *Contemporary Policy Issues*, **10**, 1992.

The Preservation and Valuation of Biological Resources, edited with G. Orians, W. Kunin and J. Swierzbinski, University of Washington Press, 1990.

'Methods for valuing acidic deposition and air pollution effects, Part A', with Mark Plummer, National Acid Precipitation Assessment Program, SOS/T Report no. 27, December, 1989.

'The economic value of elephants', with W. Henry, International Institute for Environment and Development, LEEC Paper 89-12, London Environmental Economics Centre, 1989.

'The viewing value of elephants', prepared for the Ivory Trade Review Group, Oxford, 1989.

'Optimal genetic resources in the context of asymmetric public goods', in *Essays in Honor of John Krutilla*, Johns Hopkins Press, 1988.

'Valuing Oregon salmon by using a multimarket, hedonic travel-cost method', in D. Hueth *et al.* (eds), *Sport Fishing: A Comparison of Three Indirect Methods for Estimating Benefits*, U.S. Department of Agriculture, Pacific Northwest Research Sta. Res. paper PNW-RP-395, 1988.

'Net economic recreation values for deer and waterfowl hunting and trout fishing, 1980', with M. Hay, U.S. Fish and Wildlife Service, Div. of Policy and Directives Management, working paper no. 23, 1987.

'Optimal recovery paths for perturbations, trophic level bioeconomic systems', with J. Wilen, *Journal of Environmental Economics and Management*, **13** (3), 225–34, 1986.

'Estimating the cost of oil spills: lessons from the AMOCO-CADIZ incident', with T. Grigalunas *et al.*, *Marine Resource Economics*, 1986.

'When do bells and whistles make finer music? Static versus dynamic models in fishery management', in E. Miles *et al.* (eds), *Essays in Honor of James Crutchfield*, University of Washington Press, 1986.

'Preserving endangered species and other biological resources', *Richerche Economiche*, **39**, 4 (Oct.–Dec. 1985); reprinted in *The Science of the Total Environment*, **56**, 1986.

'Harvest policies and non-market valuation in a predator–prey system', with D. Ragozin, *Journal of Environmental Economics and Management*, **12**, 1985.

'Endangered species, genetic capital and cost reducing R&D', with J. Swierzbinski, International Symposium on Economics of Ecosystem Management, September, 1983, Halkadiki, Greece; reprinted in D.O. Hall, N. Myers and N.S. Margaris (eds), *Economics of Ecosystem Management*, pp. 111–27, 1985.

'The effluent charge system in the Federal Republic of Germany', with Ralph Johnson, Office of Policy Analysis, EPA, July, 1985.

'Economic instruments: alternatives or supplements to regulations?', in OECD, *Environment and Economics Issue Papers*, International Conference, June, 1984.

'Economic instruments: review and outlook', in OECD, *Environment and Economics*, Background Papers, vol. 11, International Conference, June, 1984.

'The hedonic travel cost method', with R. Mendelsohn, *Review of Economics and Statistics*, **66** (3), 427–33, 1984.

'A model for valuing endangered species', *Journal of Environmental Economics and Management*, **11** (4), 303–9, 1984.

'Pollution control by effluent charges: it works in the Federal Republic of Germany, why not in the U.S.?', with Ralph W. Johnson, *The Natural*

Resources Journal, October, 1984; reprinted in S. Renzetti (ed.), *The Economics of Industrial Water Use*, Edward Elgar, 2002.

'Revealed preference approaches to valuing outdoor recreation', with R. Mendelsohn, *Natural Resources Journal*, **23** (3), 607–18, 1983.

'Tourists and Residents', ch.4 in NOAA, *Assessing the Economic Damage of Oil Spills: The AMOCO CADIZ Case Study*, February/March, 1983.

'Optimal harvest policies in a predator–prey system', with David Ragozin in R. Lamberson, *Mathematical Models of Renewable Resources*, Humboldt State University Mathematical Modeling Group, 1982.

Economics of Ocean Resources, ed. with J. Crutchfield, Washington Sea Grant, 1982.

'Estimating non-market economic losses from oil spills: AMOCO CADIZ, Steuart Transportation, and Zoe Colocotroni', in *The Cost of Oil Spills*, OECD, Paris, 1982.

'Steel and energy substitution in U.S. manufacturing 1947–1971', with V. Gamponia, *Southern Economic Journal*, **48** (3), 785–91, 1982.

'Recreation', in G. Brown and J. Crutchfield (eds), *Economics of Ocean Resources*, Washington Sea Grant, 1982.

'Partial and full elasticities of substitution and the energy capital complementarity controversy', with Heejoon Kang in E. Berndt and Barry Field (eds), *Modelling and Measuring Natural Resource Substitution*, MIT Press, Cambridge, 1981.

'Recreation valuation', in J. Powell and G. Loh, 'An Economic Analysis of Non-Timber Use of Forest Land in the Pacific Northwest', Forest Policy Project, Pacific Northwest Regional Commission, Vancouver, Washington (May), 1981.

'Characterizing a production or a cost function by elasticities of substitution', with H. Kang, *Review of Economic Studies*, **47** (5), 1003–4, 1980.

'An assessment of water quality management policies in selected industrialized countries', with J.Ph. Barde and P.-F. Teniere-Buchot, *Ambio*, 1979.

'Economic valuation of shoreline: a reply', with H. Pollakowski, *Review of Economics and Statistics*, **61** (4), 635–6, 1979.

'The adequacy of measures for signaling the scarcity of natural resources', with B. Field, in V. Kerry Smith (ed.), *Scarcity and Growth Reconsidered*, Johns Hopkins University Press, pp. 218–48, 1979.

'Criteria for an appropriate institutional structure', in H. Siebert *et al.* (eds), *Regional Environmental Policy: The Economic Issues*, New York University Press, 1979.

'Implications of alternative measures of natural resource scarcity', with B. Field, *Journal of Political Economy*, **86** (2, part 1), 229–43, 1978.

'The value of wildlife estimated by the hedonic approach', with J. Charbonneau and M. Hay, U.S. Fish and Wildlife Service, Division of Program Plans, working paper no. 6, Washington, DC, 1978.

'Estimating values of wildlife: analysis of the 1975 hunting and fishing survey', with J. Charbonneau and M. Hay, U.S. Fish and Wildlife Service, Division of Program Plans, working paper no. 7, Washington, DC, 1978.

'Economic valuation of shoreline', with H. Pollakowski, *Review of Economics and Statistics*, **59** (3), 272–8, 1977.

'Promising research topics regarding non-consumptive use of forest related lands', *Research in Forest and Forest Policy*, Johns Hopkins Press, 1977.

'Charge and subsidy programs of several European countries', in James B. Stephenson (ed.), *The Practical Application of Economic Incentives to the Control of Pollution*, Vancouver, BC: University of British Columbia Press, 1977.

'Mallard population dynamics and management models', with J. Hammack and Tillman, *Journal of Wildlife Management*, **40** (3), 1976; reprinted in Resources for the Future reprint series.

'Effluent charges', with A. Kneese, S. Rose-Ackerman and O. Davis, *National Technical Information Service*, 1976.

Cleaning Up Europe's Waters: Economics, Management, Policies, with Ralph Johnson, Praeger Publishers, 1976.

'Comprehensive management and effluent change systems in European water management', with Ralph Johnson, International Association for Administration, Caracas, 1976.

'Choice of tools in environmental problems: discussion', in Edwin Mills (ed.), *Economic Analysis of Environmental Problems*, NBER, 1975.

'A preliminary investigation of the economics of migratory waterfowl', with Judd Hammack, *Natural Environments: Studies Theoretical and Applied Analysis*, Johns Hopkins University Press, pp. 171–204, 1974.

'An optimal program for managing common property resources with congestion externalities', *Journal of Political Economy*, **82** (1), 163–73, 1974.

Waterfowl and Wetlands: Toward Bio-Economic Analysis, with Judd Hammack, Johns Hopkins University Press, 1974.

'Welfare-maximizing price and output with stochastic demand: reply', with M.B. Johnson, *American Economic Review*, **63** (1), 230–31, 1973.

'Dynamic economic management of migratory waterfowl', with J. Hammack, *Review of Economics and Statistics*, **55** (1), 73–82, 1973.

'Economic optimization of a single cell aquifier', with R. Deacon, *Water Resources Research*, **8** (3), 557–64, 1972.

'Pricing seasonal recreational services', *Western Economic Journal*, **9** (2), 218–25, 1971.

'Some economic aspects of groundwater use', in C. Corker, *Ground Water Law Management and Administration*; Legal Study 6, report prepared for the National Water Commission, 1971. (Chapter in monograph.)

'Economic valuation of the 1967 sport salmon fishery of Washington', with Steven Matthews, *Washington Department of Fisheries Research Bulletin*, Technical Report 2, 1970.

'Public utility pricing and output under risk: reply', with M.B. Johnson, *American Economic Review*, **60** (3), 489–90, 1970.

'Public utility pricing and output under risk', with M.B. Johnson, *American Economic Review*, **59** (1), 119–28, 1969.

'Dynamic efficiency of quality standards or charges', with Brian Mar, *Water Resources Research*, **4**, December, 1968.

'The economics of irrigated agriculture', in *Water Resources Management and Public Policy*, University of Washington Press, 1968.

'Forecasting industrial water demand: critique', in D. Sewell and B. Bower (eds), *Forecasting the Demands for Water*, Ottawa: Department of Energy, Mines and Resources, 1968.

'The California water project: is public decision-making becoming more efficient?', *Water Resources Research*, **4**, June, 1968.

'A socially optimum pricing policy for a public water agency', with C.B. McGuire, working paper no. 148, Center for Research in Management Science, University of California, Berkeley (mimeographed); published in *Water Resources Research*, **3**, First Quarter, 1967; reprinted in V. Smith (ed.), *Economics of Natural and Environmental Resources*, New York: Gordon and Breach, 1977, and in P. Dasgupta and K.-G. Maler (eds), *Environmental Decision-Making*, UNEP, 1983.

'A money flows approach to investment in game management', with James A. Crutchfield, *Proceedings of the Conference on Management of African Wildlife*, Nairobi, Kenya, July, 1967.

'The projection of Washington State economic and population growth, 1980–2020', Sec. III, 'Industry growth projection', Appendix F; 'Industrial demand for water, 1980 and 2020', Appendix C; in *An Initial Study of the Water Resources of the State of Washington*, Technical Report, Pullman: State of Water Research Center, 1967.

'Competition for water in an expanding economy: the case of irrigated agriculture: discussion', *Water Resources and Economic Development of the West*, **16**, 1967.

Index